CREATIVITY
HOLOCAUST
RECONSTRUCTION

CREATIVITY
HOLOCAUST
RECONSTRUCTION

Jewish Life in Wuerttemberg, Past and Present

by
HERMAN DICKER

SEPHER-HERMON PRESS, INC.
New York

CREATIVITY HOLOCAUST RECONSTRUCTION

Library of Congress Cataloging in Publication Data

Dicker, Herman, 1914–
    Creativity, Holocaust, reconstruction.

    Bibliography: p.
    Includes index.
    1. Jews—Germany (West)—Württemberg—History.
2. Holocaust, Jewish (1939–1945)—Germany (West)—
Württemberg.   3. Württemberg (Germany)—Ethnic
relations.   I. Title.
DS135.G37D53   1984   943'.47004924   84-10667
ISBN 0-87203-118-7

TO MY WIFE

PUBLISHED WITH THE GRACIOUS ASSISTANCE OF:
Alexander Kohut Memorial Foundation
    of the American Academy for Jewish Research
Gustav Wurzweiler Foundation
I. Edward Kiev Library Foundation
Irwin Gelbart
Jewish Theological Seminary of America
Lucius N. Littauer Foundation
Memorial Foundation for Jewish Culture
National Foundation for Jewish Culture
Rabbi Benjamin Z. Kreitman
Rabbi Myron M. Fenster
Rabbinical Assembly

PREFACE

In Germany, as in all European countries, hatred of the Jew has had an age-old tradition from the Middle Ages until deep into the Modern Era. The fate of those who professed the Jewish religion resulted in lack of rights, oppression, deprivation and very often cruel persecution. However, the most terrible inferno of all befell the Jews from 1933 until 1945, when millions of them were either tortured to death, shot, burned or gassed. Today, it is very difficult to occupy oneself with the history of the Jewish community in our state. We Germans, in whose name these horrendous crimes were committed, are deeply ashamed over what was done to the people of Jewish faith, respectively Jewish race during those calamitous years of the Nazi régime. In spite of them, however, we dare not close our eyes to events of those days. We must account to ourselves how this amokrun of nihilistic racial folly could have developed. Moreover, it behooves us to do everything possible so that such a terrible event should not recur: that our generation, as well as our children and grandchildren, should understand what a tyrannical régime means, whereby law and justice are crushed underfoot and inhumanity triumphs. For the men, women and children who were criminally brought to death between 1933 and 1945, must not be allowed to die a second time. However, this could happen if we, who fortunately live in a liberal state of law, forget them, if we are not constantly mindful of what we owe these victims of bestial power.

On the other hand, we ought to remind ourselves that in our own state a close community was created between Jews and non-Jews as a result of the Jewish emancipation in the 19th century. It was based on mutual human respect, little touched by anti-Semitic movements, and existed until the final phase of the Weimar Republic. In those days when one talked about Jewish countrymen and fellow citizens in Wuerttemberg, this was meant by it, for it was generally recognized, that, in both war and peace, the Jews of Wuerttemberg had given manifold proof of their unity with their German fatherland. The first comprehensive presentation of Wuerttemberg's Jewish history appeared from the pen of Dr. Aaron Taenzer, then Rabbi in Goeppingen, in 1937, four years after the Nazi take-over. Since that was a time of gravest suppression of German Jews, Taenzer had to be very circumspect in his evaluations, and had to give priority to dates and facts based upon primary sources. Nevertheless, this volume, reissued attractively in 1983 by the Frankfurt Publishing House of Wolfgang Weidlich, is an indispensable reference work not only by virtue of its thorough historical information, but also as an important contemporary testimony of the love of Wuerttemberg's Jews for the country which granted them unrestricted citizenship rights in the 19th century, and which was home to them as it was to their non-Jewish countrymen. Aaron Taenzer died in February of 1937, shortly before the publication of his work. This theologian and historian, who served his German fatherland so well and who was so rooted in its spiritual legacy, was thus saved from experiencing the Hitler régime's cruel destruction of the Jewish communities of Wuerttemberg and of all of Germany.

Since the downfall of the Nazi power in 1945 and rise of a new democracy in our homeland, a large number of books have appeared that deal with this history of Wuerttemberg's Jewry and of its fate during the Nazi persecution. One of the most important publications in this category is that by Walter Strauss, Chairman of the Organization of Wuerttemberg Jews in the United States. Published in 1982 by the Bleicher Publishing Company, it is entitled, *Signs of Life, Jews from Wuerttemberg*. In this volume approximately 500 former Wuerttemberg Jews, now scattered throughout the entire world, record their fate. These collected letters and reports of personal experiences are testimonies whose expressions of pain and misery make a deep impact upon the reader. One of the fellow Jewish citizens whose path we follow in "Signs of Life" is Dr. Herman Dicker, author of several books on Jewish history including *"Creativity, Holocaust, Reconstruction"* which we here evaluate.

Born in Jasina, Hungary on January 30, 1914, he came with his family to Stuttgart, where he spent his childhood and adolescent years. Even today the formative impact of his Swabian dialect can be detected in his speech. A student at the Eberhard Ludwigs Gymnasium, he obtained his Matura in 1932, and from 1932–1936 received his academic training at the University of Berlin and the Hildesheimer Rabbinical Seminary. In 1937 he earned his doctorate at the University of Zuerich, Switzerland—at that time a Jew could no longer pass his Doctorate examination in Germany—with a dissertation on the History of the Jews of Ulm in the Middle Ages. Without the possibility of a professional future in Germany, he emigrated to the United States and in 1941 entered the US Army where he served as a Chaplain until 1967. Much decorated, he retired as a Lieutenant Colonel. After graduation from the Pratt Institute School of Library Science in 1968, he found a new field of endeavor as a librarian at the Jewish Theological Seminary, New York, where today he is in charge of reference and reader services. Married to Eileen Last of London, England, they have a married daughter and a son. His parents, Osias Dicker and Sara, born Spindel, were unable to escape the Nazi persecutors of World War II, and on December 1, 1941, they were forcibly deported from Stuttgart to Riga, where they perished.

Nobody could fault Herman Dicker were he, after such

painful experiences during the Nazi persecution and particularly after the slaughter of his deported parents, to display resentment and bitterness towards his old home. However, his latest book is eloquent testimony that this is not so. We know that it has not been easy for him to begin anew, to pave the road towards understanding and ultimate reconciliation. But still, like many others of our former Jewish fellow citizens, he has chosen this path. We here in Germany should not hesitate to reach for such outstretched hands in gratitude.

Dr.Dicker addresses Jews and non-Jews alike. His lively and graphic presentation describes Wuerttemberg's Jewish history of the last century and a half. He starts with the law of 1828 which established the beginning of full equality, albeit conceded piecemeal, to Jewish inhabitants; he deals with the organization of the Jewish community within the framework of the state church; he concerns himself with the problem of "reform" from above, and the approach to Christian churches in denial of the traditional Jewish spirit. He frequently employs the biographical method to clarify the religio-spiritual currents prevailing in the historical phases of development. He shows how such developments and currents were introduced by individual personalities, decisively determined or still influenced. In his study, he pays attention to schools and education as well as to the inner life of the communities, their religious orientation, their customs and practices. He is also concerned with economic and social aspects. He leads into the First World War and the Weimar Republic by way of the growing anti-Semitism towards the end of the 19th century and the developing defense by Jews and Christians. In a crowded survey, he analyzes the brutal Nazis' schemes of extermination. And in his final chapter, he muses on Jewish/German relations not only as they appear now, but as they may develop in the future. Here, he conveys a generally optimistic view.

Herman Dicker's work is characteristic of the effort towards objectivity. It is not only the product of a scientifically trained historian, it is much more than that: it is the work of a man interested in building a bridge across the abyss of the Nazi persecution of the Jews, which could lead towards the old homeland and its people. When reading his work, a quote from the Sophocleian tragedy "Antigone" came to my mind: "We are here not to hate, but to love each other."

Stuttgart, November 28, 1983

Paul Sauer

CONTENTS

ILLUSTRATION CREDITS

Mrs. Karl Adler, Leonia, N.J., 23.
Fredy Kahn, Nagold, 12, 13, 15.
Julius Kahn, Haifa, 7, 9.
Leo Baeck Institute, New York, 4, 5, 8, 14.
Alfred Marx, Stuttgart, 11.
Ismar Schorsch, New York, 10.
Mrs. Bruno Stern, New York, 10.
Stadtarchiv, Stuttgart, 19, 20, 21.
Stuttgart City Information Bureau, 24.
Herman Wollach, Stuttgart, 6.
Wuerttemberg Landesbildstelle, 22.
Yeshiva University Gottesman Library, New York, 1.

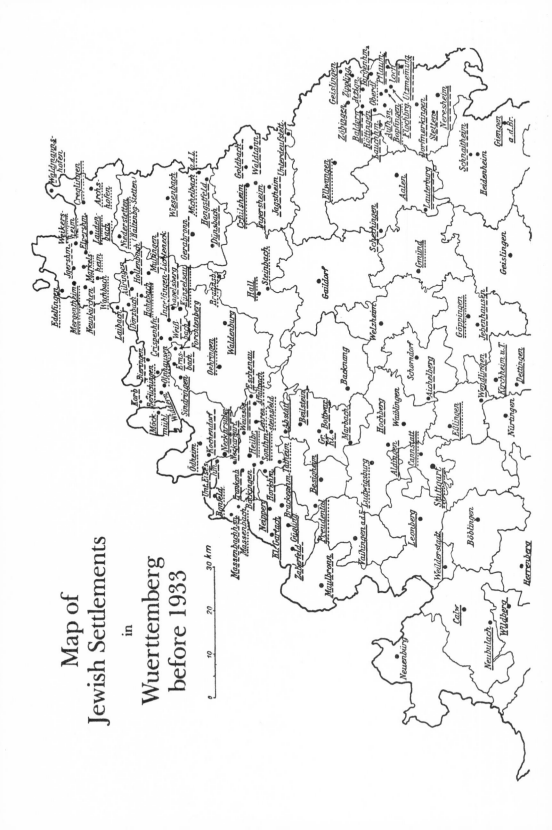

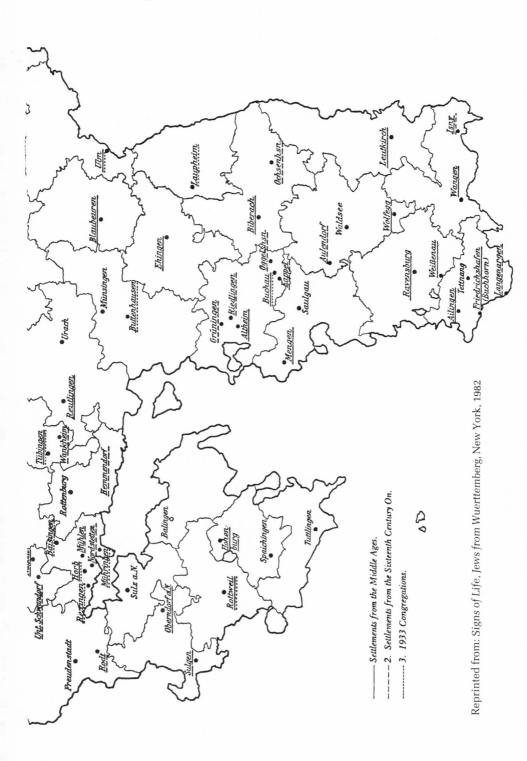

——— Settlements from the Middle Ages.
– – – 2. Settlements from the Sixteenth Century On.
· · · · · · 3. 1933 Congregations.

Reprinted from: Signs of Life, Jews from Wuerttemberg, New York, 1982

INTRODUCTION

The writing of this volume was an undertaking filled with pain and joy. Having just completed a book on Jews from the Carpathian mountains, in whose Hungarian region I was born, my publisher, Samuel Gross, suggested that I turn to Southern Germany, where I had lived from the age of one year on. One of the fortunate ones to escape to the United States in 1938, I had returned to my hometown, Stuttgart, as a U.S. Army Chaplain at the end of WW II; there I searched amidst the ruins of a bombed-out city for traces of my parents who had been deported to Riga in 1941. I found only a few survivors who remembered them, and some silver candlesticks and goblets which kind neighbors had stored pending my parents' return. But my parents did not survive, and I, too, felt like forever turning my back on the scenes of Nazi crimes.

Thirty-five years later, however, the publisher's suggestion of writing about Germany presented a challenge that slowly took hold of me. Through the search of archives, the poring over documents and periodicals, the review of existing literature and conversations with knowledgeable individuals, there unfolded a picture which provided some answers to many questions, and these, I felt, needed to be shared with others. For there were many who asked questions about what happened during the last hundred and fifty years.

Reviewing my youth in the 1920's, particularly while attending the Eberhard Ludwigs Gymnasium, I now realize that I must have been an odd person in the eyes of my classmates, most of whom were sons of elite German families. An orthodox Jew who did not write in class on the Sabbath, kept away from any after-school social gatherings and lived in humble surroundings, I had no schoolfriends who would ever want to come to nor be welcome in our Yiddish-speaking home. My father, of blessed memory, a veteran of the Hungarian army, never really felt at ease in Stuttgart. As soon as his meager earnings allowed, he would travel each year to be with his family in his native village which after World War I had become part of Czechoslovakia. My mother, of blessed memory, was far better off with most of her family residing in Stuttgart.

All the time I knew that legally I was a foreigner, although culturally I was quickly adjusting to my German environment. In the '20's I accepted expressions of anti-foreignism and anti-Semitism as part of the political climate. Still, in 1932, when the choice of a university education became an issue, I thought that as a holder of a Czechoslovak passport it would be better to begin my studies at the German university of Prague. Yet my unfamiliarity with the Czech language, a prerequisite to entrance, shifted my choice of schools. I decided to enter the university and the Hildesheimer Rabbinical Seminary, both situated in Berlin, to prepare for a rabbinical career. When the time (1936) for the Doctorate examination approached, the Nazi Dean told me that my dissertation on the Jews in Ulm during the Middle Ages was unacceptable. I can recall vividly the anger reflected in the eyes of my supervisor, Professor R. Holtzman, a renowned historian, when told about this. He immediately sent a note to his colleague, Professor H. Nabholz of the University of Zuerich, Switzerland, where I was graciously received and obtained my degree, albeit with a loss of valuable time. But what seemed a tragedy then, turned into a blessing for it convinced me that there was no future for me in Europe, and that I should take advantage of an affidavit from the United States which my parents had received from relatives, but which for personal reasons they did not want to use at the time.

And so began the saga of so many of this era: disruption of family and studies, leaving old environments and seeking a future in a new land. Fortunately, my academic credentials qualified me for a commission as a Chaplain in the United States Army, which I obtained upon becoming a citizen in 1943. Thus, the service made a traveler out of me, then us—after marriage to Eileen Last in London, England, in 1945—and sharpened my perception of events, persecution and the ills of war. Although these twenty-six years of uniformed life as a Regular Army Chaplain often caused hardship for my growing family, in retrospect I consider it a rich proving ground for serving the needs of a variety of people. After retirement from the military in 1967, I found a challenging position as a librarian of the Jewish Theological Seminary of America in New York City. Our wandering had come to a happy end.

By nature an optimist, I have never allowed myself to become bitter nor disillusioned. Perhaps this disposition has enabled me to write about the subject of modern Germany, so often avoided by others. I know that a relatively small number of Jews are again living there, which many cannot understand. I also know that new generations have grown up, unaware and often unwilling to learn about the role and fate of Jews in modern times. Thus, my purpose is to tell a story which must be told and hopefully will be listened to. I will try to give credit where credit is due, but will not be silent when truth demands the word. In my desire to present an accurate and colorful picture, I have fortunately enjoyed a great deal of assistance. I have included writings of important contemporaries, which illustrate the unique character of Wuerttemberg's Jewry, described by the revered Rabbi Max Gruenewald, formerly of Mannheim, Germany, as a combination of "roughness and sensitivity." (*Derbheit verbunden mit Ein-*

fuehlungsvermoegen.) But it was Dr. Paul Sauer, Director at the Hauptstaatsarchiv Stuttgart, who furthered my research from the very start until his thoughtful and gracious Preface and beyond. More than anyone else, his monumental works have made him the recognized authority on Jewish history of Southwest Germany. I am also indebted to Professors Utz Jeggle of the University of Tuebingen and Ismar Schorsch of the Jewish Theological Seminary of New York, whose seminal writings have illuminated difficult historical periods. Again, as in my last book, *Piety and Perseverance: Jews from the Carpathian Mountains,* I benefited greatly from the publishing expertise of Samuel Gross of Sepher-Hermon Press and the editorial assistance of Jane Salodof. Her lucid style and his careful attention to all details were of immense value to the English edition.

A large measure of support was also given to me by the archival resources and libraries of the Leo Baeck Institute, Jewish Theological Seminary, *Hauptstaatsarchiv Stuttgart* and *Wuerttembergische Landesbibliothek.* The names mentioned as pictorial credits bespeak the divergent sources of friendly interest in making the story more colorful. Needless to add, neither the English nor the German edition would have been possible without the active aid of sympathetic officials and agencies whose names are listed separately. Heartfelt thanks are also in order to the many who preferred to make anonymous contributions. Lastly, a limitless measure of appreciation goes to my wife, Eileen, and children, Anna and Eli, who each in their own way helped my work. Above all, however, I am grateful to the Almighty for having enabled me to complete this chronicle of an essential phase of contemporary history.

PART I

THE HISTORY

1. THE NINETEENTH CENTURY

The Law of 1828

Our story deals with Jewish life in the Southwest German state of Wuerttemberg, as it unfolds itself in the early 19th century.[1] Since the eleventh century, small settlements had, off and on, existed there, particularly in centers of traffic and commerce such as Heilbronn and Ulm, situated respectively at the rivers Neckar and Danube. However, by the end of the 15th century, most of the flourishing city communities had ceased to exist. The Jews were expelled and forced to seek shelter in nearby rural villages. Denied ownership of land or pursuit of vocational occupations, they had to eke out a miserable living through petty trading and moneylending. They were considered social outcasts and not acceptable members in the Christian society. Moreover, they had to pay "protection" money to the territorial authorities that granted them permission to live within their borders. In the 17th and 18th centuries a few Jews advanced by serving the financial needs of the Dukes of Wuerttemberg. Since the Dukes wanted them near their places of residence they allowed them to move into cities such as Stuttgart and Ludwigsburg. The best-known among them was Joseph Suess Oppenheimer who, ultimately in 1738 was executed, having been accused of embezzlement of state funds.

In 1806, the Duchy of Wuerttemberg became a kingdom, and the number of Jews within its borders increased from

1

approximately 500 in 1800 to approximately 10,000 in 1828. During these decades, other changes, principally legal ones, took place which led finally to the all-important law of April 25, 1828. It transformed the Jews of Wuerttemberg from the status of individually-protected persons (*Schutzjuden*) to one of a unified and state-supervised religious body. These changes were the direct outcome of the new spirit of enlightenment accelerated by the French Revolution and the Napoleonic wars. At that time, debates had begun in earnest about the status of the Jews. They were also sparked by Christian Wilhelm Dohm's book, *Ueber die buergerliche Verbesserung der Juden*, (On the Civil Betterment of the Jews).[2] Dohm had argued forcefully that "the Jew is a human being even more than he is a Jew."[3] Recognizing that most Jews lived in abject poverty, depending mainly on peddling, pawnbroking and second-hand clothes trading for their livelihood, Dohm held that this situation was a result of past policies. If these policies were changed, he argued, the Jews had the capacity to become better human beings and more useful members of society. He wrote: "I may grant that the Jews may be morally more degraded than other nations; that they are guilty of a comparatively larger number of offences than the Christians; that their character on the whole is more inclined to usury and sharp trading practices; their religious prejudice more exclusive and unsociable; yet I must add, that this admitted greater moral degradation of the Jews is a necessary and natural consequence of the oppressive conditions under which they have lived for so many centuries."[4] The view articulated by Dohm also appeared in the local chamber debates, leading to the new law in Wuerttemberg. One representative had said, "All slave nations are crafty and uneducated, and if they are Jews, their oppressors are to blame."[5] The feeling expressed repeatedly was that the Jews needed education to move into more respectable occupations, such as farming and manual labor. To the many who distrusted the Jews for religious reasons, Wuerttemberg's

Minister of the Interior Schmidlin said: "The government is neither a friend nor a foe of the Jews, it is a friend of all good people, without the anxious question: What do you believe? The government wants to favor the honest subject, irrespective of his individual religion."[6]

The law of 1828 was the result of many years of deliberations, involving not only Christians but also Jews who, at times, were extremely unhappy with the new legal stipulations. In many ways, these were more restrictive than educational; Minister Schmidlin himself termed 35 of the total of 62 articles restrictive.[7] Let us take just one example at this point. According to Article 15, citizenship could only be obtained after ten years as an independent farmer or in a vocational profession such as tailoring, shoemaking or baking.[8] But how would it be possible for Jews to obtain citizenship, if so very few of them owned farms or were admitted to the guilds which controlled the vocations and were most reluctant to take in Jews?

Despite such restrictions, the law of 1828 was a good beginning and a step in the right direction. Until then, the approximately ten thousand Jews in Wuerttemberg had no centralized voice or organization. Living in many rural villages throughout the land, they were poor, often considered outcasts by their Christian neighbors and barely making a living for their families. They must have appreciated moving out of the status of protected Jews and realizing the wish, albeit very slowly, of becoming subjects of the state with rights and duties like their Christian counterparts.

Of course, there were a few Jewish families in the land who did not have to wait until 1828 to change from the status of protected Jews to that of citizens. In 1806, for example, King Friedrich (1806–1816) permitted some members of the Kaulla family to establish themselves in Stuttgart with full *Untertanenrecht* (rights of subjects). This was done in "recognition of their many services in behalf of the country during critical times."[9] The Kaullas, originally from Hechingen, belonged to a small group of merchants who had become the bankers to the court. They and others are known in history as "*Hoffaktoren*," best described as suppliers of the King's needs, from money to jewelry, including goods and services for the military. The arrival of the Kaullas was over the strenuous opposition of the local Christian merchants who feared their competition, but this opposition was not strong enough to block the influx of the Kaullas, or other Jewish families. By 1808, fourteen families encompassing 109 persons were in Stuttgart. The name "Kaulla" was to become a household word, not only in financial circles of the state, but also in the affairs of the Jewish community. Members of the Kaulla family were very active in deliberations on the law of 1828, during which they represented the Jews living in the communities in and near Stuttgart, the capital, numerically the weakest but financially the most important.

The Jewish Oberkirchenbehoerde

It had taken a very long time to hammer out the 62 articles which constituted the law of 1828, but it would take three-and-a-half more years, until October 1831, to establish the agency that would administer the law. This body, which Taenzer calls "the soul" of the reorganization, was to function until 1912.[10] It is important that we delve more deeply into the operations of this agency, which dealt with the most sensitive affairs of the Jews in Wuerttemberg. At first let us understand the name, Royal Israelite Superior Church Authority (*Koeniglich Israelitische Oberkirchenbehoerde*). The state of Wuerttemberg was ruled in 1828 by King Wilhelm I (1815–1864), from whom all administrative authority was derived. The term "church" (*Kirche*) indicates how the government viewed the Jewish inhabitants of the state. They represented a religious group similar, but not yet equal, to Christian groups. King Wilhelm I was a Protestant; thus we see the new agency patterned according to the Protestant church organization. All administrative matters had to be approved by the King through the Ministry of Interior, to which the *Oberkirchenbehoerde* was responsible. Since religious matters were also subject to approval by the *Oberkirchenbehoerde*, one can easily foresee conflicts arising between the authority of the state and that of a Jewish community accustomed to religious autonomy.

It had been decided that the president of the *Oberkirchenbehoerde* should be a government official, which all but guaranteed that he would be a Christian, since appointment of Jews to high government office would be a long time in coming. The new president was a very fortunate choice: Dr. Johann Balthasar Steinhardt (1776–1850), a judge who had been offered the position of lay member of the Catholic Church Authority which had become vacant in 1829. Steinhardt asked for an increase in salary from 1600 to 2000 florins, which the government was willing to grant on condition that he would accept, in addition, the position of President of the Israelite Church Authority. This he did, which meant that his principal position was Catholic *Oberkirchenrat* (member of the high consistory) and his part-time position, president of the Israelite *Oberkirchenbehoerde*. The latter became functional in December 1831 after the other five members of the body had been chosen. Their selection was not easy, beginning with the clerical member whose training would qualify him to report and make recommendations on all religious matters. The choice was Rabbi Joseph Maier, whose career will be discussed later. Another decision, also not easily taken, dealt with the appointment of the authority's secretary. There were two applicants for this important position. The first was Isaak Hess (1789–1866), a native of the small community of Lauchheim. An erstwhile rabbinical student, he had given up his studies for financial reasons and become a book dealer. As head of his community, he had participated in the deliberations leading to the law of 1828, submitting a memorandum on the Jewish question and in the

1820's editing a volume of essays on Judaism.[11] In support of his application, Hess offered to move to Esslingen, the community close to Stuttgart, and to teach religion to the Jewish students at the Christian Teachers Seminary. He also pointed to his successful efforts in the care of orphaned Jewish children. Yet despite his good record and respectable credentials, Hess was not chosen.

Carl Weil was born in 1806 in Bockenheim, near Frankfurt on Main, and as a foreigner his appointment to a Wuerttemberg government post would have normally been very difficult. Weil stated, however, that the King had granted him citizenship privileges in 1826. Most likely, this had been done at the request of Solomon Jacob Kaulla of the local banking family. From an 1827 lesson plan, we can see that Weil had been the *Hofmeister* (private academic teacher) to this branch of the Kaulla family.[12] The introduction to the plan reveals Weil's concern for the education of rural youth, as well as of those in the city. Rural students should be taught agricultural and technical vocations, he wrote, whereas those in the city should learn the arts, industry and commerce. This plan, together with his booklet on the admission of Jews to civil rights, reflect Weil's major interests as secretary, a position which lasted from 1831 to 1851.[13] Prior to and during this long period, he also served as a journalist in Paris and as a newspaper editor of the *Wuerttemberg Zeitung*.[14] Weil had a fine educational background; he held a doctor of philosophy degree from the University of Heidelberg, and had passed with excellence the state examination at Stuttgart. Thus, President Steinhardt supported Weil's appointment to secretary with the endorsement of all the members of the *Oberkirchenbehoerde*; Rabbi Maier, Seligmann Loeb Benedikt, Nathan Wolf Kaulla, and Marx Pfeiffer, the latter three belonging to the affluent circles of the community.

Rabbi Joseph Maier

We now turn to the central personality of the *Oberkir-*

chenbehoerde, Rabbi Joseph Maier, who served as its clerical member from 1831 to 1873. During that period, he developed into one of the most dynamic leaders of his time. To understand Maier is to understand the many changes that occurred in the lives of the Jews of Wuerttemberg and of Germany. Maier was born on April 24, 1797, at Laudenbach, a small village in Northern Wuerttemberg. Slated to become a rabbi, he went in 1811 to Fuerth, Bavaria, the academic center for higher Talmudic learning, where his teachers included the well-known scholar, Rabbi Wolf Hamburg. He completed his rabbinical training under Rabbi Herz Scheuer in Mainz, while earning his livelihood as a private teacher, a custom of those days. Until then, Maier's training concentrated in the main on religious studies, but did not include any secular subjects. Maier strove for more; he wanted to enter a university and obtain a doctorate in theology, the ambition of many younger rabbis.[15] Since 1821, his teacher in Latin and Greek, prerequisites to the study of theology, had been Dr. Michael Creizenach.[16] Upon passing of his *Abitur* examination at Stuttgart (on a second try), he entered the University of Heidelberg which, because of its more liberal policy, attracted Jewish students from all parts of Germany.[17] Here he took courses appropriate to the study of theology, and on March 27, 1827, he passed his examination before the royal study council, with the degree of excellence. Maier finally obtained his doctorate at the University of Tuebingen with a Latin dissertation on the history of Jewish dogmas. He was wise enough to acquire all his academic degrees in Wuerttemberg, which made him a favorite choice for employment within that state. Such employment would soon be forthcoming, propelling Maier not only into the center of Jewish life in Wuerttemberg, but making him a well-known personality in many Jewish circles throughout Germany. Maier came to the attention of the royal court much like the *Hoffaktoren*, who had become bankers to the King through their economic status and financial "know-how." We have seen the Kaulla family

come to prominence as court agents. It is noteworthy that the
"*Hausrabbiner*" (family rabbi) of the Kaullas was none other
than our Rabbi Maier, a connection which probably furthered
his candidacy as the first clerical member of the *Israelitische
Oberkirchenbehoerde*. Under Maier, the *Oberkirchenbehoerde* would be challenged by the local communities as
interfering with their inner lives.

Berthold Auerbach (1812–1882), the great Swabian writer, recorded his impression about the new organization and
its clerical member. During his formative years, Auerbach
had considered a rabbinic career, and had been a close ob-
server of the Jewish scene. He wrote in one of his letters, "The
Oberkirchenbehoerde does not meet with the expectations of
some, and Maier had not received any employment as a rabbi,
although already examined, because he was accused of several infractions of the ritual law." In November 1831, one
month before Maier's appointment, Auerbach wrote: "But
listen: Dr. Maier will most likely be appointed Chief Rabbi of
the State (*Oberlandesrabbiner*). Now everything is accomplished, not just half. Maier is a very skilled, liberal man, but
too political, too stubborn and too arrogant. Recently, I have
been visiting with him often and he confirmed the above
statement with one word, although somewhat more mod-
erately. From here we have nothing to expect, for the reforma-
tion of the Jews is a job which has to be approached with
warm love and cold politics . . ."[18]

The main issue surrounding Maier's new position was
his appointment by the state, whereas rabbis had been
customarily chosen by the community. This issue would
plague him and the *Israelitische Oberkirchenbehoerde* for a
long time. Maier represented the new type of rabbis that
began to emerge in the wake of the emancipation. They were
an almost revolutionary change from the old. To quote
Schorsch: "The traditional Ashkenazi rabbi functioned primarily in a judicial capacity, as an expositor of Jewish civil
and religious law."[19] The need to enlarge the role and educa-

tion of rabbis was gradually recognized by all circles in Germany. Even the very traditional rabbis, such as Samson Raphael Hirsch (1808–1888) and Israel Hildesheimer (1820–1899), felt that rabbis should obtain secular training at universities in addition to Talmudic training. They should have a complete command of the German language, enabling them to preach to their congregations regularly. In the past, rabbis only spoke twice a year, on the Sabbaths preceding Passover and the Day of Atonement when their sermons dealt with the special requirements of these festivals. Now the new provisions of the law demanded weekly sermons in German, university training in the field of philosophy, supervision of religious education in the community, visiting the sick and comforting the dying.

Maier's selection had been preceded by a long debate on the nature of the position. At first, there was talk about the appointment of a Chief Rabbi (*Oberrabbiner*).[20] This was rejected in favor of a Superior government unit (*Oberbehoerde*), consisting of a government official (*Regierungskommissar*), a divinity scholar (*Israelitisch Gottesgelehrter*) and at least three lay Israelites as members. During the discussions, a special memorandum, dated April 10, 1827, was submitted by Jewish teachers. Reflecting the tensions between rabbis and teachers, it recommended the appointment of a capable lay person versed in "Israelitish church" and school, in lieu of a rabbi, for "He would not be bound as much by the laws of the *Shulchan Aruch* (Code of Jewish Laws) as a rabbi would, and thus, in compliance with state law, be of greater influence among the Jews." The same memorandum recommended that the *Oberkirchenbehoerde* remain independent of Jews. Three years after the promulgation of the law of 1828, Maier became the first clerical member, but only on a provisional basis. Not until 1837, after Maier had proven his worth in the eyes of the Government, did he become a permanent official with the title "*Kirchenrat*."

Maier had a formidable task, which he pursued with

great energy. In all of Wuerttemberg there lived 9991 Jews spread over eighty localities. Sixty-nine localities had Jewish communities with 57 synagogues, 51 rabbis, 67 cantors, 22 teachers, 23 cemeteries, 20,407 florin foundation money and 24,145 florin debts. Within a few short years, Maier restructured them into thirteen rabbinical districts, dismissing 45 of the old rabbis[21] for lack of "proper" educational qualifications, retaining six and finding six more who could pass the newly established government examinations.[22] These were divided into two parts. For the first, the candidate had to appear before a commission consisting of one professor from each of the Protestant and Catholic theological faculties, four professors from the philosophical faculty, and, finally, the clerical member of the *Israelitische Oberkirchenbehoerde*. The candidate was tested for his knowledge in:

1. Old Testament
2. Faith and History of Dogma
3. Talmud and Ritual
4. Pedagogy
5. Philosophy of Religion
6. Latin and Greek Philosophy
7. History
8. Mathematics

Upon successful completion of this examination, two years had to elapse, during which the candidate familiarized himself with the practical duties of the ministry, and often served a community as a substitute rabbi. Then, he appeared for his second examination before the clerical member and another rabbi, appointed by the Ministry of Interior.

To illustrate the difficulty of these examinations, particularly for the older rabbis, let us take the case of Rabbi Joseph Schnaittach of the large community of Freudental, who, at the time of his examination and subsequent dismissal in 1834, was sixty-five years of age. He was a great scholar in Talmudic law, one whose opinions were sought by many of his colleagues. These written opinions were later collected and are well known as the *Responsa of RJBM*, acronym for Rabbi Joseph ben Meir. His teacher had been the great Rabbi Nathan Adler of Frankfurt, and, like Adler, Schnaittach was well versed in the *Kabbalah*, the study of mysticism. According to the test score, Schnaittach received three "satisfactory" scores in Old Testament, Talmud and Sermon, but three "unsatisfactory" scores in Dogma, Rabbinic Business Law and Sermon Delivery, which caused his failure, since three unsatisfactory scores in major areas constituted total failure.[23]

Although it is quite difficult at this time to evaluate subject matter and score, one gains the impression that Maier was not entirely fair to the great Talmudic scholar. To give him only a "satisfactory" in Talmud seems very peculiar. Moreover, the term "Rabbinic Business Law" is very unclear; it could mean administration, of which the old gentleman had little need during his lifetime. The test rather confirms Auerbach's opinion of Maier that "he pursued the goal of reform with cold politic." Even the *Oberkirchenbehoerde* showed some compassion by granting the forced retirees a small pension. But in 1855, when the eighty-five-year-old Schnaittach pleaded for an increase, he was turned down for "lack of funds." The aged scholar stayed on in Freudental until his death in 1861, having served the community as a *Dayan* (Religious Judge). The requirement of a weekly sermon in German and the opposition of the old timers thereto must also be understood in the context of the era. German language at that time, represented intrusion of the secular into the religious way of life of most Jews, who prayed in Hebrew and spoke Judeo-German. The rabbis were concerned with protection against outside influences. While hindsight tells us that German won in the end, we must realize that this victory often required painful adjustments.[24]

Backed by the authority of the state, Maier proceeded with the reorganization of synagogue life.[25] In 1838, he issued a set of rules (*Synagogenordnung*) designed to bring order and decorum into the synagogue, an area that touched the heart of Jewish life. Maier was not the first one to do this. His new order was patterned on the one promulgated in Westphalia in 1810.²⁶ Maier prefaced his order by stating that its purpose was to strengthen the faith, and promote the ethical way of life. He claimed that the synagogue had been without supervision for centuries, and that many abuses had crept in which were a departure from the old practices. Some of the new rules stipulated the following:

-No public worship services may be held outside the synagogue approved by the state.

-Every private assembly for liturgical purposes (*Minyan*) is prohibited on pain of severe punishment. An exception is made in the case of bereavement in that the customary prayer may be said with the dying, and that, with the exception of the Sabbath, the daily prayers may be recited during the first seven days of mourning in the mourner's house.

-The beginning of the worship service is herewith fixed for all the synagogues of the state . . .

-The synagogue should be entered with decorum and without noise. He who enters must immediately go to his seat, and remain in it. Any walking around or standing together within the synagogue is prohibited on pain of punishment.

-The kissing of the Curtain hanging before the Ark on entering the synagogue during the service is prohibited; also forbidden are the following:

—leaving one's seat to kiss the *Torah* (Scroll of Law).

—knocking during the reading of the Book of Esther on the Feast of *Purim*.²⁷

—the 39 lashes administered on the Eve of Atonement.²⁸

—noisy beating of the willow branches on the Seventh Day of the Feast of Tabernacles.

—sitting on the floor on the Fast of the Ninth of *Ab* (commemorating the destruction of the Temples of Jerusalem) and removing one's shoes in the synagogue during this day.

—the procession with the *Torah* on the eve of *Simchat Torah* (festival of Rejoicing of the *Torah*); also the procession of the children with flags and candles on this day. The distribution of food and drink in the synagogue on *Simchat Torah*.

By making the synagogue and services more orderly, Maier and other reformers hoped to further the cause of emancipation. Only one of Wuerttemberg's rabbis, Gabriel Adler of Oberdorf (1787–1859), objected to the new rules.[29] Moreover, several decades later *Oberkirchenrat* Dr. Theodor Kroner, second successor to Maier's position (1894–1922), stated that the new rules were never fully accepted by the communities of the land. How could they be? To quote the historian Graupe:

> In the old synagogue or prayer room, a relaxed homely and rather informal atmosphere prevailed, although old congregational regulations were concerned with preserving a certain decorum. One was not making a formal visit when one attended synagogue. The service was frequently a disorderly medley of praying voices, drowning that of the reader. It was an expression of the individual communicating with God. And, before and after the service, the local synagogues and learning-rooms were places where different groups sat together and 'learnt' the Talmud or quite factually discussed the day's events.[30]

Busy as Maier must have been with his statewide duties as clerical member of the *Oberkirchenbehoerde*, he also found time for his own district in Stuttgart, where he began to officiate as rabbi in 1835. In his first sermon, he stressed the need for a new spirit, while respecting the old.[31] In the same year, he also married Rebbecka Auerbacher of a local family. Concerned with better education, as he saw it, Maier published several textbooks, of which the *Lehrbuch der Israelitischen Religion* (Manual of the Israelite Religion) was used for a long time.[32] These books represent the thinking of the new rabbinic breed, which saw Judaism primarily as a system of ethics and morality. Patterned like a Protestant catechism, it teaches the principles of Jewish belief in a question and answer form, using mainly Biblical references and de-emphasizing observance of religious laws and customs. The *Lehrbuch* was introduced as a guide to Jewish teacher and student, but it was written also with the Christian reader in mind; it attempted to show how much Judaism agrees with Christianity. The section "Duties towards the Fatherland and obligations of Soldiers" (*Pflichten gegen das Vaterland und Dienst der Soldaten*), in particular, was clearly designed to win favor with the government by whose authority the manual was issued. The *Lehrbuch*'s introduction claims that it had the endorsement of all rabbis in the state. In the light of Adler's protest against the "Synagogue Order," this claim seems rather doubtful. The manual's deficiencies are more in what it does *not* teach than what it does teach. Recognizing Maier's dedicated service, the King changed his temporary appointment into a permanent one in 1837, and bestowed upon him the title *Kirchenrat*. Having an official title in a status-conscious society must have meant a great deal not only to Maier himself, but to all his friends and colleagues throughout Germany. Maier's opinions were sought by many, including those in the great controversy that erupted between the Orthodox Salomon Tiktin and the Reform Abraham Geiger, rabbis of the Breslau community. To resolve the dilemma, the communal board (*Ober-Vorsteher Collegium*) of that important city invited the rabbis of Germany and Hungary to offer their views for consideration. The question as posed by the board was: "Whether Jewish theology could tolerate scholarly treatment and unrestricted research, or whether the traditional statutes as preserved in the Talmud should not be touched or even investigated."[33] Maier's thoughts were carefully outlined. He first faulted both the community and Tiktin from a legal point of view. Then, on the basis of his religious convictions, he proceeded to support Geiger.[34]

Having spelled out in detail the new synagogue order, he published in 1841 another set of instructions again under the authority of the *Oberkirchenbehoerde*, dealing with the functions and duties of rabbis and cantors. (*Amts-Instruction fuer die Rabbiner und die Vorsaenger im Koenigreich Wuerttemberg.*) Under the law of 1828, rabbis and cantors had become officials of the state; thus the *Oberkirchenbehoerde* considered it proper to instruct both on their respective functions. As a result of the reorganization in the 1830's, there were 13 district rabbis who served a total of 41 communities. The rabbis' seats were in the bigger communities, whereas the smaller ones were served by a cantor, who often also functioned as a teacher and *shochet* (ritual slaughterer). The rabbis very often found themselves on the road, covering their districts and supervising the religious activities of the local cantors. The carefully worded instructions covered synagogue, community, religous education and pastoral functions. In addition—and here we can see the guiding spirit of Maier—there was great emphasis on German prayers and sermons in the synagogue. Another new feature was the "Confirmation-Education" which was to prepare boys and girls for entry into the Jewish community. This act of entry was to be celebrated in a special service at the Feast of Weeks. The regulations noted that this was not to be considered as a confirmation of one's belonging to the community, which was determined by birth, but rather as an act of strengthening the youngster's faith. The wording was a tortuous way of admitting that the concept of a confirmation ceremony was not grown on Jewish soil, but an influence of the Christian environment. Both rabbis and cantors were members of the *Kirchen-Vorsteheramt* (Presiding Office of the Church) and, as such, were instructed to become familiar with all the functions needed to administer a community, such as taxation and welfare of the needy. All activities of the rabbis and cantors had to be carefully logged and reported to the *Oberkirchenbehoerde*, particularly when a decision could not be reached on the local level. Summarizing the detailed instructions one must give credit to the author, Rabbi Maier, for his attention to the needs of the community and the tasks of its religious functionaries. Of course, the instructions were in accord with Maier's general thoughts about Judaism, with which many of the rabbis, cantors and lay people disagreed, as we shall see later on.

Maier's administrative experience and prominent position as *Kirchenrat* made him a favorite candidate for president of the first rabbinical conference at Braunschweig in 1844.[35] He received the vote of sixteen out of twenty-two rabbis who had come from all parts of Germany.[36] While he could not be considered one of the major thinkers of his day, he had shown practical leadership in his state of Wuerttemberg and although decidedly in the Reform column, he had managed thus far to get along with Orthodox factions in his state. The prime organizer of the Braunschweig meeting, followed by Gatherings in Frankfurt (1845) and Breslau (1846), was Rabbi Ludwig Philippson (1811–1899), editor of the *Allgemeine Zeitung des Judentums*, who wanted to bring rabbis together to discuss matters of mutual interest, and to advance the cause of emancipation. One of their major concerns was the synagogue and the order of service. The proposed changes reflected their personal views of the nature of Judaism. All those attending came as individuals, and not with any mandate from their congregations. It has been rightfully pointed out that these conferences were not convened as those of Reform rabbis; they only came to be known as such because of the absence of Orthodox rabbis from the meeting.[37] Most certainly in Wuerttemberg, in the 1840's, it would be premature to speak of Reform communities.[38] At best, one can say that some of these communities had rabbis with Reform leanings.

The protocols of the conferences showed Maier not only

as a busy president, but also as head of a commission charged with a report on the new liturgy and a new prayer book.[39] In his report, Maier stated that the need for prayer reform was particularly felt by the city communities and the new generation of young people. Israel's ancient wish for the restoration of the Temple and return to its homeland was only a nostalgic longing for the past, "Now that we have found a home."

(. . . an das Land unserer Vaeter knuepfen uns teuere Erinnerungen: der Wunsch es wieder zu erlangen, ist uns, die wir eine Heimat gefunden haben, nur eine Idee, ein Schwelgen in fruehere Zeit, bei nuechterer Betrachtung geben wir das Verlangen nach ihrer Verwirklichung auf.)

Maier reiterated the need for prayers in German because: "In a few decades only a few Jews will understand Hebrew."

(Voraussichtlich werden nach einigen Jahrzehnten die wenigsten Juden diese Sprache nur mehr lesen koennen.)

Only a few principal prayers and the Reading of the Scriptures ought to be recited in Hebrew. Finally, he urged the placing of an organ into the synagogue which, as we know from later years, became the major characteristic of a Reform synagogue.[40]

The widespread criticism and protest that erupted in the wake of the conference was met head on by Maier. He published a pamphlet in which he first singled out Philippson, who said: "The rabbinical conference had instead of reviving and creating, put the critical knife at the existing." (Die Rabbiner Versammlung habe anstatt zu beleben und zu schaffen das kritische Messer an das Bestehende gelegt.)[41] Philippson's remarks hurt very much, as he had been the prime mover of the first conference and was all along considered a representative of the new, progressive, university-trained rabbi. An anonymous critic labeled Maier as unimportant (unbedeutend), and accused him of having treated the most gifted members of the conference in an insulting manner. In his rebuttal, Maier commented on his own position in Wuerttemberg: "No member left Braunschweig without assuring me of his respect and love . . . I am neither at the head of the *Oberkirchenbehoerde* nor do I have subordinate colleagues. I am only an advisor to a church body, whose members, with the exception of the president, our overall superior, are completely equal to me. The rabbis of the land are likewise not subordinates, but we are all equal and under the supervision of the *Oberkirchenbehoerde*."[42]

Maier was very bitter toward the very learned Zacharias Frankel (1801–1875), then the Chief Rabbi of Dresden, who had written him an open letter, accusing him bluntly of ignorance.[43] In his sharp reply, Maier compares Frankel with Samson Raphael Hirsch, the Orthodox rabbi, who had been afraid "to remove the old and dirty Polish garb from Judaism and to put it into new clothes." (*Er erschrak sich den alten, schmutzigen polnischen Rock auszuziehen und ihm ein neues Kleid zu machen.*) Further: "Now he covers Judaism with the Polish cowl, whose dirt he praises as jewels." (*Jetzt bedeckt er das Judentum mit der polnischen Kutte, deren Schmutz er nun als Edelsteine preist.*)[44] Maier's very strong words show not only his deep hurt, but even more, his poor judgment. The term "Polish cowl" (*Polnische Kutte*) meant being backward socially and spiritually. To place Frankel into Hirsch's corner failed to do justice to either one of them. In the 1840's, Hirsch had already established himself through the publication of his *Nineteen Letters* (1836), as the uncompromising champion of Orthodoxy, whereas Frankel had at first tried to participate in the rabbinic conference. He then left it in protest (1845) against the decision that Hebrew prayers in the synagogue were only advisable (*rathsam*) and not obligatory.[45]

Opposition in Wuerttemberg

In Wuerttemberg, too, Maier faced opposition, reflected

in an anonymous letter whose writer was introduced in an editorial footnote as "a man in office."[46] The letter points to the many violations of the new synagogue order which initially "had been welcomed by the majority of the patriotic members of the faith as a means toward restoring order and unity in public worship." The writer blames the rabbis for these violations implying they could do so only because they were financially independent of the communities. The writer is bitter about the large expenses of publishing new instructional material, song books and melodies, and then letting them go to waste by not using them.

Shortly after this report, another correspondent wrote about events in the rabbinical district of Oberdorf.[47] Here, Rabbi Gabriel Adler organized a protest meeting against the decisions of the Braunschweig conference, which, as we have seen, was chaired by Maier. Adler invited all the synagogue officials and other interested people in the district, all of whom accepted his invitation with the exception of those from the community of Pflaumloch. When it came to signing a protest declaration, some teachers refused, however, for fear that to do so could harm them. The writer, blaming Adler altogether for having approached teachers and merchants, hints that his personality was unsuited for any kind of protest.

The letter asks for periodic rabbinical visits on the part of the *Oberkirchenbehoerde*, which would eliminate some of the abuses within the communities. While it is true, the letter continues, that everyone can complain to the *Behoerde* in writing, most people prefer to spend their little time at home with their families instead of arguing with rabbis and church officials. The writer ends—probably a hidden criticism about Rabbi Adler who was not university-trained—with a call for more university-trained rabbis and a Jewish theological faculty at the Tuebingen university.[48]

We have already met Adler, who objected to Maier's synagogue rules. As a member of a distinguished rabbinic family, Adler was an old-time rabbi who, in 1834, passed his state examination and stayed on as one of the thirteen district rabbis. He was a great Talmudic scholar, whose inquiries are mentioned in the responsa of Rabbi Wolf Hamburg, the head of the Fuerth Yeshivah.[49] But it appears that Maier caused Adler's transfer after his examination from Muehringen (where he had served from 1812 to 1834), to Oberdorf, where he remained until his death in 1859. Muehringen had a much larger Jewish population, 1,576 persons, whereas Oberdorf only had 1,104.[50] Adler's replacement in Muehringen was Dr. Moses Wassermann who, at the time of his appointment, was barely twenty-four years old. This transfer shows the power of Maier who, by virtue of his position as a member of the state authority, held the fate of rabbis and teachers in his hands. Considering the shaky financial position in which religious functionaries frequently found themselves in other communities, one can readily understand the feelings of those employed in Wuerttemberg, where the state paid their salaries. This too prevented overt protests from developing. Aside from the financial security, one must constantly keep in mind Maier's and the *Oberkirchenbehoerde*'s objectives. These were to advance the legal and social conditions of the Jews, goals to which everyone subscribed regardless of religious background. This was particularly evident on April 17, 1847, when the Jewish communities presented Dr. Carl Weil with a huge silver goblet in recognition for all his work.[51] We know Weil's role as secretary and referent for administrative matters with the *Oberkirchenbehoerde*. It was, indeed, a huge undertaking to organize the many communities, rabbis, teachers and laymen into one legal organization. The struggle for civil and legal equality, which Weil had pursued with great vigor since his appointment in 1831, was far from being over, but it seems that the communities identified themselves with it. They saw the benefits and they appreciated the work of the people involved in it. One can only guess the reason why this honor was bestowed upon Weil at that particular time, but it appears that Weil was being approached to become the editor of the *Constitutionelle Jahrbücher* in Berlin. He took a leave of absence from his Stuttgart position to go there in 1848. Perhaps the Jewish community felt the honor in 1847 would keep him in Stuttgart. Upon Weil's return to Stuttgart in 1850, the Wuerttemberg government promoted him to "*Regierungsrat*," (government councillor) either out of respect for his work or to keep him in his position. But it did not help. A year later Weil left for a high position with the foreign office of the Austrian government in Vienna. His replacement was Dr. Isidor Jordan, a lawyer, who served from 1852 to 1872. Although Weil's departure must have been a great loss to the *Oberkirchenbehoerde*, the body was strong enough to continue its work on behalf of the civil equality of the Jews. The year 1850 saw also the appointment of a new president, *Regierungsdirektor* von Schmidt, who served from 1850 to 1883. There were other personnel changes among the secular members, making Maier the veteran of the *Behoerde*. To advance the cause of emancipation, he published a small pamphlet on the "*Judeneid*" (Jewish oath), a procedure that was a relic of former days, when Jewish credibility was very low and certain humiliating ceremonial acts were required to accept a Jewish oath before a civil court.[52] Another major effort of his involved a new prayerbook. This publication was characteristic of Maier's intentions.[53] In his preface, he makes it clear that he prepared this volume in his private capacity as a rabbi, and not by the authority of the *Oberkirchenbehoerde*. Further, it was not designed to replace the regular prayerbook, but only "to give a prayerbook to those who do not own one." The book itself was a collection of Hebrew prayers for the whole year. In addition, it contained a number of German prayers of personal devotion, for use either in the synagogue or at home. The book opens from left to right, while a traditional Jewish prayer volume opens from right to left, in accord with the rules of the Hebrew language. Maier's hope may have been that this new prayerbook would be accepted by communities throughout the land, but he must have soon realized that this was not to be. It was too radical a departure from tradition. And while the book lists approximately two hundred names as subscribers in and out of Wuerttemberg, this can be little proof of acceptance.[54]

Maier was wise enough to recognize opposition to this prayerbook, and he busied himself in the 1850's with a two-volume *Seder Tefilla* (Israelitische Gebetsordnung), which was published in 1861. This was done by order of the *Oberkirchenbehoerde*, and thus with the full authority of the government. This may have helped its distribution, but the major reason for its acceptance was that it was really a traditional prayerbook, with German translation plus additions for organ, choir and German prayers. Consider Maier's preface:

> The local community does not want to separate itself, in its worship, from the other communities of the country, or from the synagogue as such. What it desires is simplicity and dignity. With this, any changes affecting dogma or the transformation of the liturgy were ruled out from the beginning. The present prayerbook differed from the one in use hitherto only in the omission of the Talmudic components and of all the *piyutim* (liturgical poetry), in the abbreviation of some prayers, and in the inclusion of German prayers and hymns . . .

While Maier repeats his conviction of the need for German prayers, particularly for the younger generation, he is honest enough to say:

> It is true that German prayer and hymn have thus far been unable to acquire their right of domicile in the synagogue, and, despite the efforts in that direction of a whole generation, it still appears more or less a stranger . . .

The traditional character of the 1861 publication must have appealed to Maier's Stuttgart community, which rose from 15 families in 1832 to 547 persons in 1856, most of whom had moved from the rural communities to the capital.

The ever-increasing number of congregants made planning for a new synagogue a great necessity, although here, too, people were divided. Some preferred a school building, but a new synagogue won out, and the new Moorish-style structure was dedicated on May 3, 1861, in the presence of many dignitaries.[55] Maier must have viewed the beautiful structure, complete with organ, as a highlight in his labors on behalf of enlightened Judaism. Flushed with the excitement of the occasion, he uttered in his dedication sermon, words that would haunt him for years to come: "*Ja, dir, geliebtes Stuttgart, unserem Jerusalem, wuenschen wir Heil.*"[56] (Yes, you, beloved Stuttgart, our Jerusalem, we wish luck.) Anyone only slightly familiar with Jewish history, knows of the central role of Jerusalem in Jewish religion. It was there where the Temple had once stood, and it is from Jerusalem where Jews continued to receive their spiritual sustenance, even after the Temple's destruction by the Romans. Three times a day they turned their eyes in prayer towards their Holy City, fervently hoping that the Almighty would eventually restore the Temple to its former glory. He would send His messenger, the Messiah, to return the Jewish people from exile to Zion, establishing peace not only for them, but for all the peoples of the Earth. It was only natural that the prayers for the coming of the Messiah intensified in times of stress, and, conversely, decreased during periods of comparative security. In their drive for emancipation, the Reform rabbis reinterpreted the meaning of the messianic idea. They converted the physical concept of the return to Jerusalem into a lofty idea whereby, in some distant future, God would be accepted by the whole of mankind.

We have seen that throughout Maier's career there was sporadic opposition to his stewardship. It was, however, never really organized or very outspoken. This was about to change, due not only to the local conditions in Wuerttemberg, which the traditional elements criticized more and more, but also as a result of national developments. The ascendancy of Samson Raphael Hirsch in Frankfurt produced an eloquent spokesman for Orthodox Judaism.[57] In addition, a weekly newspaper, the *Israelit* started to appear in 1860 in Mainz. Its editor was another Orthodox rabbi, Dr. Marcus Lehmann, whose aim was to counterbalance the influence of the *Allgemeine Zeitung des Judentums*, which was edited by Rabbi Ludwig Philippson and was ideologically close to Reform Judaism. The religious situation in Wuerttemberg—particularly Rabbi Maier—would become a favorite target of the *Israelit*. Thus, we see a whole series of lead articles in this paper under the heading, "The Israelite Conditions in Wuerttemberg, Particularly Stuttgart," which appeared in 1863 and 1864.[58] At about the same time, three pamphlets by an anonymous writer who called himself Gabia ben Psisah, and a rebuttal by an anonymous writer, who called himself Rabbi Schimon Hazaddik, appeared on the scene. They reflected a debate between the two personalities, Rabbi Maier alias Rabbi Schimon Hazaddik and Ludwig Stern alias Gabiah ben Psisa.[59]

Ludwig Stern: Champion of Orthodoxy

Stern, a teacher from Freudental, had prepared himself for his profession in a very thorough manner. His pamphlets are proof that he was well-versed in Scriptures and Talmud. He had passed the state examination and, before coming to Freudental, served in several small communities. During his studies, he lived for a while in the house of Isaak Hess of Ellwangen, the dedicated champion of Jewish causes, who in turn had been the unsuccessful candidate for secretary of the *Oberkirchenbehoerde* in 1831. The Jewish community in Freudental itself had had a long history of dissatisfaction with Maier. It had maintained Rabbi Joseph Schnaittach, the great scholar, as religious judge in its midst until his death, although he had not passed the state examination in 1834 and was no longer their official rabbi. Undoubtedly, members of the community were supportive of Stern's efforts against Maier. But his major support must have come from the circle around the *Israelit* at whose publishing plant, the LeRoux Company, his own three pamphlets were printed. If one compares the articles in the *Israelit* with the pamphlets, one is struck by the close similarity in style and content, which makes one believe that they were written by the same author.[60] The language used by both is very polemical and abusive. Stern accuses Maier and the Jewish members of the *Behoerde* of not being representative of Wuerttemberg's Jewry, which was three-fourths traditional, whereas they were not concerned with religious observance, but more interested in pleasing the government. Another complaint was the matter of appointment of rabbis and teachers in individual communities. They were being chosen and examined by the government, with no regard for the wishes of the communities they were to serve. There was no proper training of teachers and thus a low standard of Jewish education prevailed. The critics mentioned, of course, Maier's remarks: "*Stuttgart ist unser Jerusalem.*"[61] To be exact, these were not the words uttered as we have read before. But Maier, too, was not accurate in his rebuttal.[62] He claimed to have said: "*Heil sei in deinen Mauern Stuttgart Jerusalem*" (Blessed be in Thy walls Stuttgart Jerusalem) which he interpreted to mean: "*Gott moege Stuttgart das Heil widerfahren lassen das er ehemals Jerusalem hat zu Theil werden lassen*" (God may bestow upon Stuttgart the same blessing which He once gave Jerusalem). Whatever the words and their interpretation, this is what Maier said about Israel's hope in the Coming of the Messiah

> Until then (i.e. the Coming of the Messiah) we view Wuerttemberg, which, according to its location, fertility, wise gov-

ernment and harmony between different religious groups, is
equal to the former Palestine, as our fatherland and love it as
much as our fathers loved theirs . . .[63] (*Bis dahin (d.h. das
Kommen des Messiah) betrachten wir aber Wuerttemberg,
das hinsichtlich seiner Lage, Fruchtbarkeit, weiser Regierung
und Eintracht unter den verschiedenen Bekenntnissen dem
ehemaligen Palästina an die Seite gestellt werden kann, als
unser Vaterland, lieben es so innig wie unsere Vaeter das
ihrige lieben . . .*)

With words like these, mixing political concepts with religious beliefs, it is no wonder that Maier became the principal
target of the opposition. The drive for civil and political
equality had been ongoing ever since the law of 1828 came
into being. We know that Carl Weil, the secretary of the
Oberkirchenbehoerde, had all along struggled by submitting
petitions to remove the legal restrictions in this law.[64] However, there were many favorable voices within the members
of the *Staendeversammlung* (Assembly of the Estates), which
supported these efforts for legal equality. The legal development within Wuerttemberg received a big boost from the law
of the German National Assembly, whereby religious creed
should not limit nor condition the enjoyment of civil rights.
(*Durch das religioese Bekenntnis wird der Genuss der buer-
gerlichen und staatsbuergerlichen Rechte weder bedingt
noch beschraenkt.*) After further deliberations, the King of
Wuerttemberg finally approved on July 21, 1864, the law that
granted the Jews equal rights in all civil matters. One of its
benefits included the abolishment of the special Jewish oath,
which had so long impaired the credibility of the Jews before
the courts. It also permitted marriages between Jews and
Christians.

In the light of these civil improvements, many voices
asked for the removal of the *Oberkirchenbehoerde* altogether.
In the main, they emanated from the rural communities
which considered many of the state agency's rulings to be an
interference in their communal life. In the past, the opposi-

tion had frequently softened, because it was felt that the agency wanted to advance the civil rights of the Jews. Now in the 1860's when there were general legal advances, the opposition began to bear down on Maier himself, for it saw in him the prime champion of religious reforms. A strong gathering met in June 1864 at Hohebach, and submitted a petition to the state for revision of the *Oberkirchenbehoerde*.[65] This led to a meeting in December 1870 under the auspices of the Minister for Church Affairs. This was the first time that the grievances of the critics were officially aired at the highest level. The opposition combined Orthodox groups and those who argued in behalf of the communities' autonomy on legal grounds.[66] One representative of the Orthodox was Ludwig Stern, who had battled Maier in the early 1860's and left Freudental in 1864 to become a teacher in the newly founded *Israelitische Lehrerbildungsanstalt* at Wuerzburg, Bavaria.[67] It seems that Stern had retained his interest in the communal affairs of nearby Wuerttemberg, as well as his citizenship in this state. This enabled him to become an official spokesman for the community of Mergentheim. Discussion centered around such questions as: which communal institutions should be carried by the state, and which should remain the responsibility of the local community. A draft had listed synagogues, rabbis and cantor-teachers in the first category, with institutions such as ritual slaughter, ritual baths for women (*Mikvaot*), and cemeteries falling into the second. The Orthodox faction argued that a "pompous synagogue service" was less important than purity of family based on the availability of a ritual bathing facility. One rabbi argued, that in order to pray one need not attend services at the synagogue, but could do so at home. Others said that as long as membership in the community was compulsory, the religious needs of all the members, even though in a minority, must be met. Other areas of criticism included the rules of the synagogue, the selection of rabbis and the education of teachers.

Despite all these criticisms, Maier's person continued to

enjoy the respect of the government. In 1867, on the occasion of his seventieth birthday, he received a high decoration which conferred upon him the status of nobility. Henceforth, he could add the word *"von"* to his family name, which made him the first rabbi in Germany so honored. In the last few years of his life—he died on August 19, 1873—Maier was in failing health, which prevented him from being as vigorous as he had been during the earlier part of his forty-year tenure.

Rabbi Moses Wassermann

It appears that the authorities had been searching for a successor to Maier, even before his demise. Only two months later, Moses Wassermann, Rabbi of Muehringen, was appointed by royal decree to fill Maier's vacancy as the clerical member of the *Oberkirchenbehoerde*, and as rabbi of the Stuttgart community. This quick decision was designed to avert the complaints that it was improper to combine these positions in one person. The clerical member was technically the supervisor of all the rabbis of Wuerttemberg, including the one in Stuttgart. Thus Maier's successor would again be the target of the opposition. Printed petitions to the Ministry of Church and School Affairs had urged a delay in the appointment of the clerical member, since a hasty decision would hinder the revision of the *Oberkirchenbehoerde*, long under discussion.[68] It was argued that Stuttgart was a Reform community; if its rabbi would also serve as the clerical member, he would of necessity impose his opinions on communities with different views, or otherwise have to go against his own convictions. The petition also pointed to the neighboring Grand Duchy of Baden, where the office of the clerical member of the *Oberrat* was separate from that of the Karlsruhe community. The same argument is repeated in an editorial of the *Israelit* signed by G.b.P., the initials for Gabia ben Psisah, alias Ludwig Stern, which makes one assume that Stern was once again the center of the organized opposition.[69] Fortunately for the establishment, Moses Wassermann was available to follow Maier on short notice. This decision was made easier for many reasons. First, Wassermann was well-known in Wuerttemberg. His father, a native of Oberdorf, had been a rabbi in Laupheim (1825–1835) and Mergentheim (1835–1858), which meant that he had passed the examination of the 1830's and stayed on as one of the thirteen district rabbis.[70]

Young Moses, born in 1811, had his Hebrew training from his father and Rabbi Abraham Bing of Wuerzburg. For his general education, he had finished Gymnasium in Ulm, and obtained his doctorate from the University of Tuebingen. During his student days, he became friendly with Leopold Kaulla who studied law at Tuebingen and later, as a director of the *Hofbank*, served as a member of the *Oberkirchenbehoerde* from 1849 to 1883. Since 1835 he had been the rabbi of the prestigious community of Muehringen, where he stayed until his appointment to the Stuttgart position in 1873. As a young rabbi, he had participated in a meeting of rabbis called by Abraham Geiger in Wiesbaden in 1837[71] and had written in behalf of Geiger during Geiger's struggle with Rabbi Tiktin of Breslau.[72] Wassermann drew a line between a rabbi's duties towards his community and his rights to private opinions: a rabbi must be concerned with the prevailing sentiments of his community, but in his private research he should be free. Concern with the sentiments of his traditional district may have prevented Wassermann's attending any of the three rabbinic conferences in the 1840's, although basically he leaned to the side of Reform. A fine preacher, he was much beloved by Jew and non-Jew alike. His contacts with the authorities enabled him to quell the anti-Semitic outbursts of 1848 which occurred in Baisingen, a village in his rabbinic district. During the 1860's, Wassermann was one of the supporters of the *Oberkirchenbehoerde*, although he too was displeased with the poor education of the teachers.

While at the University in Tuebingen, Wassermann was a favorite of the poet Ludwig Uhland (1787–1862), who recognized his student's writing skill, and encouraged him to develop it further. Wassermann produced fictional works such as, *Die Maedchen von Chaibar*, published in 1859, and *Juda Touro, Ein Gentleman, semitischer Abstammung*, which appeared in 1877.[73] Interestingly enough, both novels deal with Jewish characters outside of Europe; the first with Jewish life in the days of Mohammed (570–632), and the second with an American Jewish personality of the eighteenth century. Both works show their author as a careful researcher, with a fine style and a rich imagination.

When called to Stuttgart, Wassermann was plunged into a set of responsibilities quite different from his Muehringen duties. As the clerical member, he now had to deal with the religious activities of all the communities and, as a rabbi of the capital's fast growing population, he ran into many problems of city life. Sixty-two years of age, thirty-eight of them spent in the more sedate surroundings of Muehringen, were not exactly the best preparation for a new lifestyle. Still, he approached his new tasks with great dedication, although as Maier's successor, he had to contend with all the criticism leveled against his predecessor. This applied to the synagogue order, but even more so to the status of religious education in the community. Already in the 1850's there had been petitions to establish a public Jewish school for the growing number of children in Stuttgart's community. These were, however, of no avail, as we know that Maier and his supporters felt it more important to erect a big synagogue which took a great financial effort.[74] Religious education of the young was left to a congregational school (*Religionsschule*) that held classes on Sundays, and after the conclusion of the regular school day. A teacher's report in 1868 lists a whole set of complaints about improper lesson plans, absenteeism, lack of parental support, inadequate facilities and poor teachers' pay. In addition, an attempt was made to provide religious education in the various secondary schools of the city, but many students avoided religious classes altogether. To help the aging Wassermann, a new rabbi was engaged in 1881, Dr. David Stoessel of Lackenbach, Hungary. His principal duty initially was to assist Wassermann in his teaching responsibilities at the secondary schools. (In 1886, Stoessel was promoted to Deputy Rabbi and in 1893 to Associate-city and district rabbi.) Still it is reported that the status of religious education in Stuttgart of the 1880's compared unfavorably with that in other Wuerttemberg communities.[75] A sign of the general dissatisfaction within the community appeared in 1878, when a small group of traditional Jews formed their own congregation: they eventually would play a major role in the spiritual life of Stuttgart's Jews.

While this development shows a desire to strengthen religious ties, the episode of Rabbi Jacob Stern is a case in reverse.[76] Stern had been born in 1843, the son of a very pious family in Niederstetten. His mother, a native of Oberdorf, belonged to the Frankfurter family, one of whom, Dr. Naphtali Frankfurter, became a rabbi, first in Wuerttemberg and then at the Reform temple in Hamburg. For his Talmudic training, young Stern, together with his cousin Jacob, had gone to the *Yeshivah* (Talmudic Academy) of Pressburg, Hungary, which was one of the finest centers of traditional Jewish learning. After completion of his Talmudic studies, he entered the University of Tuebingen to prepare himself for the rabbinate as prescribed by Wuerttemberg law. We have a report whereby Stern had come back from Pressburg as a follower of Chassidism, wearing sidecurls and speaking with a Polish accent.[77] This, of course, made him immediately suspicious in the eyes of the correspondent, who probably had little understanding of Chassidism and the customs of its followers. In addition, Stern began to study Kabbalistic works and pursued a life of abstinence and fasting. During that phase he attacked *Kirchenrat* Maier as a bad influence in Judaism. But then, this report continues, he turned to the writings of Spinoza, denied positive religion and became a friend of Maier, whom he only recently had attacked.

Another account, signed by E.R. Rosenbaum of Wuerzburg, deals with the Jewish situation in Wuerttemberg and especially with Jacob Stern, who in 1874 had become rabbi of Buttenhausen.[78] It refers to an exchange of letters between Stern and Rosenbaum in 1869; in them Stern expressed resentment at being called a person without religion, at a time when his major concern in life was to spread the Jewish religion among the people. He did not object to being attacked openly, and he admitted to reform views and lack of observance of ritual laws. He stressed that he completed his scientific-theological training in six years. A few issues later, an open letter was addressed to Stern by Rabbi Menco Berlinger of Braunsbach (1860–1900), a leader of the Orthodox faction, who also attacked Stern for his disregard of Jewish law.[79] He particularly rejected Stern's insinuation that Orthodox Jews were not loyal to the King and the laws of the land.

To assign Stern to Buttenhausen, the smallest district rabbinate of Wuerttemberg, proved to be a poor decision. There soon developed mutual distrust between the Rabbi and his flock. He accused them of shoddy business practices, and they criticized him for his deviation from traditional observances. There were official investigations before the court and the *Oberkirchenbehoerde*, which led to Stern's dismissal from the position in 1883.[80] A few days later, he left the Jewish community altogether and became an editorial writer for the *Schwaebische Tagwacht*, a Socialist newspaper in Stuttgart. His subsequent writings included a pamphlet against the practice of *Shechitah*, the ritual slaughter of animals.[81] Stern's career from Chassidic Talmud student to Reform rabbi, Spinoza translator to Socialist writer, must have been a deep blow to his family and the Jewish community at large. The former Rabbi tried to return to the Jewish fold in his later years, but failed. When he died in 1910, a prayerbook was found before him, open at the page of the *Kaddish*, the Hebrew prayer for the dead.[82]

In 1884, almost as if to compensate for the Stern episode, the Jewish community, joined by many Christian friends, celebrated the 50th anniversary of Wassermann's appointment. Like his predecessor, he received in 1884 a high decoration from the King, which conferred upon him the status of nobility. A final highlight of Wassermann's career was his appearance before a court in Ulm—only a few days before his death in 1892 at the age of 81—to give testimony about the Talmud.

Hans Kleemann, a former clergyman and editor of the *Ulmer Schnellpost*, had published a series of derogatory articles about Jewish ethics.[83] When charged in court with libel, he defended himself by claiming that his information was based on the works of August Rohling (1839–1931). Rohling, a Catholic priest, had written a great deal of anti-Semitic literature, including *Der Talmudjude*, which was widely used as a source of anti-Jewish propaganda.[84] Wassermann appeared in court as an expert witness. In his presentation, he pointed to the many distortions in Rohling's book, which claimed that Jews were told to mistreat non-Jews and that Jews were permitted to perjure themselves in cases against Christians. Wassermann brought along books on ethics used in the Jewish schools in Wuerttemberg, and read them to the court as evidence against Kleemann's accusations. He added that all schools were under the supervision of the state and the local Christian clergy.

It was important for Wassermann to join the fight against anti-Semitism, which had been on the rise in the last decades of the 19th century. While Rohling befouled the atmosphere with his distortions about the teachings of the Talmud, the Berlin preacher, Adolf Stoecker (1835–1909), founder of the Christian Social Workers party, spread the anti-Semitic gospel in mass rallies throughout Germany. He came to Stuttgart, where he spoke to an overflow crowd in the *Liederhalle*, a very large hall in the city.[85] To counteract Stoecker and other such influences, a branch of the Christian *Verein Zur*

Abwehr des Antisemitismus, (Association for the Defense against Anti-Semitism) was formed locally.[86] Both Rohling and Stoecker were Christian clergymen, who argued that Jews could not be trusted and had no place in the Christian (i.e. German) state. For Rabbi Wassermann, who had labored so hard for religious equality, these accusations by fellow theologians must have come as a painful blow at the end of his long life.

Rabbi Theodor Kroner

More than a year passed before Wassermann's successor was selected. Ultimately, the choice fell upon Dr. Theodor Kroner. Wassermann, like his predecessor, had occupied two positions, an administrative one as clerical member of the *Oberkirchenbehoerde*, and a religious post as rabbi of the Stuttgart community. The first one had to be filled by appointment of the King, and the second by the Minister of Church and Schools. We are fortunate in having the document that describes the intricate selection process, and the careful considerations preceding the nomination of Kroner.[87] First, the authorities wanted to find a candidate among those eleven rabbis who were either native Wuerttemberger or already in a post in the state. None, however, seemed to fit the requirements of this double assignment, whether due to age, health or ability. Then there were 19 applicants classified as "foreign" (*Auswaertige*), rabbis, among whom Kroner seemed to be the most outstanding. Born May 12, 1845 at Dyhernfurth, Silesia, into a rabbinic family, he had obtained his training at the Jewish Theological Seminary and the University, both at Breslau, where he also visited the Catholic Teachers Seminary to prepare himself for the *Rektoratsexamen* (principals' examination). He had occupied important rabbinic and teaching positions, the last as director of the Jewish Teachers Seminary at Hanover. His good references were enhanced when Dr. Nathan Schmal, the legal member of the *Oberkirchenbehoerde*, visited with the authorities at

Hanover. Kroner was known to be both a good preacher and scholar as well as pleasant in appearance. Moreover, he was a supporter of national policy and the monarchy. There was some concern that Kroner was theologically too Orthodox, and would not be tolerant towards others. Kroner, however, had been able to lay such fears to rest during his own visit to Stuttgart. Thus, the road was cleared for royal and ministerial approvals.

It was high time that a new and strong personality, such as Kroner, took over leadership in religious affairs. Ever since 1892, the authorities had been dealing with a problem created by Dr. Samuel Gruen, district rabbi of Oberdorf since 1877.[88] Born in 1841 in Brod, Hungary, he had obtained his doctorate in Vienna and, prior to coming to Wuerttemberg, had been rabbi in Hohenems, Vorarlberg, Austria. Married however, and the father of two children, he seemed to have marital difficulties. Moreover, the official reports state, he had a chronic lung and heart condition, and had sought help twice in a sanatorium for nervous diseases. Gruen had petitioned the King for support in his drive for reform of Judaism, asking a trip to the Holy Land whence Gruen's new message should originate. While the selection of Kroner was still pending, Gruen petitioned the King to condition any appointment upon the following:

a. abrogation of prayers for return to Palestine and animal sacrifices.
b. establishment of a Sunday service, principally in German, in order to further the religious and patriotic sentiments.

This, he wrote, was the only way to shake the Jews out of their lethargy, and bring the religion of their fathers in harmony with the modern view of the world. This would not only help Jews in their desire to bring God's rule for all mankind, but more important, bring immortal credit to the King himself. In his petition, Gruen referred to articles in the *Schwaebische Chronik*, in which his ideas on the reform of Judaism were described.[89] We also know that he gave theosophical lectures in Stuttgart entitled; "What prevents Jews from acknowledging evangelism?" and "How can Israel renew itself from its degradation?"[90] Gruen finally was dismissed from his position in 1894 and died later in Vienna. While Gruen had urged the appointment of a Reform rabbi, there were others who called for a more conservative one.[91] They renewed the well-known request to separate the position of clerical member from that of communal rabbi of Stuttgart. Aside from these religious problems, there were also anti-Semitic speeches made by an agitator named Lenz, which must have added to the difficulties facing Kroner at the beginning of his assignment.[92] But it wouldn't take very long before one could see the effect of the new rabbi. Being a graduate of the *Juedisches Theologisches Seminar*, whose founder had been Zacharias Frankel, Kroner must have been a representative of the historical school, which did not object to reforms, as long as they did not conflict with historical Judaism. Stuttgart, a fastgrowing city community, had been for fifty years under the leadership of Reform rabbis, whose major objective was legal equality for their fellow Jews. They preached more ethics than traditional observance, and were often more interested in form than in content. In addition, it should be realized that city life, with its greater anonymity and economic opportunities, had loosened the traditional cohesiveness of its Jewish population, which, in the main, came from a rural environment. It would have been just short of a miracle had Kroner been able to immediately change the basic character of the community. Thus, he began to strengthen existing practices creating opportunities for training and study. For example, he converted ritual slaughter from a free enterprise by butchers, into a religious communal institution under the supervision of the rabbi. This eliminated abuses which had occurred in the past.[93] He enlarged the communal religious school and formed new associations for the young, who needed better education.[94] In 1894, he recommended to the *Oberkirchenbehoerde* the establishment of extension courses for teachers and cantors. These were funded by the *Central Kirchenkasse*, the *Behoerde*'s financial arm, and participants who came in for the Sunday afternoon sermons from the rural communities were granted a travel allowance. A year later, Kroner founded a *Talmud Torah* (group to study Judaism), all in all a sign of remarkable activity which drew praise even from the Orthodox *Israelit*, a newspaper not kindly disposed in the past towards the religious life of Wuerttemberg.[95] A few years later, the same paper again extolled the virtues of Kroner and his concern for the religious life of the community.[96] The fact of his being a disciple of the Breslau seminary—the Orthodox objected to their graduates in principle—did not diminish his stature. Not only Judaism in Wuerttemberg, but throughout Germany would be better off with rabbis like Kroner, the report maintained.

Another very important organization, instituted by Kroner, was the *Verein Wuerttembergischer Rabbiner* (Association of Wuerttemberg Rabbis), which began functioning in the mid 1890's. It must have been a great personal satisfaction to the founder to see his own son, Hermann, a member of this group.[97] To have the support of this group was particularly helpful in strengthening religious life throughout Wuerttemberg. Moreover, the struggle against the anti-Semitic forces was ongoing. The "*Schwaebische Reform Partei*," a small anti-Semitic party, had petitioned the state to have the *Shulchan Aruch* (Code of Law) translated, to show "that the Jews adhere to secret teachings, which allowed them to damage their fellow Christians." We know already that Wassermann tried to expose the falsity of these accusations based on Rohling's writings. Kroner, too, had been writing against Rohling, while director of the seminary in Muenster, Westphalen.[98] Now, in 1897, a debate took place before the Diet in Wuerttemberg in the presence of Dr. von Sarvey, Minister of Church and School who headed the government agency in charge of the *Israelitische Oberkirchenbehoerde*. Fortunately, wisdom prevailed and the petition for a translation was turned down because, "there had never been any complaint about Jewish books used in the schools of the land."[99]

In the area of teachers' appointments, unity of the rabbis also was important. Articles appeared in the press critical of Kroner, whose policies were allegedly robbing the communities of their former peace: In the days of Maier and Wassermann, harmony had reigned between Christian and Jewish authorities but Kroner, the non-Swabian, was trying to push Jewish life back into the Middle Ages.[100] Whereas his predecessors had reduced religious differences for the sake of fuller citizen rights, Kroner was emphasizing rituals and ceremonies in order to keep better control of the Jews. Such an attitude displeased many a Wuerttemberger, for it was strange to the character of the land. A second article put the blame less on Kroner than on the general situation, the shrinking of the rural communities, and the need for a general reform of the *Oberkirchenbehoerde* which had been so long delayed. A third article expressed full confidence of the association of Israelite teachers in the leadership of Kroner.[101] It further hailed the good relations between him, and all teachers in the many districts with which he has close contacts. Any criticism was only sporadic, this article concluded.

The many associations founded and developed by Kroner clearly show his objective of strengthening the community's religious fiber by building bridges between all factions in the land. Kroner was a man of peace who disliked confrontations, although he did try to maintain the authority of his high office. In his historical review Kroner only reports the positive, without mentioning the problems he faced at the beginning of his ministry.[102] He could have easily criticized his predecessors, Maier and Wassermann; instead he credited them for trying to adjust Jewish living to the realities of large city communities. He related the traditional rural communities to the influence of the three large Orthodox strongholds to the north of Wuerttemberg: Fuerth, Wuerzburg, and Frankfurt. But even cities such as Stuttgart and Heilbronn had small Orthodox congregations. He must have realized that the majority of his own community had moved into the liberal column but, Kroner maintained, there existed a third party—in addition to liberal and Orthodox—of great influence in the community. This was the party of unity and peace within. Apparently, this was Kroner's party, which, though never formally organized, exercised its influence through individuals.

Kroner showed religious flexibility when needed, but also firmness when his authority was challenged. Early in his assignment, he forbade the previously practiced participation of rabbis and cantors at cremations. Years later, he yielded to the request of the *Oberkirchenbehoerde*, leaving attendance to the discretion of the individual.[103] As for his firmness, the following incident is especially characteristic.[104] It not only shows Kroner's desire to reinstate old synagogue practices, but also the lack of religious autonomy of an individual community. The issue revolved around the *Bar Mitzvah* ceremony, which signifies the coming of age of a Jewish boy. It was traditionally observed by the youngster being called to the *Torah* (Holy Scroll) and his reading of a portion from it. The 1838 synagogue order had abolished this custom of *Torah* reading on the grounds that it was not a religious requirement and that the time for learning to read the *Torah* could be used for more practical pursuits. We know that this order, as well as other changes, were never fully accepted, however, and the incident of 1905 became known only because it reached the highest state authorities for a decision. In this year, Mr. David Reis obtained the approval of the rabbi and the community to celebrate his son's *Bar Mitzvah* in the old tradition, meaning for his son to read the *Torah* in the synagogue. But his petition to the *Oberkirchenbehoerde* in Stuttgart was twice turned down as being in violation of the order of 1838. The decision had been three to one, with the dissenting vote cast by Kroner, who favored the traditional ceremony and stated his reasons in a long memorandum to the Ministry. He contended that disapproval would be a gross interference in the religious life of the community. The vote showed lack of responsiveness to religious requirements on the part of the Jewish members of the *Oberkirchenbehoerde*, who, as a rule, had been chosen from the very affluent sector and had often been criticized for being disinterested in tradition. The incident itself made people understand why, in Jewish circles, there was a frequently cited comment that the best Jew in the *Oberkirchenbehoerde* was its president who, by law, had always been an official of the Christian faith. As a result of his dissatisfaction, Reis, an Orthodox Jew, became, in 1911 one of the founders of a separate religious association, called "Adass Jeschurun," with Dr. Jonas Ansbacher as its first rabbi.[105]

A similar argument against interference into the religious affairs of community associations was advanced in 1910, but this time at Kroner himself. The documents reveal enough to present the outlines of the incident, although not all details can be determined.[106] We have previously learned that an Orthodox association, the *Israelitische Religionsgesellschaft*, had been formed in Stuttgart in 1878. Although small in numbers, it had established its own synagogue—considering the main synagogue with its organ to be ritually unacceptable—religious school, ritual bath (*Mikvah*) and slaughterer (*Shochet*). The association had never separated itself from the community legally, although spiritually it considered itself apart. Thus Kroner, at least in the eyes of the government, was the religious head of this portion of the community, and part of his responsibilities was to certify the qualifications of its *Shochet*, J. Sulzbacher. It seems that Kroner initially approved this man, but when the approval came due for renewal, Sulzbacher refused to appear before Kroner and lost his certification as a communal *Shochet*. The Orthodox became greatly aroused and submitted a petition to the Ministry charging that Kroner, a non-Orthodox rabbi, was not qualified to pass judgment on an Orthodox slaughterer. His action, they held, constituted interference in the religious life of the individual, a matter in which the state, by whose authority Kroner acted, would not want to become involved. The issue developed into a larger controversy, as traditional elements throughout Wuerttemberg, organized into the Association for the Interests of Law-Abiding Judaism, supported the position of the Orthodox Stuttgart association. This attack against his personal integrity must have hurt Kroner deeply. At the onset of his assignment in Stuttgart, he had reorganized the procedures of ritual slaughter and made it an integral part of communal functions. For the sake of strictly religious observance, he had taken the slaughtering away from the butchers, and made supervision a responsibility of the rabbi. In 1901, he had taken over the then *Shochet* of the *Israelitische Religionsgesellschaft,* Jacob Hirsch, and placed him on the communal staff because the Orthodox association was unable to pay him an adequate salary. At the same time, he allowed Hirsch to continue worshipping in the association's synagogue, although by law he could have insisted on his attendance at the communal house of worship. Kroner's concern for traditional values and religious harmony was evident from his leadership in the association of Wuerttemberg rabbis.[107] This group consisted of all communal rabbis, some of whom were either Orthodox or Neolog.[108] They played an important role, thanks to their inner harmony, in raising the level of religious observance and Jewish education throughout the land. The rabbis represented a united front; this helped them not just in their relations with the authorities, but even more so in dealing with a group of teachers who were frequently very critical about their functioning. As can be seen in letters to local newspapers and subsequent comments by the *Oberkirchenbehoerde,* the teachers charged that there were too many rabbinic positions—there were a total of 13—and too many visitations on the part of the district rabbis.[109] The number could easily be reduced to six, and the resulting savings could be utilized for an increase in teachers' and cantors' salaries. The teachers claimed that in neighboring Bavaria, Baden and Hessen, one district rabbi took care of 2000 to 3000 persons, whereas in Wuerttemberg the ratio was one rabbi to 950 persons. In his comment, *Ministerialdirektor* Dr. Hermann von Habermaas, president of the *Oberkirchen-behoerde*, pointed to the fact that, unlike other states, the rabbis of Wuerttemberg were the presiding officers of their local church bodies; this required a great deal of their time.[110] Moreover, their academic training allowed them to teach in the upper classes of the secondary schools. At the same time, the visitations and examinations of the synagogues and schools in their district were of utmost importance to the religious life which again makes a reduction of the rabbinical strength unwarranted. With understanding personalities like Habermaas and especially his successor Dr. Karl von Baelz, who served as the last president until 1924, the long-desired revision of the *Oberkirchenbehoerde*, came to fruition. Kroner himself was actively engaged in all deliberations; they, however, were seriously interrupted with the outbreak of World War I in 1914.

2. | EDUCATION

Schools

A special characteristic of the Jewish people is their concern for education. Biblically ordained—"And you shall teach your children"—it gave vitality to their existence and sustained them throughout their long and often painful history. In the Middle Ages, the ideal of Jewish education in Germany was mastery of Hebrew, Bible and Talmud.[1] The Middle Ages was a time when the state did not concern itself with the education of its Jewish residents. Education of Jewish youngsters was handled by private teachers, paid for by the parents and in cases of dire need by the community. The quality of education was uneven, often limited by a community's poverty and the lack of qualified teachers. Higher Jewish, i.e. Talmudic training, in southern Germany, could be obtained at the academies of Frankfurt and Fuerth. Attendance at these centers was mainly reserved for the intellectually and financially able, however, and most youths had to be satisfied with whatever local opportunities presented themselves. Secular subjects were not taught at all, vocational training was non-existent, and earning of one's daily bread depended upon petty trade. Yiddish was the language spoken by Ashkenazi Jews from the tenth century to the nineteenth century. Gradually, voices, both Jewish and non-Jewish, could be heard urging Jews to study German as one of the best ways of social and legal advancement. To this end, the eighteenth-century Jewish philosopher, Moses Mendelssohn, translated the Pentateuch, a text familiar to most Jews, into German, using Hebrew letters for their understanding. Although this was considered an abuse of the Holy Text in traditional quarters, the translation contributed greatly to the knowledge of German and the cause of enlightenment.

In Wuerttemberg itself, the government attended to the education of its Jews through an order of King Wilhelm on November 18, 1817.[2] It directed the establishment of committees under the Protestant and Catholic school councils, which were then in charge of education. In 1825, both councils issued further administrative instructions that amounted to compulsory education of all Jewish boys and girls, age six to fourteen. Instruction was to take place either in existing local schools or in newly formed Jewish schools with state-recognized teachers. Both church councils made provisions to free Jewish children attending local schools from Christian religious instruction. Isaak Hess, whom we have met previously in the deliberations about the *Oberkirchenbehoerde*, was very actively engaged in the drive for secular education. His petition of 1817 had resulted in the issuance of King Wilhelm's directive. We also know of his forceful presentations to the Diet, charging them with responsibility for education of the Jews, who would then be prepared for a productive life in society. Another driving force was Rabbi Gabriel Adler of Muehringen, who in 1821 announced a plan for compulsory education of boys and girls, age six to fourteen, which would include secular subjects in its curriculum.[3] Designed for the Schwarzwald region, which was Adler's rabbinic district, the plan called for rabbinic supervision of Jewish schools. In this respect it did not succeed, because the Christian state authorities insisted on retaining supervision of all schools. Since most Jewish parents preferred to send their children to institutions of their own, the major communities in the 1820's, established schools in Nordstetten, Muehringen, Esslingen, Pflaumloch, Laupheim, Jebenhausen, Buttenhausen, Oberdorf, Baisingen, Buchau and Hochberg.

The lesson plans of the Jewish schools corresponded to those of other elementary schools in the state. In 1827, Dr. Carl Weil, the private academic teacher of Solomon Jacob Kaulla, proposed to organize a *Realschule*, i.e. high school classes, for rural and city communities. Weil's proposal never became a reality, however, as rural communities seem to have been satisfied with elementary schools,whereas the city communities were not strong enough to support such a school during the 1820's and 1830's. Moreover, the city parents preferred to send their children to the Gymnasium, upon whose completion students could enter the university.

The new school laws represented a great step towards legal equality of the Wuerttemberg Jews, but it must be pointed out that initially the cost for new schools had to be borne by the Jewish communities alone. Not until 1840 did the local community pay for the school, and then, only if 60 or more Jewish families resided in the area. All other schools, named voluntary religious, had to be financed by the Jewish community, which often created great financial hardships for teachers and parents. Still, these voluntary schools continued to increase, until they reached their peak in1838 when there were twenty-eight throughout Wuerttemberg.

Teachers

In time, teachers came to play a very important role in the Jewish life of Wuerttemberg. As state supervision necessitated a more formal type of training, Jewish students were admitted to the Christian Teachers' Seminary in Esslingen in 1821. The three-year course was free; indeed, earlier students had received an annual stipend of 75 florins from the King's private treasury. One of the first Jewish graduates in 1825 was Leopold Liebmann (1805–1893), who then remained as the teacher of the newly formed Jewish school. His career would become intimately involved with the development of Wuerttemberg's educational life. His duties were manifold: he conducted religious services, which included weekly sermons

and educational talks to the youth; when confirmation became an important phase of education, he prepared an appropriate booklet. At first, he gave private lessons in Hebrew
and Jewish religion to all Jewish students at the seminary;
these lessons later became an official assignment of seven
hours weekly, eventually increased by the *Oberkirchenbehoerde* to twelve hours. In another chapter we will look at
Liebmann's role as Head (*Hausvater*) of the Jewish Orphan
Home in Esslingen and founder of the "*Verein Israelitischer
Lehrer und Vorsaenger*" (Association of Jewish Teachers and
Cantors). Suffice it to say here that at his retirement in 1873,
Liebmann had trained over one hundred teachers from
Wuerttemberg and its environs. We also know that some
Jewish applicants were privately prepared with the full approval of the authorities by both Catholic and Protestant
teachers, an indication of the authorities' interest in helping a
fledgling Jewish teachers' profession. It took quite a few years
until properly certified teachers began functioning, for in
1828 there were only 22 in the official statistics of Wuerttemberg.[4]

The same statistics reveal that the *Vorsaenger* (cantors)
also became involved in teaching. They were very important,
inasmuch as they had for a long time been the liturgical
leaders of all religious services. Until the rabbi's new role
emerged, as described previously, the cantor led all services.
The rabbi's role had been one of religious judge, who only
spoke twice a year to the community in preparation for
Passover and the Day of Atonement. With the reorganization
of the Jewish communities, based on the law of 1828, the 51
rabbis of Wuerttemberg were reduced to 13 district rabbis
and the 67 cantors to 41. This was done by a process of state
examinations, which both rabbis and cantors had to undergo.
It followed that in communities without a rabbi, the cantor
assumed many of the rabbi's functions. In 1831, the young
Oberkirchenbehoerde issued a ministerial directive to the
Oberschulbehoerde: to combine the position of the cantor

with that of the teacher. Interestingly enough, the initiative for such a move came from the school authorities, because it was the teacher who held a state position, whereas the cantor did not yet enjoy such a status. These were the years when *Kirchenrat* Maier was busy reorganizing communal life for the Jews of Wuerttemberg, which made many cantorial positions shaky and some even superfluous.

The supervision of Jewish schools by Christian authorities continued until the twentieth century. In places where the Protestants were stronger, it was the local minister, and in Catholic areas, it was the priest who exercised supervisory functions. Rabbis and other Jewish community officials had a role in administrative matters only.[5] The authority of the Christian clergy extended even over the religious education in Jewish schools, although this was modified in 1851, when the Israelite *Oberkirchenbehoerde* obtained for rabbis a share in the supervision.

In 1848, *Kirchenrat* Maier attempted to place Jewish schools under rabbinic supervision.[6] To this end he had called a meeting that was attended by fifteen teachers. The teachers' response, however, was not as Maier had hoped. They objected because the limited number of rabbis would preclude their supervising all schools. Not all rabbis had enough pedagogic training, they argued, although pedagogy had been part of the state examination for rabbis under the law of 1828. Another, more understandable, point was that the Christian inspectors had been a very friendly group, which did not interfere with their teaching. They acted, the Jewish teachers said, as representatives of the state, and not as clergymen of different faiths. Moreover, these inspectors protected the teachers from improper demands of the local Jewish community.

This last argument is a very revealing one, as it points to the role of the Jewish teachers in relation to the rabbis and the community. Tensions in all sectors were sure to exist in places where teachers also functioned as cantors. In 1841, the

Israelite *Oberkirchenbehoerde*, with *Kirchenrat* Maier as the principal organizer of communal affairs, issued a detailed list of duties of the cantors.[7] They were in length and content similar to the one issued at the same time for rabbis, which made good sense. For the cantor was, in the absence of a rabbi, the religious leader of the community. Obviously these instructions were of an ideal nature that only an extraordinarily gifted and motivated individual would have been able to follow. Aside from his liturgical, preaching, and teaching roles, the cantor was to be a member of the *Kirchenvorsteheramt* (church presidium). This was the selected group of three to five elected community officials, whose job was to oversee the general administration, particularly its financial and welfare affairs. Their job was to assess individual taxes, to prepare the budget, and to submit it to the district office (*Oberamt*) which in turn forwarded it to the *Oberkirchenbehoerde*. These were indeed very complicated tasks and very time consuming. The rabbis and the cantors were the presiding officers and also the record keepers. With the rabbis frequently absent on district visits, it stands to reason that the major workload fell upon the cantor, who, particularly in rural communities, was often the most educated individual. Does it then come as a surprise that a regular teacher was reluctant to assume the additional duties of a cantor who was frequently caught in the struggles between rabbi and community? On the other hand, a cantor who was subject to the authority of the *Oberkirchenbehoerde* was anxious to acquire the status and financial security available to the teacher, whose superior authority was the *Oberschulbehoerde*. There were other problems which made the teachers' position difficult. There were limited classroom facilities, frequently reminiscent of the old *Cheder*, aptly translated into the German word *Winkelstube*, i.e. a hole in the wall, where boys and girls perched together for daily school work. The parents' attitude toward the teacher was frequently very low—a holdover from the eighteenth century. At that time, it was assumed that anyone versed in Talmud could become a teacher. The new teacher, seminary-trained and examined, was a novelty. His job was not only to educate the children, but also their parents. Thus, the government's interest was very helpful in establishing a better atmosphere for teaching, through official recognition and financial security.

Another and perhaps more important problem was the type of school books available. Since all elementary education in Wuerttemberg was controlled by Protestant or Catholic authorities, the schools used books oriented toward these religious persuasions. The Jewish teachers often found themselves either adapting these books to their own needs, or publishing books of their own. We have seen that the Israelite *Oberkirchenbehoerde* had issued a number of school books in the 1830's, mainly with the help of *Kirchenrat* Maier.[8] It is doubtful that these publications were accepted by all the teachers, many of whom were traditionally oriented.[9] The format and contents, moreover, were often patterned according to Protestant examples. The Jewish teachers' criticism came to light in connection with a directive issued on November 19, 1855, by the Protestant consistory.[10] It ordered that Jewish candidates for entrance to the seminary, memorize a selection of songs and Biblical passages similar to those in the book used in entrance examinations of Protestant candidates. The *"Volkslehrer"* report complains that none of the Biblical passages had to be known in Hebrew, only in German, which had been taken from Martin Luther's Bible translation and was often incorrect. Moreover, although published twenty years earlier, the book from which the songs were selected really never found a home in the synagogue or family. Songs for Jews should be composed by Jews, contended *Volkslehrer*, and not borrowed from another religion. The report concludes with criticism reflecting the religious reservations of Jewish teachers in rural schools. It tells of Rabbi Wassermann of Muehringen who traveled to Frankfurt at the request of the *Oberkirchenbehoerde* to discuss the publication of a *Lesebuch* (reading book) with Doctors Stern and Jost, two well-known teachers of the *Israelitische Real-schule*, the high school recognized for its reform orientation. The report expressed fears that a book edited by these men would be too rationalistic in religious outlook, and too sophisticated in approach for Wuerttemberg's rural schools.

The criticism against the *Oberkirchenbehoerde* and its clerical member, *Kirchenrat* Maier, reached its peak in the 1860's. Although carried on anonymously, everybody must have known that *Lehrer* Ludwig Stern was the erudite leader of the opposition. Yet even this very strong confrontation between rabbi and teacher did not basically change the course of events. Other more powerful social forces ultimately influenced the fate of rural communities: emigration to the United States and flight to the cities were prime factors which will be discussed in further chapters. Here it is of interest that *not* a rabbi but a teacher, would attack the reform leader in Wuerttemberg. This type of opposition would have been unlikely, unless the teacher was firm in his convictions and sure of his position. Indeed, Stern's attack represents the strongest confrontation between the forces of Orthodoxy and Reform in Wuerttemberg's Jewish history. Wuerttemberg's Jews more often demonstrated a spirit of cooperation among different factions, who banded together in pursuit of common causes.

The Waisenhaus

A fine example of this spirit is the "Association for the Care of Poor Israelite Orphans and Neglected Children," out of which grew the "Israelite Orphan and Education Institution Wilhelmspflege of Esslingen."[11] Its history is a shining example of general concern on the part of Jews and non-Jews for the less fortunate in their midst. The association was the brainchild of Isaak Hess of Ellwangen, who, in 1831, obtained official permission to organize the care of orphans. In this noble endeavor he received support from all segments of society, including the royal family; succeeding chairmen of the association represented the social elite of the Jewish community of Stuttgart. [12] Moreover, the prolonged tenure of their presidencies alone is a reflection of their dedication to this worthy cause. During the first ten years, 57 boys and girls age six to eleven, were placed in teachers' homes throughout the state. When this proved unsatisfactory, the association purchased a building which was dedicated in 1842. Officially known as *Wilhelmspflege*, in honor of King Wilhelm I, it was popularly called the *Waisenhaus* (Orphans' Home). Its financial success for close to one hundred years depended upon the voluntary contributions of rich and poor throughout Wuerttemberg and abroad. A special contribution was solicited from all communities on the Sabbath before the Day of Atonement *(Shabbat Shuvah)* and all annual reports attested to the solvency of this ever-expanding institution which educated over six hundred youngsters during its existence. The lions' share of credit for its success must be reserved for the three men, called *Hausvaeter* (Fathers of the House) who were responsible for its internal operation. They were Leopold Liebmann from 1842 to 1873, Leopold Stern from 1873 to 1899 and, finally, his son-in-law, Theodor Rothschild from 1899 to 1939. The *Waisenhaus* was ransacked on November 10, 1938, the infamous *Kristallnacht*, and the children dispersed.[13] It was reopened for a short while, but then closed entirely. Rothschild himself continued teaching in Stuttgart until 1942, the year he was deported to the Theresienstadt concentration camp where he died in 1944.

All three housefathers were unique personalities. Liebmann, as already noted, was one of the first Jewish graduates of the teachers seminary at Esslingen. He remained in that community from 1825, first as teacher of the newly organized Jewish school and instructor of Hebrew and religion at the Seminary. In 1842, he became *Hausvater* of the *Waisenhaus*, initially providing a home and education for 26 orphaned boys and girls. The curriculum went beyond that of an average primary school in the teaching of a foreign language, either English or French. The class routine and discipline were severe, although one could notice signs of modern pedagogic methods. This strictness prevented a close relationship between staff and children. There also was frequent infighting among staff members. Religious life was strict, with Liebmann delivering a sermon every Saturday which the children had to write from memory the following day. When he retired amid great honors in 1873, he had provided shelter and education to over 140 orphans, giving them vocational training and preparing them to stand on their own feet.

Liebmann's successor, Leopold Stern, had also been a graduate of the Esslingen seminary and a teacher at Braunsbach, before becoming *Hausvater* at the age of twenty-eight. He was less of a disciplinarian and more progressive in his educational program. His goal was to convert the institution into a family-style home. In this he was greatly helped by his wife Sara Essinger, daughter of a physician from Oberdorf, who was also well learned in Talmud.[14] They were parents of five children who were treated like all the other youngsters, attending the same school in the *Waisenhaus*, eating at the same tables and playing together in their leisure time. There were now over forty orphans in the house, which Stern not only enlarged by building a third floor, but also arranged a special place for worship. As his curriculum included much free time in which to pursue personal interests, he built a swimming pool and expanded the garden where the children could plant and enjoy their own fruit. At Stern's twenty-fifth anniversary the King honored him with the rank of *Oberlehrer*. Unfortunately, a year later, in 1899, he died at barely 54 years of age.

Landflucht (Flight from the Country)

Before the story of the *Waisenhaus* leads into the twentieth century, let us turn our attention to important developments in the second half of the nineteenth century. These affect not only the role of the teachers, but also, and even more so, the rural communities of Wuerttemberg with repercussions for the Jewish situation in all areas. These developments, generally classified under the heading *Landflucht*, involved two movements: First, away from the country through emigration overseas, and, second, movement from the rural communities to the cities within Germany. Emigration principally led across the Atlantic to the United States, although there was emigration to other states within Europe as well. The latter was small and difficult to pinpoint. Detailed statistics exist for those Jews who left Wuerttemberg for the United States between 1848 and 1855.[15] A portion of these statistics are reproduced in the Appendix, as they constitute a valuable resource for family history. They are based on official information gathered by the districts where emigrants applied for an exit permit. Although not complete, we learn names, ages, places of origin, occupation, family status, assets and reasons for emigration. Most of the people leaving did so to improve their personal circumstances. The majority were young single males, although quite a few females emigrated, all seeking better opportunities for matrimony. There were also men with large families as well as widows with children.

The rural community of Jebenhausen is a specially illustrative example of a once flourishing Jewish settlement and its dissolution through emigration overseas and moves into the cities.[16] Between 1830 and 1870, more than 300 persons left for the United States, reducing the community to less than 60 families. Parallel with these departures occurred moves to nearby cities, particularly Goeppingen, which became a big textile industry center with many prominent Jewish firms.[17] These departures led to the closing of the elementary school in 1865, because it did not have the required 15 students. Subsequent moves to establish a religious school ten years later also had to be given up. The district rabbinate was relocated to Goeppingen in 1868, and the community finally dissolved in 1899, with only the cemetery remaining as a reminder of the past.

This brief outline of the Jebenhausen story may be seen in many communities, particularly the smaller ones. Frequently, emigration to the cities or abroad was undertaken by the younger and more affluent residents, who left behind them the older and poorer population. The financial solvency of the community underwent upheaval, affecting the status of its only paid official, the teacher and his family. Relatively speaking, the elementary level teacher was in a good position if he could stay in a Jewish school throughout his lifetime. His salary, including pension, was paid by the state, as pointed out by Leopold Liebmann of Esslingen and Isaak Weil of Kochendorf, both teachers and cantors, in their memorandum to the Diet on August 6, 1862: 300 florins for rural teachers and 400 to 500 florins for city teachers. For this sum, the duties of a Jewish teacher often included those of a cantor, leading religious services once or twice on weekdays, and two to three times on the Sabbath. Moreover, many teachers were responsible for sermons each Sabbath and holiday, religious education, administrative duties and visiting the sick. And while the teachers were pleased to perform all these duties, little time was left for anything else. For instance, unlike Christian teachers, they could not derive any side income from agricultural work, and there was seldom benefit of property connected to the position of a Jewish teacher.

The situation of the religious school teacher was even worse, according to the memorandum. Although he may have spent many years in such a school, this teacher's chances for promotion to an elementary school position were very slim. If his school should be dissolved he usually would be forced to take a cantorial job, with neither a proper pension nor provisions for his widow. Poor salaries and retirement benefits tended to attract the unqualified, to the detriment of religious and educational standards with which the state was presumed interested. In the end, the memorandum recommended continued state supervision of the Jewish schools.

In order to further the common interests of all the teachers, Liebmann organized the Association of Israelite Teachers and Cantors in 1862. Three years later, this group had more than fifty members. One of its objectives was to raise funds for needy teachers and their families, which was a direct reflection of their poor pay and retirement benefits. Liebmann headed the association until 1887 when his advanced age (he was 82) forced him to decline reelection. The group itself was very active, meeting frequently in committees and plenary sessions. Its activities were regularly reported in Jewish newspapers such as *Israelit* and *Allgemeine Zeitung des Judentums*.

The problems faced by the teachers were not only financial. There were questions involving curriculum, textbooks and school facilities. Additionally, they had to explain the role and duties of a Jewish teacher to the Christian supervisory authorities. And while the teachers always expressed their appreciation to the state for its support, one has to realize that Jewish communities had special needs based on their long tradition. These needs changed in intensity from year to year and from community to community, as is evident from two memoranda from the teacher's group to the Ministry.[18] Each reflects changes since the previously cited memorandum as well as difficulties within the teaching profession. The teachers urged that preference in hiring be given to those trained at the Esslingen seminary. This, in turn, would ensure that candidates were familiar with Wuerttemberg's elementary education. The teachers also recommended that the number of candidates be related to the number of vacancies; they also complained that the authorities did not announce vacancies, which prevented local candidates from competing for these positions. This was particularly important for teachers in the small rural communities where the future life span was limited. Opportunities for employment in the city were reduced by the urban practice of hiring temporary teachers, who sometimes had not passed all the required examinations. This was particularly the case for cantors, who according to law could be appointed directly by the communities themselves. The freedom occurred not through a loophole, but as a holdover from early custom where the cantor was the only one to lead the services. As the public services leader of the community, he carried a special religious responsibility and position. Thus, he was often chosen by the members directly. Direct elections were frequently influenced by personal interventions on behalf of the candidate, however, making choices subject to the influence of relatives, a process disruptive of communal harmony. The teachers preferred appointment of cantors by higher authority such as the *Oberkirchenbehoerde*, which would be aware of candidates' qualifications and eliminate undue local pressure.

Another serious consideration was the fate of the elementary schools themselves. As we have seen in places with more than 60 Jewish families, the general community paid for their upkeep. With the decline of the rural communities, there were by 1911 only six locations in Wuerttemberg with one-class Jewish elementary schools. They were: Laupheim, Rexingen, Buchau, Buttenhausen, Oberdorf and Crailsheim.[19] The teachers urged that the minimum number of Jewish families be reduced from sixty to thirty. They feared losing their publicly financed positions, inasmuch as the prevailing system of church control over elementary schools in Wuerttemberg precluded the appointment of a Jewish teacher at a Protestant or Catholic school.

Similar problems affected the voluntary schools, which were mainly financed by the Jewish community with a small contribution from the state. By 1911, their number had shrunk to sixteen, located at Edelfingen, Laudenbach, Hohebach, Nordstetten, Baisingen, Niederstetten, Muehringen, Creglingen, Sontheim, Michelbach, Ernsbach, Braunsbach,

Olnhausen, Talheim, Freudental, and Archshofen. The state threatened to withdraw its limited support if the number of Jewish schoolchildren would go below twelve. The teachers urged that the number be lowered to six or eight, lest most of these schools disappear and with them Jewish education as a viable profession.

One compromise was to allow Jewish children to attend Christian schools, while receiving religious training from communal Jewish teachers. This was tried, but the results were not satisfactory for a number of reasons. Such instruction was done outside the regular classrooms in places maintained by the Jewish community. School hours were after regular hours at the elementary school, giving them the character of being less important. Moreover, attendance was not obligatory, causing much absenteeism due to poorly motivated children or parents.

Stuttgart

While the rural communities and their state-supported educational programs suffered from population flight to nearby cities, these cities did not generate Jewish elementary schools of their own. The best example of this is Stuttgart, which derived its numerical increases from the rural communities. The need for religious education was met with the establishment of a communal religious school. Its development is carefully recorded and shows slow and often unsatisfactory progress.[20] In the 1850's some urged the founding of a Jewish elementary school, but other circles considered this unnecessary, and some even called the 'unsuccessful' proposal a return to the ghetto. At a time when political and social advance was foremost in the people's minds, there was more interest in sending children to public schools that could ultimately lead to high schools and universities. There were also open conflicts between Maier and Wassermann, the rabbis of Stuttgart, and some of the community leaders. Maier's interests were mainly directed towards integrating the community into the body politic, a goal that countered efforts to strengthen Jewish identity. By the time Wassermann came upon the scene in 1873, the educational pattern of the Stuttgart community was already too well established to allow for basic changes. The battle for an improved religious school was led by Gottlieb Sontheimer, who served as one of the elected community officers from 1866 until his death in 1897. The challenge was not only to improve the community religious school, particularly in the area of Hebrew training and student attendance, but also to provide religious education for the boys and girls attending the high schools of the city. Christian Heinrich Dillmann (1829–1893), founder and rector of the Stuttgarter *Realgymnasium* was very helpful in the latter area.[21] His cooperation led to the beginning of religious classes for Jewish children in the high schools of Stuttgart. Teaching at these higher institutions required an academically trained person, which necessitated the appointment of another rabbi to assist Wassermann, who, due to his advanced age, was unable to assume these new responsibilities. The choice fell upon Dr. David Stoessel (1848–1919) from Lackenbach, Hungary, who began his duties as assistant rabbi and teacher of religion in 1881. In spite of all attempts toward an improved curriculum and new teaching staff, the quality of religious education remained very thin. One need not read through the lines of a report on education, prepared by Rabbi Th. Kroner, in order to understand the author's criticism. His report for the period 1880 to 1894 states, in part:

> Religious instruction is given at the community religious school and the public schools. At the religious school there are three teachers for forty-two boys and forty-two girls. They are divided into five classes, with eleven hours of instruction . . . there is no proper lesson plan . . . the children do not become sufficiently acquainted with the religious service or religious obligations . . . Only two classrooms are at their disposal . . . At the higher schools there are one hundred and

four boys and eighty-one girls . . . Instruction covers biblical
and Jewish history and teaching of religion. Of the higher
school students, eighty-four take Hebrew lessons at the community religious school. Thus, one hundred and one students
did not receive any training in Hebrew. Considering a community of seven hundred families with only one hundred and
eighty-five children receiving religious instruction, of whom
the larger number did not participate in Hebrew, and compar-
ing this with the religious instruction in other communities,
one can understand why the church elders desired a thorough
improvement.[22]

The final phase of Kroner's report covers the period from
1894 to 1911, coinciding with the author's own rabbinic
leadership. One can see why his extensive experience enabled him to develop coordinated lesson plans for both the
communal religious school and public high schools. Kroner
enlarged the number of classes, providing for advanced education by forming two associations: the *Berthold Auerbach*
and the *Talmud Tora Verein*. His aim was to stimulate the
interest of students and their parents by impressing them
with the importance of Jewish education. His individual
efforts were greatly helped by a directive of the Ministry,
making religious instruction obligatory for boys and girls,
age six to fourteen, attending high schools.[23] This must have
been a great struggle for Kroner, as is evident from his report
which sounds like an indictment against certain attitudes
within the community:

The efforts to allow religious instruction at the high schools
were met by one special obstacle. This was the all too great
caprice shown by some parents and some children towards
religious instruction. A very considerable number stayed
away from this instruction, and in some classes even the most
skillful teacher was unable to establish a discipline similar to
the obligatory subjects. This bad situation grew even worse
with the introduction of Hebrew into the high schools and the
entrance of Galician and Russian children into the commu-

nity school. Both kept practically all children of native German Jewish families away from the community school. It had become an urgent necessity to obtain for religious instruction at the high schools the required equal status which would allow for respect on the part of parents and children . . .[24]

Years later the obligatory status of religious instruction was extended to the upper classes also, but only for biblical history. The study of Hebrew remained optional, as interest in Jewish education in Stuttgart was generally on the decline despite all Kroner's efforts. Those families who desired a more traditional lifestyle and intensive instruction for their children turned to the *Israelitische Religionsgesellschaft*, a small Orthodox association which had been operating in the city since 1878.

3. | THE PEOPLE AND THEIR CUSTOMS

Our narrative now turns to the people and their development in the rural and city communities. In presenting pictures of their life styles we will better understand the changes which transformed them from "Jews living in Germany" to "German Jews." In this chapter we will concentrate on rural communities and subsequently evaluate the forces which molded the people in the cities. The "Jew in Germany" lived his personal life in a restricted setting governed by the laws and customs of Jewish tradition. His community was like a "state within a state." He accepted the fact that he was considered an outsider without the rights and opportunities granted to Christian citizens. When the rabbis moved from country to country, as they often did, they moved within a Jewish sphere independent of political and geographic borders. The Jews did not like this state of affairs which denied them the security of living in peace with their neighbors. They accepted it as a part of their being in exile, ultimately to be returned to the Holy Land by the intervention of the Almighty.

Then the gates of the ghetto began to open. In Wuerttemberg, we have taken the year 1828—although in individual cases it occurred sooner—as the beginning of a new order when the Jews began to achieve, with the consent of the authorities, a new status. The speed with which Jews adopted the German language and culture is evidence that they saw in it an improvement over their old conditions. They shed the national contents of their Jewish tradition and replaced it with German nationalism. At the end of the nineteenth century they called themselves "*deutsche Staatsbuerger juedischen Glaubens*" (German citizens of Jewish faith), thereby trying to show that any difference between themselves and their fellow citizens of the Christian faith was only a matter of confessional preference. In Wuerttemberg a Swabian ingredient was included in the new status. When the Jewish Orphans Home in Esslingen, the pride and joy of a charitable state, celebrated one hundred years of its existence, in 1931, Dr. Otto Hirsch, then president of the *Israelitische Oberrat*, congratulated the institution by saying: "that he saw in it a genuine Jewish and Swabian spirit."[1] These were sincerely expressed words, reflecting his faith in a symbiosis between Germans and Jews.

The Community

Ever since the destruction of the Temple in Jerusalem, Jewish communal life had always revolved around the synagogue. For our own narrative about synagogue life, we have selected Niederstetten, in northern Wuerttemberg because we are fortunate in having a carefully documented account written by Bruno Stern, whose ancestors lived in this community for many generations.[2] Its Jewish settlement dates back to 1675 and the community had become in 1807, due to political realignment, a part of Wuerttemberg. We will single out from Stern's report those events that seem characteristic of other settlements of the state. Throughout the nineteenth century Niederstetten's Jewish population ranged from 100 to 200 persons, but its community, though small, was well organized thanks to its long existence and its relative affluence. This is evident from the fact that, in 1824, this small group was able to build a new synagogue and a community house out of its own resources. The total cost of these buildings was close to 8,000 florins of which one thousand was donated by one Laemmlein Loew with the stipulation that each year fifteen florins be spent on wood for the poor and three florins, on the anniversary of his death, for the poor and for prayers. Each member, male and female, had a synagogue seat and prayer stand for their ritual belongings. There was, of course, strict separation of the sexes.[3] The entrance to the seats had to be used by men and women, which caused so much disagreement that some were reputed to have stayed away from the dedication ceremonies of the new synagogue.

The law of 1828, as we have seen, set in motion the changes from *Schutzjude* to citizen. It placed the previously independent communities under the *Israelitsche Oberkirchenbehoerde*, which at first was responsible to the Ministry of Interior, later the Ministry of Church and School Affairs. One of its first directives ordered the community of Niederstetten to use, instead of Yiddish, German for all its entries into the book of records. A reorganization creating thirteen district rabbinical positions for all of Wuerttemberg in the 1830's, assigned Niederstetten to the district of Weikersheim. The new order, making appointments of rabbis and teachers subject to state examinations, forced Niederstetten's old rabbi and its teacher out of their positions. However, a loyal community made arrangements to pay both of them a pension out of its own funds. The rabbi, a man by the name of Essinger, stayed on as a legal authority to advise the congregation on religious law.

The community, now called *Kirchengemeinde*, was governed by three elected officers known as the *Kirchenvorsteher*, and presided over by the district rabbi, when he was present, and the local teacher. This meant that for the most part the latter was the presiding officer at their meetings. The teacher's salary of 225 florins annually was the biggest item of the budget. It is most difficult to evaluate today whether this sum was sufficient for a family. As was common practice, the teacher received a house to live in, paid reduced taxes and derived some income from being a ritual slaughterer. Still, as we have seen, the teacher's lot was not an easy one and his individual circumstances varied from community to community.

The budget also shows us that Niederstetten had to make an annual contribution toward the salary of the district rabbi at Weikersheim. Another item deals with the thirty-four school children, who had to pay two florins annually as school fee. There were other expenses, such as support of the poor and maintenance of the synagogue buildings, including the ritual bath for women *(Mikvah)*. It was the responsibility of the *Kirchenvorsteher,* most of whom were selected from the more affluent members of the community, to assess the taxes for each member.

The Synagogue

Enforcement of the strict synagogue rules announced by the *Israelitische Oberkirchenbehoerde* in 1838 must have caused a lot of headaches. A hitherto independent group of Jews were suddenly told in detail when to appear at the synagogue, what to pray and how to conduct themselves while there. Any infraction of the rules, either by coming late, leaving early or conversing during services, could be punished by the *Kirchenvorsteher.* Theoretically, a fined member had a right to appeal to the royal *Oberamt* (i.e. the higher civil authority), but this rarely occurred.

The new synagogue order required the cantor to sing a German song before and after the sermon. This did not meet with the approval of many of Niederstetten's Jews. To show their displeasure, they left the synagogue service before the sermon and returned at its conclusion. Close to twenty members submitted a petition to the *Kirchenvorsteher* to eliminate such singing lest they be compelled to stay away from services altogether. They would be willing, so they said, to listen to the sermon in German, but not to participate in the singing of German songs which frequently were copies of

Protestant chorales.[4] The Niederstetten group then asked that a higher authority relieve the cantor of his duty to sing German hymns during religious services.

In reviewing this conflict, the modern reader should remember that synagogue ordinances were designed to bring uniformity to synagogue activities. Yet these ordinances dictated exactly those customs where disagreements existed between those who advocated a new order and those who defended the traditional manner by which they lived. We now have to introduce a term which is very important to the understanding of the clashes between the *Oberkirchenbehoerde* (in particular, *Kirchenrat* Maier) and the rural communities. This term is called *Minhag* in Hebrew and is best translated as 'way of life'.[5] Dispersion of the Jewish people throughout many lands and over centuries had resulted in various interpretations of traditional laws by the rabbis, which, in turn, led to diverse local customs. Important codifiers of law, such as Rabbi Moses Isserles (1510–1572), incorporated many customs into the law books, giving them the status of binding authority. Jewish laws as well as customs must be viewed as living entities; they grow and develop together with the people that live by them. When Reform Judaism came upon the scene in the nineteenth century, its leaders tried to reduce the importance of rabbinic law and local custom. They held—this was emphasized in the introduction to the official synagogue order—that many abuses had entered the synagogue services as a result of persecution in previous generations. Moreover, the introduction stated, the diversity of customs was disturbing to the dignity and order of the public service. Thus, the need for uniformity among synagogues, which, in turn, would preserve the faith and stimulate a moral way of life. By establishing uniformity the reformers hoped to move the Jewish community out of their spiritual isolation and pave the way for an easier entrance into the society around them. The reformers, however, underestimated the depth of tradition as observed in rural communities. Thus, the opposition in Niederstetten and elsewhere throughout Wuerttemberg.

As we have read, some of the new synagogue rules ordered congregations to forbid kissing the curtains before the Ark of the Holy Scrolls upon entering the synagogue, to suspend the annual children's procession on the festival of *Simchat Torah* (Rejoicing of the Torah) or to eliminate the chanting of the *Haftorah* (prophetic portion) by a youngster reaching *Bar Mitzvah* (son of commandment) age. Many Jews considered these rules to be attacks on customs developed over the centuries. To the unsophisticated Jew, such customs were essential parts of his Jewish life style. For the synagogue was not only a place to meet one's personal God, but also the place where one could rejoice at meeting his fellow Jew in a fashion that was both spiritual and physical. This could involve singing, dancing and eating together in celebration of certain festivals. Thus, the Jewish people vehemently objected to the new rules of the *Oberkirchenbehoerde*, which were seen as dangers to Jewish existence. Similarly, the introduction of organ music into the synagogue during the Sabbath service was opposed as a product grown on spiritually foreign soil. Praying in a synagogue that had an organ was not considered praying at all, which explains why many city dwellers returned to worship in their rural synagogues during the High Holidays. They preferred the sometimes discordant singing of the congregation to the exact, but impersonal harmony created by a technical instrument.

The Torah scroll has always held the central place in Jewish religious life. It contains the five books of Moses, from which public reading dates back to Biblical times. Synagogue building and services were structured to underline the importance of the Torah and its message to the people. There was the Holy Ark, which housed the scrolls, and the *Almemor*, the place in the center, to which the scrolls were carried in procession for the purpose of reading from them. A detailed protocol had developed over the centuries dictating the number of persons called to read publicly the portion earmarked for each Sabbath and for other occasions when the Torah was read: holidays, major or minor, and special weekdays. The honor of being called up *(Aliyah)* was regarded very highly, with the first honor always given to a member of the priestly class *(Kohen)* and the second to a *Levite* (member of the tribe of *Levi)*; the sequence signifies that the synagogue service was a replica of the Temple service of old, where these two groups were in charge of all proceedings. Following these two honors were others that could be given to the rest of the people. These were limited, however, with the number determined by whether the service was for a holiday or weekday. Distribution of these honors came to be a very complicated matter. Suffice to state here that each member took his turn. There were occasions, however, particularly in connection with rites of passage, when the order of turns had to be interrupted. We quote from the Niederstetten synagogue order as recorded by Stern and dated January 1, 1846.[6]

"A. to avoid strife within the community, the following was decided by the presiding officers: the following are considered *Chiuvim* i.e. persons to be called to the Torah outside their regular turn:
1. the bridegroom on the first Sabbath after his engagement, on the Sabbath prior to his wedding day, on his wedding day, on the Sabbath after his wedding day;
4. (our record does not list 2 and 3) the father, upon his son becoming a bridegroom or his daughter a bride, on the Sabbath prior to the wedding and on the wedding day. Incidentally, on this day the distribution of the Torah honors is at the discretion of the bridegroom;
4a. the father on the Sabbath before his son's circumcision;
5b. the husband on the Sabbath on which his wife completes her weeks of afterbirth impurity . . . whether her child is still alive or not;

6. a man on his *Yahrzeit* (anniversary of death of next of kin) if it occurs on a day, on which the Torah is read in the synagogue—if the *Yahrzeit* falls on a Sunday, then the man will be called to the Torah on the Sabbath afternoon service;

7. the godfather, the father of the child and the *Mohel* (circumciser), if the circumcision takes place on a day when the Torah is read . . . the distribution of honors is at the discretion of the child's father;

8. a person rescued from an accident, if he wants to pronounce *Gomel* (blessing after danger overcome);

9a. the person blowing *Shofar* on New Year's day and the cantor on New Year's and the Day of Atonement, if he performs his functions without remuneration;

9b. the person who has built or bought a house will be called up on the first Sabbath after moving in;

10. an honor may be made up only if one was unable to keep his turn due to sickness or being in a mourning period;

11. a member who had been absent half a year, on the first Sabbath of his return—if under eighteen at the Sabbath-afternoon Torah reading, from eighteen up on Sabbath morning;

12a. any married stranger, who is here on Sabbath and has local relatives, should be called up during the morning services. Afterwards he will not be called until three months have passed. If he doesn't have any local relatives, his being called is at the discretion of the official in charge of honors;

12b. a bridegroom who married a girl from the community and visits the community for the first time on a Sabbath or holiday. Beyond that his being called up is optional;

B. any person, entitled to honors, must tell this, prior to the service to the officer in charge so there should not be any talking, quarreling or any bad temper during the service and the call-up. If there is no notification, the officer cannot be accused of any oversight.

C. the officer in charge of honors who violates this directive will suffer a fine of eighteen *Kreuzer*.

D. this directive will be publicized at the first communal meeting.''

It should be realized that this careful attention to an equitable distribution of Torah honors was also motivated by economic considerations. Effective January 1, 1842, everyone, except the rabbi, cantor or strangers, had to pay six *Kreuzer* for an *Aliyah* received on Sabbath or holiday mornings. Moreover, it was customary to offer a donation to the community or other worthy cause at the time of the *Aliyah*. Some honors, particularly those on holidays, were sold in advance to the highest bidder which left the poorer members out of the picture.[7] Bidding used to take place in the synagogue itself, but this practice was strictly forbidden in the new synagogue order of the *Oberkirchenbehoerde*. In Niederstetten the bidding took place in the community room nearby. Many of the above customs are recorded in the *Sepher Minhagim* (Book of Customs) of the Fuerth community which, as a center of learning, set the standard for many communities in Southern Germany.[8] In some areas, however, local communities were even more detailed in their customs. A good example is Niederstetten itself. Tradition has it that the first *Aliyah* at the Torah reading be given to the *Kohen* (Priest), with the second to a *Levite*. Since Niederstetten had a large number of *Levites*, the *Kohanim* used to leave the services prior to the reading of the Torah, which enabled the *Levites* not only to receive the second, but also the first *Aliyah*. This explains why local customs came into being. They frequently originated as a result of local situations and often remained with the communities even though the original cause had disappeared.

As we have seen, the synagogue stood in the center of all communal activities. Religious services took place regularly, mornings and evenings, with all the men attending, provided, of course, they were not absent in the pursuit of a living for their families. The *Shamash* (beadle) used to call the men to worship by knocking at their doors, but this practice was denounced by the new synagogue order as too noisy and undignified. Instead, a uniform time schedule was announced for all services throughout the state. Some discretion was left to the local rabbi in conjunction with community officials about the time of summer services, but none could start later than eight in the morning. Of special interest is the time for the New Year and Day of Atonement services, which began at five-thirty in the morning to ensure enough time to conduct the very lengthy liturgical rites of these days.

An unorthodox method of calling Jewish people to worship was established at the synagogue in Buchau, a community in the south of Wuerttemberg. Here, it was decided to place a bell in the tower of the building, where it rang at the time of worship and other important community occasions. Rumor had it that the bell had been a present from King Wilhelm I, who was unfamiliar with Jewish tradition. Once the gift was received, rumor continues, the community felt too constrained to turn the royal gift down. On the bell was a Hebrew inscription taken from verse one of psalm 122 which reads: "I was glad when they said unto me, Let us go into the house of the Lord."

The Family

Important as the synagogue was in the life of every Jewish community, it must be clearly understood that the strength of the synagogue was a direct reflection of the strength of the Jewish family. Indeed, the rural communities' strength was based on the fact that all considered themselves part of one family. This is not to say there weren't any quarrels, but they were family quarrels. People living in a limited area were close to each other physically and spiritually. Their closeness was particularly evident in the celebration of family events, blessed as well as sad. Let us begin with the birth of a child.[9] At such a blessed event, the whole community was notified by school-age youngsters sent as messengers. Deliveries normally took place at home with the assistance of a midwife; only on rare occasions was a physician present. The pregnant woman's room had Kabbalistic drawings on the walls, which were supposed to protect mother and child against Lilith and other evil spirits.[10]

If the infant was a boy, special arrangements were made to prepare for the circumcision, a hallowed commandment anchored in Biblical Scriptures themselves. Our spokesman's father, Max Stern, happened to be a *Mohel* (circumciser) who performed this sacred ritual as a matter of honor, traveling far and wide in performance of this act. Once he was even called to Paris, France, where a former resident of Wuerzburg, Bavaria, desired Stern's services for his child. In the states of Wuerttemberg and Baden, anyone who wanted to become a *Mohel* had also to be trained by a doctor and pass an examination before the district medical officer. The circumcision itself took place in the presence of a doctor, frequently of the Christian faith, as few Jewish doctors were available. Grateful parents who offered Stern a remuneration were told to send it to the *Waisenhaus* in Esslingen. If, on the other hand, families were poor, Stern used to come with gifts and money to help with the celebration.

Three days before the circumcision, women relatives of the mother brought candles into the house where the candles burned until three days after the circumcision. At the ceremony itself one candle, twisted out of twelve strands of wax, was lit, symbolizing the twelve tribes of the ancient Jewish people. On the Friday night after the baby's birth, male members of the community gathered in the house for a special celebration called *Sochor*, meaning male, during which they studied and were served refreshments.

The circumcision, being the sign of the Covenant, was usually performed in the synagogue before the conclusion of the regular morning service. Father, grandfather, godfather (*Sandek*) and circumciser (*Mohel*) wore their finest clothes and, in the event that the Torah was read, they all received an *Aliyah*. There were two seats, one for the *Sandek* and the second for the prophet Elijah, the champion of religious purity, who was symbolically present at such ceremonies.

Upon completion of all the rituals, the guests returned to the house for a festive meal. Three days after the circumcision, the baby was given its first bath, which was attended by the women of the community.

A special event took place four to six weeks after birth, when the mother left her house for the first time to attend the Sabbath services at the synagogue. On the same afternoon, boys and girls under thirteen years of age came to the house for the *Holegrasch*.[11] The ceremony gave the baby its secular name, the Hebrew name already having been given at the circumcision or when the father of a girl was called up to the Torah. The baby was placed in a basket and was lifted up three times by the people who exclaimed: What shall the baby's name be *(wie solls Kindle heisse)*? The name was then announced by the father whereupon all children received sweets to take home.

Another ceremony—which also ranked high as a Biblical commandment—was the redemption of the first-born son *(Pidyon Haben)* on the thirty-first day after birth. It symbolized the release of a first-born Israelite from temple service by a *Kohen* (Priest), which was done by giving the *Kohen* a token sum. Although strictly observed, it was not as popular an event simply because in small communities it did not occur too often.

Finally, a very colorful ceremony in connection with the birth of a boy was the carrying of the *Wimpel* (linen band) into the synagogue. A piece of linen, placed under the baby during the circumcision, was kept until the boy was approximately two and a half years old. It then was cut into long pieces and sewn together into a band. Then the name and birthday were woven into the *Wimpel* together with blessings for the boy's future. On the holiday, after the boy's third birthday, he was brought to the synagogue for the first time. At the end of the Torah reading, the father took the boy to the *Almemor* and turned the *Wimpel* over for binding around the Torah scroll. This ceremony marked the beginning of the boy's attendance at synagogue, where he was permitted to sit on one of the seats reserved for children.

Ten years or so after the *Wimpel* ceremony, another rite marked the youngster's entry into the adult community. It is called *Bar Mitzvah*, meaning son of commandment, indicating that henceforth the youngster would have to observe Jewish laws and customs. The preparations for this event, which took place on the Sabbath after the boy's thirteenth birthday, were very extensive. One of the first and most impressive obligations for the youngster was that from then on he would have to fast a full day at the major fast days of the religious cycle. For that, however, preparations had started long before. Shortly after their sixth birthday, all children, boys and girls, fasted half a day. Then, the last three fast days before his *Bar Mitzvah*, a boy had to fast a full day. It seems that Niederstetten did not pay any attention to the synagogue order of the *Oberkirchenbehoerde*, which had sought to eliminate a youngster's Torah reading at his *Bar Mitzvah* ceremony. We read in Stern's report of the careful preparations for Torah reading that he and his brothers had to make prior to their *Bar Mitzvah*. Like most boys, young Stern was glad when the day's rituals were over, and he could change from his new blue suit with long pants and hat into short pants and cap. After all, he had performed well, displaying his knowledge of Hebrew text and music. Now it was time to examine the presents which had arrived from relatives, friends and neighbors, be they Jewish or Christian. All shared in this happy community event.

The next important celebration took place on the day when a boy or a girl became engaged to be married. It stands to reason that a society as family oriented as the Jews, would do everything in its power to bring about such happy events. And while a legend has it that God Almighty in Heaven was using His time to arrange matches, the people below did everything to assist in this noble task. Very often the families used the services of a *Shadchan* (professional matchmaker) whose wide contacts facilitated the get-together of the proper parties. It was his, sometimes very arduous, task to convince each side that the proposed match was the ideal one. Once the heads of families met, there were many items to be discussed, including the dowry of the bride-to-be. The services of the *Shadchan* were rewarded by two to three percent of the dowry. A part of the preliminaries was the meeting of the young people, always chaperoned, to look each other over. All was done in strict secrecy to avoid any loose talk or embarrassment in the event that the proposed match would not come to pass. If negotiations proceeded smoothly, there were more visitations (Stern calls them "inspections") in the homes of the two families. Throughout, the families tried to maintain the fiction that the match was a result of an accidental meeting of the young people and of their falling in love with each other, but everyone knew that many negotiations had been needed to move the "accidental" meeting to a firm commitment. It should be noted that each well organized community had an association which helped poor families in finding matches for their daughters.

Once the engagement had been agreed upon, all the members of the community were notified by a specially selected boy or girl. This set off a full round of visits and family celebrations. First the groom's visit to the bride's home with presents, to be followed by the return visit of the bride. Then there was the *Spinholtz* celebration of the Friday before the wedding.[12] A day later, at the Sabbath morning service in the synagogue, the male members of both families, headed by the groom, received their *Aliyah*. They wore their finest holiday clothes including mantle and collar.[13] Stern also mentions a celebration called *Polterabend* (Nuptial eve), on the evening before the wedding, when the families gathered for dancing and merrymaking.

We are guided by Stern's outline of how weddings were observed in his community. It should be realized that neither his nor ours can be a very detailed account as there are so many customs surrounding this ancient ritual. In reading what Stern remembers of the wedding procedures in his home community, we can see that it too did not follow rules laid down by the synagogue order of 1838. Stern speaks about weddings also having taken place in the home, whereas the order designates only the synagogue for such occasions. As to the fasting of the young couple on their wedding day, mentioned by Stern, the order is completely silent. The ceremony took place under the *Chuppah* (bridal canopy) held by four boys, not yet *Bar Mitzvah*. The couple's heads were covered by a *Talit* (prayer shawl), a custom the order no longer permitted. Other well established customs not recorded by Stern—for example, music at the procession to the synagogue and breaking of the glass at the ceremony's conclusion—were also frowned upon by the rules of 1838 designed to eliminate practices that the reformers deemed noisy and undignified. This is not the place to explain all the many customs surrounding Jewish weddings; suffice to say that most were meaningful. They were certainly no barrier to better understanding between Jews and Christians for we know from Stern that there were always many visitors of all faiths who crowded the synagogue and the streets to enjoy these festive occasions.

Death and Mourning

This general community participation in happy occasions carried over to times of sickness and death. Since all of Niederstetten had only one trained nurse (a Protestant deaconess), men and women took over the night watch of the dying. When the end approached, appropriate prayers were said and a *Minyan* (quorum of ten men) was provided. Outside the house where a person died, a bucket of water and towels were placed for washing of hands upon leaving. In compliance with city ordinances the interment took place forty-eight hours after death.

Depending on the sex of the deceased, the men or the women prepared the body, which was placed in a wooden coffin with a morsel of earth from the Holy Land. Brief prayers were also recited asking forgiveness for any injustice done to the deceased during his lifetime. The coffin was carried by six men to the municipal funeral carriage, which was drawn by two horses. Behind the carriage marched the teacher followed by male and female mourners, all in black. They were followed by people of all faiths from the community.

Most people walked to the cemetery, which was far and on top of a mountain; some carriages were provided for those in need. Niederstetten's cemetery dated from 1741 and was surrounded by a stone wall. The tombstones showed the Hebrew name and dates of the interred and some laudatory remarks about the person's life. There were also symbolic drawings for a *Kohen, Levi* or *Mohel*. The backs of the stones contained German inscriptions. There were no decorative flowers, only a few trees and bushes. Family plots were unknown; interments followed in the order of their occurrence.

After the coffin had been lowered, the teacher (or the rabbi when present) delivered a eulogy and a prayer. Then came the ceremony of *Kriah* (the tearing of one's garment as the outward symbol of mourning) and the *Kaddish* (prayer for the dead). All participants threw three spades full of earth onto the coffin and formed two rows through which the mourners returned from the grave.

At home, the mourners sat on wooden cases covered with a pillow. They were served hard boiled eggs without salt, which had been brought by a neighbor. For three days there was no cooking, all meals were prepared by members of the community, which did everything to share the grief and to ease the pain. Morning and evening services were held at home throughout the *Shivah* (the seven days of mourning), with the teacher holding a study session in memory of the departed. On the Friday night during *Shivah*, the mourners went to the synagogue, but did not enter until after the singing of the Sabbath song *Lecha Dodi* (Come My Friend). Throughout the year of mourning a person did not sit in his regular seat, but sat further removed from the *Almemor*. His prayer shawl (Talit) had a black ribbon at the collar, which he covered on the Sabbath when there is no mourning. A tombstone was placed by the time the year was over. Then on the anniversary of the death, also known as the Yahrzeit, the mourners went to the cemetery where they recited the Kaddish in the presence of a Minyan. It was customary to visit graves at Yahrzeit and before the High Holidays. Prayers were said, and, upon leaving, one placed a handful of freshly plucked grass and three stones on the tombstone.[14]

Sabbath and Festivals

We now turn, if only briefly, to the ways in which the Sabbath and holidays were observed. Again, we are following Stern who has written with such great love about his own community. There are other chroniclers, such as Schwab, Picard, and Jeggle, however, all of whom have tried to recapture this bygone era and to relate it to its rural environment.[15] In reading these accounts, one is immediately struck by the strict attention to religious tradition that gave followers direction to their daily lives. Weekdays became a preparation for the Sabbath, and the Sabbath strengthened the individual physically and spiritually to measure up to his daily responsibilities. We have seen that synagogue services were central to the festive spirit, but a great deal depended upon the wives and their preparation in the home. Meat for the Sabbath meals had to be bought early in the week from the butcher and chickens had to be slaughtered by the Shochet. Dough consisting of white flour, potatoes and water—in the East, eggs and oil were added—was kneaded and left overnight to rise. On Friday mornings the risen dough from which the challah portion had been taken, was divided into twelve strands, corresponding to the twelve tribes, and twisted into braids. The dough was then brought to the baker—there were no Jewish bakers in Niederstetten—who was careful not to bake anything else together with the Berches.[16]

In connection with the baking, Stern tells a delightful

story that shows the piety of a Niederstetten woman named Hanne Goldstein and her family. Hanne had assumed the task of supervising the bakers although they were known to be very respectful of Jewish ritual requirements. One day—a Friday—her sister traveled by train from Nuremberg to Niederstetten, a relatively short distance even when trains were not too fast. In Crailsheim she had to change trains, but since the other train was delayed, she began saying her afternoon prayers. Just then the train arrived. Her piety did not allow her to interrupt her devotions, however, and she missed her connection. She also could not take the next train since it would not have brought her to Niederstetten before the beginning of the Sabbath. Thus, she remained in Crailsheim and continued on her journey on Sunday, arriving two days late, but happy.

As the Sabbath was holy, no work or travel was permitted. Mother Stern, her son tells us, used to get nervous on Fridays for fear that she would not be able to complete her many household chores in time. But when father and children returned from the synagogue, everything was ready. The house was clean, the rooms were brightly lit by candles from the Sabbath lamp, and the table was set for the family. Father and mother greeted each other and the children received their blessing from her, as father had already blessed all of them at the synagogue. Then came the ritual washing of the hands, *Kiddush* (sanctification of wine) and the blessing over the *Berches*. The Friday night meal usually consisted of noodle soup, potted meat, sauce, potato salad and cake. Sometimes fish was served as an in-between dish, but never "gefillte fish," which was unknown. After Sabbath songs and grace, father and mother usually took a little nap while the children played. Later in the evening father studied the Scriptures of the week and explained their meaning to everyone present.

On Sabbath mornings one had to rise early. In the summer, synagogue services began at eight and in the winter, at eight-thirty. For breakfast there was coffee, *Berches* with butter or jam, and often cake. The highlight of the morning worship was the reading of the Torah with the question of who would receive an *Aliyah* and who would be called to chant the *Haftorah* (prophetic portion). After the service the teacher conducted a study session.

Since ritual law forbade the lighting of a fire on the Sabbath, another means furnished a hot noon meal for the day. This was through a metal chest with twin compartments. On Fridays a pot was filled with rice, peas, beans, meat or chicken and covered with water. The pot was placed in the upper compartment, while the lower one contained coals that were lit on Friday. The pot simmered all night, so that by noon the family could enjoy a hot and nutritious meal. The dish was called *cholent*.[17] The rest of the day was spent visiting, napping and enjoying coffee with cake, following the afternoon service. The last was very important to youngsters under twenty years of age as they were allowed to receive an *Aliyah* at that time. After conclusion of the Sabbath, the men went to the restaurant where they played cards until deep into the night.

While preparations for the Sabbath required a few days, those for the Passover holiday took weeks if not months. Again the burden fell upon the women whose task it was to clean out the house from *Chametz* (leavened bread) to make room for the special Passover food. This not only involved all grain products, but also certain vegetables that were forbidden during Passover. It also meant replacing the dishes used throughout the year with special Passover utensils. The whole operation necessitated an entire cleaning of the house from top to bottom to make sure that no forbidden foods were left. The Passover dishes stored in the attic were brought down and placed in the kitchen, which had been divided into Passover and regular sections. The highlight of the cleaning was the search for bread the night before Passover. This was more symbolic than real since the house had been thoroughly cleansed during the preceding days. Therefore, mother placed small pieces of bread on the table of each room so that father could collect them in a merry procession of the whole family. Stern tells of a teacher named Oberndoerfer, who had been influenced by the strict Orthodoxy of Frankfurt and who said that this search was not proper. He held that father should open each drawer and look into every closet for *Chametz*. Father followed the Fuerther custom, however, for it would have been impossible to clean out the whole house in one evening. In the morning, the family had to eat breakfast in the hallway since the kitchen had already been converted for Passover. Afterwards all the *Chametz* collected the night before was burned. If there was still some left, mother gave it to the cleaning women who quickly removed it from the house.

Stern's loving narration continues with the first two evenings of the holiday, each called *Seder* meaning "order." We will not go into all the details of this ancient ceremony nor will we discuss at length the *Haggadah* (narration), which is the Hebrew text read and chanted prior, during and after the meal. Suffice to say that it is the story of the Exodus from Egypt which is interpreted and symbolized reflecting all ages. What we will mention here is only what we consider special to this holiday and others in a small village of Wuerttemberg. Father Stern used to conduct the *Seder* both in Hebrew and German because quite often non-Jewish friends came as guests and, of course, were interested in all the ceremonies. A special chore reserved for the children after the first two days of Passover was the carrying of *Matzot* (unleavened bread) to Christian neighbors. The *Matzot* were carefully wrapped in table napkins and brought to the people. The children used to make a little speech saying that their parents were sending the *Matzot* or *Osterkuchen* (Easter cakes) to be tasted. The neighbors acted "surprised," went into a room and came back with a few raw eggs as a return present. For all knew that Jewish people were not allowed to accept during the week of Passover any other food but eggs. In Christian circles, *Matzot*, when eaten with honey and sugar, were viewed as a great delicacy; some even considered them a protection against lightning and hail.[18]

A playful occupation during Passover was the coloring of raw eggs. Since regular dye was forbidden on these days, the eggs were placed into onion peels and boiled, which gave them a brown color. The children used them for "egg throwing" in the grass and, when the peels cracked, they ate them.

Seven weeks after Passover the community celebrated the *Shavuot* (Weeks) festival. It coincided with the spring season which was evident in the synagogue. With permission of the city authorities, small birch trees obtained from nearby forests were placed along the seats. Around the *Almemor* stood many vases with flowers, especially lilacs and peonies. While synagogue decorations reflected the happy spirit of this spring festival, the absence of any ceremonial display was characteristic of *Tishah B'Av* (Ninth of Av). This was a fast day commemorating the destruction of the Temple and other calamities in the history of the Jewish people. In the three weeks before, no festive events took place because they were considered a period of mourning. The synagogue was darkened with only a few lamps flickering. The curtain before the Ark and the covers on the *Almemor* and pulpit had been removed; the rugs on the floor were rolled up. The men took off their shoes and put on felt slippers. Then the teacher sat down on the steps leading to the Ark and chanted the service in the wailing melody of the day.

In the fall, preparations began for the *Rosh Hashanah* (New Year) festival. The *Shofar* (ram's horn) was blown throughout the month of *Elul* to alert the community to the importance of High Holy Days. The Christian neighbors used to say: *Jetzt faengt das Winterhoernle zu blasen an* (Now the little winter horn starts to blow). Special prayers were said, particularly during the week before *Rosh Hashanah*, and the whole family received new clothes, which had been ordered from the tailors weeks before. An important activity was the writing of letters to families and friends to keep them abreast of developments and to wish them all the best for the coming year. Father did most of the writing with mother only adding a few lines.

On the holidays, mother wore the customary white dress. Many women still wore the white bonnet which had been traditional in years gone by. Father had his black suit with white tie and top hat. Together with the special prayerbooks he took to the synagogue the *Sarjenes* (shroud), which was worn under the *Talit*, symbolizing this season of God's judgment about "who shall live and who shall die."[19] Although few in the community were learned, all were sensitive to these grave questions. They participated in the prayers with pious concentration and expressed the hope that the Almighty would bless them and their families in the year ahead.

When father returned from the synagogue, a surprise awaited him. On the table, hidden by the *Berches*, lay a number of letters written by his children under the teacher's guidance. In them were thanks to their parents for the past and promises of good behavior in the future. The next day everybody rose early, for the service began at six in the morning. The early start perhaps explains a custom described by Stern as an "*Unsitte*" (bad habit). The blowing of the *Shofar*, characteristic of *Rosh Hashanah*, usually took place during mid-morning; any prior intake of food was not permitted. Thus people must have developed the habit of sneaking out to their nearby homes *after* the *Shofar* blowing for a cup of coffee and then returning to synagogue. One can be sure—as Stern reports of his father—that the more observant in the community frowned upon this practice, but even his own children managed to leave in the name of tradition.

Of course, no such infraction of the rules would have been possible on the Day of Atonement, the holiest day of the religious year. Here it was fasting from the night before until the night after. Some people even remained in the synagogue throughout the night, busying themselves with additional prayers and appropriate studies on the meaning of the holy day known in Hebrew as *Yom Kippur*. Others denied themselves the comfort of sitting down, but showed their devotion by standing for all the services. In reading Stern's account of his home community, one can be impressed with the thought that similar observances took place throughout Jewish communities everywhere. True, there were different melodies and customs based on country and environment, but prayers and spirit were essentially the same, a powerful demonstration of religious unity.

No sooner was *Yom Kippur* gone, when the preparations for the *Sukkot* festival began. *Sukkot* means "booths" in Hebrew; in Germany the holiday was called *Laubhuettenfest* (Feast of Tabernacles). Historically, this festival was a reminder that the Almighty had liberated the Jews from Egypt and that they had lived in temporary dwellings while wandering in the desert. In addition, it was the season of thanksgiving for His harvest that brought food to nourish men and animals. These sentiments were expressed in the colorful decorations of the *Sukkah* which became the home for eight days. There was a happy competition in the community to determine whose booth would be the most beautifully decorated. Some homes, including that of the Stern family, had a built-in *Sukkah*, which meant an area on the second floor, which had a removable roof. Wooden sides were erected here with a lattice covered by branches and foliage. Most people did not own such well constructed *Sukkot* and had to build each year anew. All activities normally carried out in the house—for example, eating, studying and sleeping—took place in the *Sukkah* in order to be constantly aware of the holiday's meaning.

Simchat Torah (Rejoicing of the Torah) was the finale of the festive season. It also marked the beginning of the regular cycle of synagogue services. End and beginning were evident in the many events crowded into a twenty-four-hour period. In the afternoon the whole community of men, women and children attended the auctioneering of the special honors connected with *Simchat Torah* and with year-round needs in the synagogue. The term "auctioneering" is used deliberately because that was the exact purpose of the event, namely to raise funds for the good of the community.[20] The honors for which there was animated bidding involved the scrolls: who would take them out first from the Ark and who would receive the *Aliyot* connected with the reading of the end and of the beginning of the Scriptures. The man called for the final portion was the *Chatan Torah* (bridegroom of the Torah) and the one called for the reading of the first chapter of Scriptures was the *Chatan Bereshit* (bridegroom of Genesis). Then there was the honor of donating the wine for services throughout the whole year and of who would take care of the *Wimpels* (bands) around the scrolls. The latter, Stern reports, was often bought by his mother. The bidding reflected religious zeal and financial affluence mixed with communal politics.

The evening witnessed a big get-together at a nearby restaurant with dancing and entertainment to which non-Jewish youth were also invited. The children recited poems while the teacher spoke about the meaning of the occasion. According to Stern, ultimately these gatherings were discontinued at the insistence of the teacher Oberndoerfer, who viewed them as not in accord with the spirit of *Simchat Torah*. For him all activities should be centered around the Torah itself with the highlight being the morning processions. A joyous spectacle it was, indeed, when all the scrolls were taken out of the Ark and carried around the synagogue where everyone touched them with hands and lips. It was a great day for young and old, as everyone had the honor of carrying a scroll, which was the concrete symbol of living Judaism.

By singling out the small community of Niederstetten we have tried to show how a typical rural group in Wuerttemberg organized its life. Of course, all Jews had their special problems, but almost all in the rural communities tried to retain their spiritual identity as Jews. Our Niederstetten community had 217 persons (general population 1537) in 1847, 146 (general population 1731) in 1905, and 100 (general population 1800) in 1925. Still the shrinking group upheld basic institutions such as the synagogue, cemetery, women's bath, school and teacher. Most men were engaged in commerce connected with cattle, produce, furs, hide and hardware. Some had stores, but there wasn't enough of a local economy to provide a living. Thus, most men had to be on the road for a livelihood, which kept them away from home for the whole week, and they only spent the Sabbath with their families. If one would want to characterize these Jews of Niederstetten and similar rural communities, the word "loyal" would be most appropriate. They were loyal to their families and faith. The same attitude showed itself in their dedication to their friends, Jewish and non-Jewish alike. They had their own religiously oriented associations, but were also members of local sports, song and commerce groups. During the first World War (1914–1918) many served in the army, some even volunteering their service inspired by the call: "Fuer Kaiser und Reich, Koenig und Vaterland." (For Kaiser and (German) Empire, King (of Wuerttemberg) and Fatherland.) Stern tells the story of a Moritz Wolfsheimer from nearby Weikersheim who found himself in the United States when the war broke out. He signed on as a fireman on a ship bound for Europe and reached Germany via Switzerland to be ready for military duty. He survived the war and its turbulent aftermath, but he and his son lost their lives in a concentration camp.

Hindsight tells us that this loyalty to home and community made these rural Jews lose sight of the bigger picture and the clouds that were gathering on the German horizon. Otherwise one is at a loss to explain why in the mid 1920's many Niederstetten Jews cancelled their memberships in the *Centralverein deutscher Staatsbuerger juedischen Glaubens*, the national defense organization.[21] Another revealing episode took place at about the same time in the life of young Bruno Stern. One of his teachers in Bad Mergentheim had persuaded him to place blue and white colored boxes into the Niederstetten homes. These were the means by which the Zionist movement raised funds for the upbuilding of Palestine. When the teacher Oberndoerfer learned of this, he was very upset and ordered the young boy to give up his efforts. He told him that the building of Palestine would have to await the coming of the Messiah. As a result of this admonition the monies in the boxes were never collected.

4. | ECONOMY AND SOCIETY

Occupations

In the previous chapter we tried to give a picture of one rural community in 19th-century Wuerttemberg as a sample of similar communities throughout the state. At the outset we posed the question of how a Jew living in Germany changed in the course of this century into a "German Jew." What took place to change him from a person with very few rights into one of many rights? We took the year 1828 as our principal point of departure because that was when the King of Wuerttemberg issued the "*Law pertaining to the public situation of members of the Israelite faith*" (*Gesetz in Betreff der Oeffentlichen Verhaeltnisse der Israelitischen Glaubensgenossen*). We have seen that the major motivating force for this new law was the belief of those in power that the Jews had to be brought into the mainstream of society. Before integration could be accomplished, the authorities held, more education was necessary to change the occupations of the Jews from unproductive to productive ones. Heretofore, the majority of the Jews had eked out a meager livelihood by peddling and petty trading. Thus, article fifteen of the new law stipulated that a Jew would have to work ten years in agriculture or handicraft to become eligible for citizenship. To encourage a change to handicraft, the *Oberkirchenbehoerde* stated in 1833 that it would be prepared to pay the cost of apprenticeship, but only for those willing to become a smith, carpenter or wheelright.[1] Lighter craft, such as baking, butchering and tailoring, were not considered worthy of support.

It stands to reason that the conditions for citizenship could not be easily fulfilled. First of all most Jews were too poor to buy agricultural land even if it had been readily available. As for handicraft, the situation was also difficult. One had to find a *Meister* (master) willing to teach the craft to a young Jewish lad.

If we accept the official statistics, by 1852 there were 1,300 artisans and 405 farmers and agricultural workers among 4,000 productive Jews.[2] Among the artisans were 412 butchers, 274 weavers, 121 shoemakers, 86 tailors and 50 soap boilers.[3] It appears that in some areas the authorities were very strict in their requirements for citizenship. We read about a Jewish physician from Muehringen, who applied for citizenship in the community of Rottweil, south of his hometown. After his application was turned down, he complained to the Ministry, but was rejected on the ground of not having been engaged for ten years in a productive occupation.[4] Toury points out that the campaign for Jews to enter agricultural and artisan occupations was illtimed.[5] He holds that colonialism and industrialization made it irrational for newcomers to enter these fields. The pressure coincided, however, with the people's desire to move out of the category of *Schacherjuden* (hagglers). That so many became butchers was due to the ritual needs of the communities themselves. As for weavers and tailors, these were popular crafts because proficiency in them facilitated moving into manufacturing and industry.

The history of the Jebenhausen-Goeppingen area is a case in point showing the move of Jewish weavers into large-scale manufacturing.[6] Jebenhausen was a strong rural community whose 500 Jews constituted more than 46 percent of the total population in 1840. It was the seat of one of the thirteen district rabbis in Wuerttemberg. While most Jews were engaged in petty trade, some had learned the weaving craft even before the law provided an incentive to pursue agriculture or handicraft. They learned their skill in nearby Goeppingen, the district seat, where a large number of Christian weavers were situated. The woven merchandise was usually sold directly by the producers to the consumers until 1828 when a few young Jews formed the firm A. Rosenheim and Company, distributing on a larger scale. They accomplished this by visiting textile fairs in and out of Wuerttemberg. When some of the Goeppingen weavers felt that they were not receiving an adequate price, they began distributing their products on their own. This created stiff competition and forced the Rosenheim company to move into the production of cotton goods. In turn, the weavers countered with an official complaint that Jews were not permitted to do so as this work was reserved for weavers belonging to the guild. The Rosenheim company proved that cotton weaving did not fall under the jurisdiction of the guilds, however, opening the door for rapid expansion of the Jewish firm. By 1842 it employed 400 workers; in 1844 it had its own dye workers—twelve in Jebenhausen itself and the rest in outside communities. Their yearly production was two million *ellen* (an ell is seven tenths of a yard). The Rosenheim company was dissolved upon the death of its founder in 1847, which resulted in the formation of other firms employing in 1852 approximately 3,000 home workers. Some of Jebenhausen's Jews were also engaged in the optical industry; the Koch family was very prominent in it.[7] When in 1847 Goeppingen became a part of the new railroad system, many of the Jebenhausen firms moved into this nearby city and helped make Goeppingen a center of the German textile industry. The manufacture of corsets, originally imported from France, became a specialty of newly established Jewish firms. Like cotton goods before, it was not subject to the control of the guild and therefore easier for Jews to enter.

The move to Goeppingen caused, of course, the decline of rural Jebenhausen. Another reason for its downward trend was the large scale emigration of its youth to the United States of America. Most of the emigrants appear to have been unable to establish themselves in their home community or in nearby Goeppingen. Statistics tell us that between 1830 and 1870 more than 300 Jewish persons left Jebenhausen to seek their fortune overseas. Many were artisans who gave "settling" as the reason for leaving their home community.[8] These figures must be kept in mind lest we assume that the integration of artisans into the industrial sector of Wuerttemberg was a smooth one.

Another weaver story which ultimately ended in success, describes the great difficulties of youngsters trying to provide for their families. It concerns the Elsas family, which moved from Aldingen to the south of Ludwigsburg, where Jews had lived since 1731. Moses Elsas, born in 1814, was only thirteen and the eldest, when his father died, leaving Moses' mother with seven young children to support.[9] Moses helped support the family through peddling, while sending his younger brothers Benedikt and Louis to learn the weaving craft. Benedikt, born in 1817, was such a good apprentice that he soon found work as a journeyman in the famous flag factory of Weigle. Whatever he earned, he turned over to his family, but it was not enough to feed the many hungry mouths. Thus permission was obtained from the district of Ludwigsburg for Benedikt to take the guild examination for weavers. Benedikt was only twenty-one years of age. Normally an applicant for the master examination had to be three years on the road as a journeyman and twenty-five years of age. Benedikt had to pass before the head of the weavers' guild who gave him a very difficult assignment, almost as if to trick him, but he completed the job in record time. As a certified master he was permitted to weave cotton and linen products on his own account, hire apprentices and sell his merchandise on the Ludwigsburg market. One of his first apprentices was his own brother Liebmann, later known as Louis. After a few years in Aldingen, they moved their firm to

Ludwigsburg which was connected to the railway system.

Benedikt married the sister of his brother-in-law while his older brother Moses still had to postpone his wedding until he became thirty-six years of age. This was the law for those who were not actively engaged in handicaft. The whole family finally moved to Ludwigsburg where they bought a house big enough for the business plus three married brothers, their families and their aged mother.

The firm continued to expand and introduced the first mechanical weaving chairs in Wuerttemberg. In 1863 it changed its residence to Cannstatt where they bought a large building, which, situated near the Neckar river, had its own waterpower. Here the firm, Elsas and Company, continued to flourish until its dissolution by the Nazis in 1938.

Upward Mobility

The few examples cited show the upward mobility of Wuerttemberg's Jews. It coincided with their move from the rural communities into the cities where greater opportunities existed for economic advance and higher education. As Monika Richarz has pointed out, the policy of directing Jews into specified occupations was directly opposed to the free choice of occupation for the rest of the population. Therefore, it could not be sustained in the long run. In the middle of the nineteenth century it also became clear that occupations in craft and agriculture were declining; these were the areas from which the urban and rural proletariat would originate. Thus, Jews moved into newly created occupations or those in greater demand, especially in commerce. A rapidly expanding population, growing productivity and improved transportation led to an enormous upswing after 1850. Between 1850 and 1872 the yearly total of German exports grew five-fold. The prospects for manufacturing and banking were equally favorable. Although industrialization came late in Germany, with continued expansion there was an ever increasing need for capital. For these reasons, the advancement of the majority of Jews can be attributed to their flexible adaptation to the changing structure in commerce and industry.[10]

These observations apply in a modified form to the situation in Wuerttemberg. Here the change from an agrarian to an industrial society occurred slowly. Although by 1861 there had been a general increase in the urban population, really big cities did not exist as yet.[11] Between 1834 and 1861, Stuttgart had grown from 38,000 to 61,300 persons, Ulm from 15,100 to 22,700, and Heilbronn from 10,700 to 14,300. The state's Jewish population of about 12,000 shifted only gradually from the country to the city, with 60 percent still living in rural communities as of 1864. What movement occurred led to new Jewish communities, of which Stuttgart was the largest with 1,500 persons. Most of those who resettled found their way into commercial and industrial occupations.[12] The number of Jewish university students also was on the increase, which reflects not only the economic affluency of their parents, but also the youngsters' desire to break away from commerce and move into the academic professions.[13] While Jews in Wuerttemberg were theoretically equal since the law of 1864, admission to a prestigious civil service career was still beyond their reach.

We have the story of Robert Hirsch (1857–1939), who studied law at the University of Tuebingen and applied for a position as judge.[14] Although armed with excellent credentials, he had been turned down several times when he finally appealed to Dr. von Faber, the Minister of Justice of Wuerttemberg himself. The minister urged the young man to become a lawyer instead, since as a judge he would face too many prejudices. A lawyer, the minister said, is not evaluated by his religion, only by his qualifications, whereas a judge had to administer oaths in which the name of God is invoked and the religious feelings of the public respected. What the minister implied was that public prejudice would impair a Jew's functioning as a judge. Indeed, in all of Wuerttemberg there were only three low-level judges until 1918. Hirsch settled in Ulm as a lawyer, in which capacity he held forth from 1886 to 1933, when his name was stricken from the list of lawyers admitted before the court, an anti-Jewish action by the Nazis.

Hirsch was not the only one to suffer from anti-Semitism; his whole generation was made to realize that the Jewish struggle for equality had not come to an end as yet. The Jews' social advance during the second half of the 19th century had not kept pace with their economic advance. Strong political forces developed which tried to slow the integration of Jews into the body politic. The new wave of anti-Semitism hit especially hard the urbanized Jew who had left the comparative shelter of the rural community in search of improved economic and social status. He had given up most of his distinctive Jewishness to prove that he was a person worthy of the privileges of citizenship.

5. | ANTI-SEMITISM BEFORE WORLD WAR I

As Michael Meyer has pointed out, two anti-Semitic groups opposed the full integration of Jews into Germany.[1] The first was represented by Adolf Stoecker, the Prussian court preacher, who maintained that Jews could become fully German only by conversion. Jews, according to this latter day advocate of the Christian state, enjoyed equality in Germany by the good will of a generous Christian nation. As long as Jews believed in their own religion and the future of its role in the world, they could not aspire to political equality. The other group of anti-Semites was headed by the secularist writer Wilhelm Marr, founder of the Anti-Semitic League. For Marr, Jewishness had a racial characteristic which no conversion could wash away. He devoted special attention to Reform Jews whose Jewishness was least apparent. He is quoted as having said: "The Reform Jew is a creature of which one never knows where the Jew begins and where he ends. . . . God save German representative institutions from Reform Jews. Better the most orthodox Polish Rabbi!"[2]

Berthold Auerbach

These anti-Semitic attacks constituted a severe blow to all those who believed in the progress of emancipation and the complete integration of Jews into Germany. One of these was Berthold Auerbach (1812–1882).[3] We have met Auerbach early in his life when, as a student in Stuttgart and Tuebingen, he considered becoming a rabbi. Born in Nordstetten, a small village in the Black Forest, he was thirteen years old when sent by his parents to a preparatory school for higher Talmudic learning. Auerbach became neither a rabbi nor a lawyer (a profession he also considered for a while), but a writer instead. He made a name for himself in this field, but his road to national and international fame was not easy. While a student he had become involved in activities critical of the government and was jailed from January 8, until March 8, 1837 in the mountain prison of Hohenasperg near Ludwigsburg.[4] At this time he had already completed his pamphlet "*Das Judentum und die neueste Literatur.*" (Judaism and the Latest Literature.) He had also begun publishing portraits of prominent Jewish figures, which he edited with N. Frankfurter, in *Gallerie der Ausgezeichneten Israeliten aller Jahrhunderte* (Gallery of Eminent Jews Throughout all Centuries) from 1834 until 1838. From these sketches grew two novels, one on the philosopher Benedict Spinoza (1632–1677) and one on Moses Ephraim Kuh, a lesser-known Jewish poet of the eighteenth century.[5] Auerbach translated Spinoza's works from Latin into five German volumes which appeared in 1841. Pazi suggests that this fascination with Spinoza may have been stimulated by common personal experiences.[6] Both had been destined to become rabbis; Spinoza made his name as a philosopher and Auerbach as a writer. In one of his letters he speaks about writing something not connected with Jews.[7] This probably was a draft of his first twelve rural stories, which appeared in 1843 as the *Schwarzwaelder Dorfgeschichten* (Black Forest Rural Stories) and immediately propelled their author to national fame. In these stories, Auerbach conveys rural life and personalities in a manner that touches the reader's heart. It is the milieu which Auerbach had been born into and which his pen brought to the attention of an astonished and receptive public. He read his masterpieces to many audiences while traveling through Germany and Austria. Thus, he wrote that in Karlsbad he met

the philosopher Friedrich Schelling, a fellow Wuerttemberger (1775–1854), who told him that the Swabians ought to
crown him for the rural stories, which Schelling often read to
refresh himself.[8] Auerbach was happy. Offers for his works
were pouring in from publishers. In one of his letters from
Weimar he wrote that he would need ten hands and three
heads to use all the material about which he wanted to write.[9]
Here in Weimar, the great German cultural city, he was offered the prestigious court position of chief librarian by the
duke and duchess who showered the highest attention upon
him. The position was very enticing, but Auerbach refused.
He felt that life in court surroundings would not go well with
his own nature.

　　Anton Bettelheim, Auerbach's diligent biographer, calls
the years 1843 to 1848 the sunniest period of his life.[10]
Traveling through Germany and Austria, Auerbach found
many admirers and made many new friends, who were impressed by his writings and pleasing personality. In Berlin he
was flattered by Jakob Grimm, the great folklorist, who remarked that Auerbach had freed him from a prejudice. He
would never have believed that a Jew could enter so deeply
into the German character.[11] During this period, Auerbach
published the *Gevattermann* (1845–1848), a folk almanac,
which was widely acclaimed for its stories about the lives
and problems of people in all areas of endeavor. But while
Auerbach's writings made him more and more a spokesman
and poet of German country life, he was always conscious of
being a Jew.

　　On October 10, 1847, Auerbach arrived in Breslau. The
next day, a Saturday, he went to the synagogue to listen to the
sermon of his friend, Rabbi Abraham Geiger. By chance he sat
next to Moritz Schreiber, sharing a song book with him. It
was Schreiber's daughter Auguste, age 22, with whom Auerbach—then 35 years old—fell in love, became engaged, and
married on May 30, 1948 with Geiger officiating at the wedding ceremony. It was a happy match. Auerbach took his

young bride on an extended honeymoon to meet all his
relatives and friends, ending up in Nordstetten to introduce
her to his aged mother.[12] Ecstatically he wrote his father-in-
law about their new home in Heidelberg. Since his childhood, he explained, he had been a wanderer, but now for the
first time in his life he had found a place to sit in peace. When
on October 31 of the same year he wrote to Schreiber that
Auguste was expecting, Auerbach's joy was overwhelming.
"I want to kneel down in tears and let all of God's glory pass
over me." ("*Ich moechte weinend niederknien und alle
Schauer mich ueberstroemen lassen*"). On March 4, 1849,
Auguste gave premature birth to a healthy son; one month
later she died from heart failure. Auerbach was crushed.
These weeks of personal tragedy coincided with revolutionary movements, which fought for more freedom; these conflicts led to anti-Semitic outbursts in various cities in West-
ern Europe, including Heidelberg.[13] A year later Auerbach
married Nina Landesmann from Vienna. She bore him a
daughter and two sons, but it appears from all his letters that
Auerbach never overcame the loss of his beloved Auguste.

A sensitive author, Auerbach drew inspiration for his
prolific writings from people he met and the interpretation of
current events. Until 1859 he made his home in the Saxon
city of Dresden, but then moved to Berlin, the busy capital of
Prussia, soon to become the political center of a united
Germany. In one of his letters Auerbach describes this move
as a stupid act (*dummster Streich*), since what he needed for
life was nature and not a city.[14] Nevertheless these years from
1860 until his death in 1882 proved to be most productive,
both in literary output and social position. This account
cannot attempt an adequate evaluation of his writings. Many
of his rural stories, novels and calendars appeared in multi-
ple editions and translations. He was often invited by the
Royal Family at Berlin to read his stories and, wherever he
went, he was well received by the public. In short, he was a
great success.

Auerbach was an ardent patriot who advocated the unification of Germany under the leadership of Prussia. When this state defeated France in the War of 1870–1871, and Alsace-Lorraine was returned to Germany, no one was happier than Auerbach. One of his close friends was Eduard Lasker, (1829–1884), an eloquent member of the German Reichstag, who emerged in the early 1870s as one of the strongest supporters of a unified Germany.[15]

Ever since the appearance of his *Dorfgeschichten* in the 1840s, Auerbach chose general topics for his work. During the 1870s he expressed the wish of composing Jewish rural tales,[16] but he never succeeded in carrying out this wish just as he never wrote his autobiography. This is to be regretted for they would have shown him committed to Jewry, which to him meant his Nordstetten home, his family and his friends. While he held that science would ultimately take the place of all religions, he assured his cousin Jacob, that in his contemplated writings about Judaism, he would not want to enter into its inner dialogue for lack of sufficient knowledge.[17] In Berlin he was active in an association to help poor Jewish students and very concerned about the plight of Jews in Rumania and Russia.

The last years of his life were extremely painful. In failing health, he sought a cure by spending much time in spas. Even more than his physical condition, the deteriorating political and social climate distressed Auerbach. The very same people with whom he had friendly contacts participated in the anti-Semitic propaganda of the 1870s. There was the Viennese surgeon Theodor Billroth (1829–1894) who wrote against Jews in medicine, provoking Auerbach to reply in an open letter.[18] About the historian Heinrich von Treitschke (1834–1896) who joined the anti-Semitic forces, he would say: "How could a man like him join this mob. I can no longer visit our Thursday-society because I don't want to meet and greet him."[19] In vain he tried to find an explanation for this *Furor Teutonicus* (Teutonic wildness). Perhaps, he wrote, it is due to a re-awakening of the German self-consciousness, but then again Jew hatred existed earlier, during the years of reaction, 1812–1830.[20] After witnessing a two-day debate in parliament against the Jews, he wrote: *Vergebens gelebt und gearbeitet* (Lived and labored in vain).[21]

His many friends in high places tried to assure him that these anti-Semitic movements were of a very temporary nature.[22] Particularly, Empress Augusta (1811–1890) and her family continued to belittle the importance of these anti-Jewish attitudes. It is not known how much this reassurance eased Auerbach's pain in the last year of his life; he had written an essay—never published—against the court preacher Adolph Stoecker, one of the most ardent enemies of the Jews, but he resented the fact that the missionary society took up the struggle against Stoecker. This society was a public institute whose single purpose was to convert Jews to Christianity. Their struggle, he realized, had an ulterior motive: the society would have a difficult time in their conversion efforts if anti-Semitism were rampant. Their attitude also was evident in a letter written by Empress Augusta and posthumously published.[23] She considered anti-Semitism as un-Christian and detrimental to the reputation of Christianity. She feared that such an intolerant attitude would prevent Jews from joining a religion suspected of intolerance.

The life of Auerbach provides some answers to our question of how the early 19th-century Jew living in Germany without rights moved to the status of a "German Jew" i.e., a person with many rights. Even more than the liberal legislation of enlightened lawgivers, the deep yearning of the individual Jew for equality inspired these changes. Upward social mobility brought fortune and fame to many Jews. An expanding industrial society offered tremendous opportunities for enterprising individuals, who only recently had been small time peddlers and shopkeepers. In Auerbach's case he had delved deeply into the life of the rural communities and became an internationally acclaimed interpreter of the German countryside. Auerbach, like many of the Jewish intelligentsia, was aware of the obstacles to complete integration, but like many of his friends he hoped that the forces of anti-Semitism would eventually disappear. He did not see nor did he want to accept any tension between his being a Jew and being a German.

We have seen that Auerbach began avoiding any social contact with Treitschke, the nationalistic historian. It was he who said of Auerbach's rural stories that its peasants were only Jews in disguise. They were artificial creations, for a Jew could have no genuine relationship to the tillers of the soil.[24] The philosopher Moritz Lazarus (1824–1903), one of Auerbach's Berlin friends, articulated the views of most German Jews in opposing Treitschke.[25] Lazarus identified himself as a German of the Jewish faith, not ashamed to profess publicly his loyalty to both *Deutschtum* (Germanism) and *Judentum* (Judaism). He claimed that the attachment of the Jews to their fatherland was unquestionable. The Jews, Lazarus held, were ideally suited to be good Germans because they shared language, birthplace and residence, devotion to the state, obedience to the law, education and culture with the non-Jewish Germans. Ancestry could not be the crucial factor, Lazarus argued, otherwise the great German philosopher, Immanuel Kant (1724–1804) could not be considered a good German because his ancestors came from Scotland.

Anti-Semitism in Wuerttemberg

While organized German anti-Semitism had its major seat in Berlin, the propaganda waves from Stoecker also entered the Wuerttemberg area. His sermons, mailed weekly to many individuals, and his lectures in Stuttgart were bound to influence people. It should be remembered that the total Jewish population of Wuerttemberg was rather small, only about 12,000, of whom a large percentage still lived in rural communities. While we hear of anti-Semitic incidents such as the destruction of tombstones at the Niederstetten cemetery[26] and a physical attack against a young cattle dealer of Buttenhausen,[27] relations were generally good between Christians and Jews in these communities. There was general jealousy caused by the quick economic advance of the Jews, but this jealousy was mainly a city phenomenon. In the countryside there was greater harmony among Jews and Christians, based on the recognition of their religious differences, which no one tried to belittle. For example, Rothschild wrote of Buttenhausen, his native village, where in 1870 more than half of the population was Jewish (442 persons):

> I do not remember that the good relations between the two faiths were ever seriously troubled. At the end of the village we had a joint school building. In it were two schoolrooms and two apartments for the teachers, both with separate entrances. In one room the Christian youth became big and strong and familiar with the art of reading and writing, while in the other, Jewish boys and girls grew into mature and complete human beings. On Saturday our schoolroom was closed. We went in festive clothes to the synagogue, which stood on a hill and was for us a sanctuary full of secret mysteries. Then on Sundays we went with our satchels to school, while our Christian comrades went to church, situated on the opposite mountain. Church and synagogue faced each other peacefully above the valley as two places of human respect for God.[28]

Contrary to reports of religious peace in the rural communities, accounts from the cities show clear evidence of anti-Semitism. We read of an incident where an officer from Berlin, on reserve duty in Stuttgart, took exception to another officer's sitting in a restaurant with one of his Jewish classmates. The gentleman from the big city remarked in a loud voice that it was an insult to the fatherland for a Christian officer to sit at the same table with a Jew. He should be deprived of his sword which should be broken into pieces and thrown into his face; moreover, he should have to give up his uniform. When this Berlin gentleman repeated the same remarks a few days later, the people present gave him a good beating and threw him out of the restaurant. The story concludes that this visitor from Berlin must have realized that such anti-Semitic Jew-baiting was detested in Stuttgart, even by those who did not consider themselves friends of the "Semites".[29]

However, Berlin was not only the headquarters of German anti-Semitism; it also produced the first organization that tried to fight against it. In 1891, some five hundred leading Christians formed the *Verein zur Abwehr des Antisemitismus* (Association for the Defense against Anti-Semitism), which quickly established branches throughout Germany.[30] We have already noted that Stuttgart too had a group of prominent Christians who tried to defend the legal rights of Jewish citizens. One of its most effective defense methods was the publication of a weekly information sheet of four to eight pages called *Mitteilungen* (Communications), which had about 6,000 subscribers. It covered anti-Semitic activities, including court cases, and rebuttals showing the flimsiness of the accusations and accusers. The leading anti-Semitic newspaper in Wuerttemberg was the *Ulmer Schnellpost* (Quick Post of Ulm), whose editor, Hans Kleemann, had written several articles making derogatory statements about Jewish ethics and morality.[31] In 1892 the *Israelitische Oberkirchenbehoerde* sued the editor for libel which brought the anti-Semitic case before a jury. Kleemann had written about the "low ethics of an already debased human race which considered the *Talmud* as its 'Holy Book' for morality." Thus the major issue before the Court was whether the *Talmud* contains unethical statements, especially those that are derogatory of Christianity. The prosecution had brought in two experts: the 81-year-old Rabbi Wassermann (he died shortly after the trial) and a retired 74-year-old Protestant clergyman by the name of Pressel. Wassermann's testimony was somewhat peculiar. He first tried to convince the jury that the

Talmud did not contain anything unethical, but then he proceeded to belittle the *Talmud's* significance. He said that during the last 100 years the *Talmud* had lost three-fourths of its importance; he also reported a diminution of the authority of the *Shulchan Aruch*, the code of Jewish law. There were whole Jewish communities that had never seen a *Talmud*, he said, and regarding the principle of brotherly love, Judaism teaches the same as Christianity. He brought Jewish school books used in Wuerttemberg to prove that Jewish ethics did not discriminate against non-Jews. The other expert, Reverend Pressel, cited his long experience as a school inspector of Jewish schools, stating Jewish confirmation lessons were often patterned after Protestant samples.

The accused editor replied that his articles were based on Professor Rohling's book *Der Talmudjude* and only to be viewed as criticism of those who still adhered to the *Talmud*. He had not intended to slur the Jewish religion, but had acted in good faith and had only expressed a critical opinion. The jury found Kleemann "Not Guilty," which could be interpreted as either the prosecution presenting a weak case or the defense bringing up a strong rebuttal. The Orthodox *Israelit* tried to blame Wassermann's testimony for the judgment of innocence.[32] In belittling the value of the *Talmud*, he played into the hands of the defense, it held. Moreover, by claiming that the Jews of Wuerttemberg broke with the *Talmud* since receiving equal rights, the prosecution made it easy for the defense to argue that Kleemann too was justified in his criticism.

In the same year, another anti-Semitic episode is reported from Heilbronn, where Victor Hugo Welker, president of the Association of Swabian Peasants, lashed out against dishonest Jewish businessmen during a public gathering.[33] He was challenged by Mr. Gumbel, a local Jewish resident, who tried to point out that dishonesty was not reserved for Jews. The report tells that the 400 to 500 listeners present supported Welker with great applause, whereas Gumbel barely escaped a beating by the riotous crowd.

Bad as these reports from Ulm and Heilbronn were, it must be said that the strength of the anti-Semitic movement in Wuerttemberg was very limited. During the elections to the *Reichstag* (German parliament) of 1893, only 400 votes out of 31,524 were given to anti-Semitic candidates and none was elected.[34] While the *Ulmer Schnellpost* continued with its journalistic diatribes, in 1894, it lost its position as the official newspaper of Wuerttemberg's *Deutschnationale Antisemitische Partei* (German-national anti-Semitic Party). Instead, the Berlin newspaper *Volksrundschau* (People's Review) was chosen. Apparently the work of the *Schnellpost* must have been unsatisfactory to the local party members.

Generally speaking there is little evidence that the *Verein zur Abwehr des Anti-Semitismus* had to be active in the state of Wuerttemberg. Its *Mitteilungen* bring few reports about open outbreaks against Jews, and a Wuerttemberg branch of the defensive *Centralverein Deutscher Staatsbuerger Juedischen Glaubens* (Central Association of German Citizens of Jewish Faith) came into being rather late.

Begun in 1899 as a small group led by Dr. Gustav Feldmann, a Stuttgart physician, it grew by 1906 into a statewide organization with fifteen local chapters.[35] To ascribe the lateness of the Wuerttemberg organization to a lack of anti-Semitic incidents is not sufficient. Until 1893, when the *Centralverein* was formed in Berlin, the Jews living in Germany did not have any national defense organization. They were aware of the anti-Semitic forces that stood in the way of complete integration, but they were reluctant to publicly oppose them. They preferred to rely upon well-meaning Christians to battle for their political rights. As a case in point, Schorsch's detailed study about the Jewish reactions to German anti-Semitism, quotes Berthold Auerbach. When the Berlin city delegates issued a declaration against anti-Semitism in November 1880, Auerbach wrote his cousin Jacob:

"In this instance one is joyously revived; here one sees that the concern of the Jews is not their own concern but at the same time that of freedom of humanity. What we have so long wished and hoped for, that we Jews should not have to defend ourselves, that instead Christians would take the initiative, has happened and in the best manner.''[36]

When in 1891, the *Verein zur Abwehr des Anti-Semitismus* came into being, many Jews were happy that the battle would be carried on by Christians, to whom they lent moral and financial support. Thoughtful Jewish leaders realized, however, that the efforts of the *Abwehrverein* were of limited value. While it helped by exposing anti-Semitic acts, it also looked askance at Jewish activities in behalf of their own identity.

Its major concern was the character of the German state, which the members of the *Abwehrverein* viewed as a *Rechts-staat* (law state) where every citizen was bound by the same obligations and entitled to the same rights. To limit the rights of Jews was undermining the existence of the state. The *Abwehrverein*'s members were adherents of the German liberal tradition, which encouraged the assimilation of the Jews for the sake of German unity. Some of their leaders even urged an increase of mixed marriages and the discarding of Jewish ritual practices, which they viewed as being among the causes of anti-Semitism.[37] The *Abwehrverein* also viewed with displeasure the formation of separate Jewish students and sports associations which were the result of Jewish exclusion from German groups. Thus, many Jews soon recognized that they could not depend upon outsiders alone for defense of their political rights and particularly not for the protection of their spiritual identity. Such considerations led to the formation, in 1893, of a previously mentioned association that called itself: *Centralverein Deutscher Staatsbuerger Juedischen Glaubens*. Its publicly stated principles read:

1. We German state citizens of the Jewish faith stand firmly on the soil of German nationality. We have with the

Jews of other countries no other relationship than have the Catholics and Protestants of Germany with the Catholics and Protestants of other countries. We joyously fulfill our duties as German citizens and hold firm on our constitutional rights.

2. As Jews we belong to no political party. The political opinion as well as the religious one is an individual matter.

3. We have no other morality than that of our fellow citizens of other faiths. We condemn the immoral behavior of an individual regardless of faith.

4. We protest against the generalizing with which careless or malicious critics charge the entire body of Jewish citizens for the behavior of the individual Jew.[38]

The slowness of Wuerttemberg's Jews to associate with an organization whose membership by 1903 had risen to 12,000 individuals and 100 affiliated bodies totaling more than 100,000 Jews was due to a number of factors.[39] Foremost, of course, was the relatively harmonious relationship between Christians and Jews. This was particularly the case in the rural communities, but also in the cities there seemed to have been little occasion for the Jewish defense organization to go into action.

In Goeppingen the local group, formed in 1908, became really active only after World War I.[40] When, in 1902, a member of the Wuerttemberg parliament indulged in anti-Semitic remarks about Jewish business practices, the incident was reported in the Jewish press as "an intermezzo and a novum" (something new) for this body.[41] Another member, a country squire, countered that in his long experience as a farmer he sometimes found it easier to do business with Jews than his own associates. He added that he was not a friend of the Jews, but he could not tolerate talk about them in this (anti-Semitic) fashion for they too, in God's name, are human beings.

Another reason for the slow start of the Centralverein in

Wuerttemberg was that the Jews of this state were parochial and often viewed with suspicion any activity that originated from Berlin and the North. Moreover, its communities were still state-controlled with the *Oberkirchenbehoerde* as their supervisory body. It would have been very difficult, if not technically impossible, for a community that was a local state body to join a private organization. Thus association with the *Centralverein* became a choice of individual membership, which for Stuttgart, the largest community, amounted in 1910 to 378 (i.e. approximately 20 percent of the community).[42] No doubt these members should be considered more actively Jewish with the remainder not really concerned with the question of anti-Semitism and Jewish identity. They were more interested in the support of charitable activities, organized mainly to promote local and state welfare programs. They were also contributing to the support of the Jewish community of Palestine, particularly its old age homes and hospitals. They knew that their political equality had not reached the point where they were able to pursue socially prestigious government careers. On the other hand, the Jews of Stuttgart and Wuerttemberg were very pleased when new laws of 1912 gave the Jewish communities more freedom from the state authority and more control over their own affairs. The more than eighty-year struggle for religious autonomy was coming to an end. While ultimate control was still a matter of state authority, henceforth the Jews would no longer constitute a state church, but an *Israelitische Religionsgemeinschaft* (Jewish Relgious Community) and become a corporation of public law.[43] There was not much time for the Jews of Wuerttemberg to enjoy their newly won autonomy, before World War I broke out on August 1, 1914. A loyal citizenry heeded their government's call to arms and hurried to serve their country. Inspired by all their leaders they prayed for the welfare of the *Kaiser* of Germany and the King of Wuerttemberg, hoping for victory of the *Fatherland*.

6. THE 20th CENTURY TO THE ADVENT OF NAZISM

World War I

The outbreak of World War I in August 1914 united the Jews of Wuerttemberg in support of the Fatherland's war efforts. Their participation in the military services has been carefully recorded.[1] Of 10,413 Jewish citizens, 1,610, i.e. 15.4 percent served at the front; two hundred and sixty-three died, 509 were wounded, 568 promoted, 467 decorated once and 573 decorated several times. One hundred and five were promoted to officers: ninety-eight to lieutenants and seven to first lieutenants. Two hundred and six volunteered, seventeen were pilots, forty-four were doctors and six were dentists.

Rabbi Aron Taenzer, a chronicler of Wuerttemberg's Jewish history, exemplified the community's patriotism. Born in 1871 in Pressburg, Hungary, he came to Goeppingen in 1907. At the start of the war he was already forty-three years of age, a busy community leader and a local historian. He also was the father of six children, of whom two sons were later wounded in battle. Nonetheless, he immediately volunteered for duty as an army chaplain. At first, his application was turned down because only six rabbis had been scheduled for service with all the German armies. In addition, the *Oberkirchenbehoerde* had designated the mobilized cantors of Wuerttemberg to provide religious services for its troops. Taenzer, however, continued to press his application, until July 1915, when he was assigned to duty at the Russian front.

Taenzer's memoirs provide a vivid picture of his three

and a half years in the military.[2] This writer, a former chaplain himself, has a special appreciation for Taenzer's work under most trying circumstances. Like his Christian colleagues, he was entitled to a carriage with two horses, a driver, free food and quarters, rations for the horses and the use of a military automobile, whenever one was available. His orders do not mention any remuneration, so that it may be assumed the *Oberkirchenbehoerde* took care of this while he was in the service. Although assigned for Jewish troops only, Taenzer immediately offered his support to all, regardless of faith. A man of the Book, he writes that he had taken riding lessons and instruction in the use of a revolver, both of which proved very useful in the war. Humorously, he tells how a service at the front was delayed because someone had stolen his horses and carriage. Taenzer even tried to ease the hunger of the civilian population, by establishing a public kitchen in the war zone, which was used by military and civilian alike. He received many decorations for his valiant service.

German Jews had hoped their loyalty to the Fatherland would reduce the forces of anti-Semitism. They had believed the *Kaiser* when he proclaimed in 1914: "I do not know parties any more, only Germans."[3] Consequently, they were bitterly disappointed when the collapse of the German war machine precipitated a resurgence of anti-Jewish feelings. As had happened so often in the past, Jews suffered the role of scapegoat and were blamed for Germany's defeat by being accused of having shirked their duties in the military. They were dubbed "the misfortune of the German people," and categorized either as capitalists who had become rich from war profits, or as communists who had overthrown the imperial government. Even in Wuerttemberg, where anti-Semitic agitation had been minor prior to the war, there was heated discussion about the so-called Jewish question. This prompted Christian leaders to issue an open appeal for calm and unity, in order to assist in the reconstruction of the Fatherland.[4] Among those active in the struggle against anti-

Semitism was *Stadtpfarrer* Eduard Lamparter (1860-1945) who, as president of the *Abwehrverein*, worked tirelessly for a better understanding of Judaism. The Jews also received support from the *Centralverein*, which had been in existence before the war, and from a new organization, the *Reichsbund juedischer Frontsoldaten*, formed after the war to defend the honor of the 100,000 Jewish men in uniform, particularly the 11,000 killed in battle.

Internal Reorganization

The end of World War I brought to fruition changes, proposed before the war, in the internal structure of the Jewish community. In 1924, a new constitution converted the *Israelitische Oberkirchenbehoerde* to the *Israelitische Religionsgemeinschaft*. In essence, it meant that the Jewish community administered its affairs autonomously. Power resided with the people and their elected representatives, who constituted a *Landesversammlung*. The representatives elected the *Oberrat*, which functioned as the executive. It consisted of a president, (who also acted as the legal member) and a clerical member; both of whom were salaried.[5] They were assisted by five honorary members and a salaried secretary, Julius Wissmann.[6]

By 1924, the center of Jewish life had moved to Stuttgart where 6,000 Jews were living. They constituted half of the Jewish population in Wuerttemberg, with the other half remaining in smaller cities and rural communities. The financial strength of the community also was concentrated in Stuttgart. It had been said, that all through Germany ten percent of the population was financially able to support ninety percent of the budgetary needs of all communities.[7] Although not quite in the upper ten percent, many Jews belonged to a middle class of business people and academicians. Jews also belonged to a very large group of small shopkeepers, artisans and employees who eked out a living as best as they could. Stuttgart, like any other large community, had a welfare department (including an employment service) to take care of the many needs from all backgrounds.

The fifteen years after World War I also brought changes in the people, groups and institutions which influenced Jewish life in Wuerttemberg. Rabbinical leadership passed from Dr. Kroner to Dr. Paul Rieger in 1922. Kroner, who throughout his life had endeavored to form bridges between all factions, had spent the last years of his ministry preaching peace and healing to a torn nation. Conscious of internal division among Jews, he expressed the view that only anti-Semitic agitation was capable of bringing all Jews together.[8] Rieger, like Kroner, was not a native Wuerttemberger; he came from Dresden. He, too, was a graduate of the Breslauer Theological Seminary, but more liberal than Kroner. Early in his academic life, Rieger had made a name for himself with a *History of the Jews in Rome* which he wrote in collaboration with Hermann Vogelstein.[9] This writer had the privilege of attending his classes in Jewish religion at the Eberhard Ludwigs Gymnasium for many years, and knows how this eloquent teacher could make Jewish history come alive. Rieger had come to Stuttgart rather late in his rabbinical career; he was already fifty-two years of age and had held important posts at Potsdam, Hamburg and Braunschweig. An ardent champion of the *Centralverein*, he served as its chronicler,[10] while stimulating the life of all Wuerttemberg communities as editor of the *Gemeindezeitung fuer die Israelitischen Gemeinden*. Founded in 1924, this newspaper provided a much-needed forum for information and education.

Otto Hirsch

The most important lay leader of the postwar era was *Ministerialrat* Dr. Otto Hirsch (1885-1941). Much has been written about this extraordinary personality, whose roots were deeply imbedded in his Jewish faith and the Swabian soil.[11] Concern for community and public welfare was a tradition in the Hirsch family. Otto's father, Louis (1858-

1941), a wine merchant, had been a member of many communal organizations, including, since 1911, the *Oberkirchenbehoerde*, which was followed by the *Oberrat* where he served as vice-president.[12] Otto's mother, Helene Reis (1860-1939) came from the rural community of Niederstetten. With his brilliant mind, Otto received an appointment to the municipal government of Stuttgart on the day of his marriage to Martha Loeb in 1914. Due to his essential civilian position, his application to serve in the military during World War I was turned down. After the war he transferred to the State Ministry of Interior, received an early promotion to *Ministerialrat*, and became executive director of the semi-governmental Neckar River Agency, charged with the responsibility of river traffic.

Despite his heavy governmental duties, Hirsch found time to devote himself to the needs of the Jewish community, and was chairman of the committee that drafted the 1924 constitution. A fair-minded person and a liberal among Jews, Hirsch made sure that those who were Orthodox would be treated equitably and be permitted to organize their own communities. This assured them religious autonomy, yet did not interfere with either their continued flow of financial support nor the maintenance of a unified community.[13]

The new constitution created a framework for the communal life of Wuerttemberg's Jewry. However, a vehicle to promote its inner cohesiveness was still needed, since the majority of liberal Jews were mainly interested in preserving their political rights and fighting off attacks by anti-Semites. This was the major objective of the *Centralverein*, to which many, including Otto Hirsch, belonged. However, Hirsch realized that any defense against outside attack would have to be strengthened from within through the love and knowledge of Judaism. In 1924, Hirsch met the Jewish philosopher and educator Martin Buber (1878-1965), whose thinking greatly impressed him. Together with his friend Leopold Marx (1889-1983), a cultured industrialist, Hirsch saw the need to establish a platform from which Judaism could be taught in a neutral, non-political manner.[14] This led, in 1926, to the formation of an association called *Juedisches Lehrhaus*, patterned after a similar institution, established a few years before in Frankfurt-am-Main by Franz Rosenzweig (1886-1929). With Hirsch as its chairman as well as student, the *Lehrhaus* developed into a thriving educational activity. For courses in Jewish history and language, it turned to rabbis and educated laymen throughout Wuerttemberg, while its major attraction was Martin Buber, whose guest lectures appealed to a large number of Jews and non-Jews.

Among the many other personalities who contributed greatly to the spiritual texture of the Jewish community during the 1920's, foremost was Dr. Simon Bamberger, spiritual leader of the orthodox *Israelitische Religionsgesellschaft* from 1925 to 1939. This association was founded in 1878 when a few individuals, dissatisfied with the liberal trends of the main synagogue, tried to organize a community of their own. The religious functions of this association were carried out by a teacher-cantor who also acted as a *Shochet* until, in 1919, its first rabbi, Dr. Jonas Ansbacher, arrived after having served a similar group in Heilbronn. However, he only stayed until 1925, as his relationship with the Eastern European members of the congregation was not a smooth one.[15] The total membership of this congregation was fifty families, of which half were of Eastern European origin. But with the arrival of Rabbi Bamberger in 1925, whose ancestor Seligmann Baer Bamberger (1807-1878) had been the champion of those who battled for Orthodox Judaism within the establishment, any thought of separation disappeared. Bamberger's major opponent had been Rabbi Samson Raphael Hirsch of Frankfurt, the fiery protagonist for a separate orthodox community (*Austrittsgemeinde*) in Germany. Young Rabbi Bamberger—he was only 26 at his arrival—quickly captured the hearts of all the members of his congregation, as well as of many others. Meticulously observant, he was totally dedicated to the cause of traditional Judaism and education. He and his wife maintained a very hospitable home, which was always filled with people seeking his counsel and teaching.

The "Ostjuden"

Since the turn of the century, Jews from Eastern Europe, often called *Ostjuden*, had begun arriving in Stuttgart in larger numbers, and by 1933 they constituted approximately ten percent of the 4,500 Jews of the city. The bulk had come from Galicia which, until 1918, had been a part of Austria-Hungary, the German ally. While some attended the liberal or orthodox synagogues, the majority preferred to form their own groups, both for worship and social activities. When Galicia, their place of birth, again became a part of Poland after World War I, these Jews acquired the status of Polish citizens living abroad. Some went through the arduous and long process of acquiring German citizenship—each state had to approve every application—but most of them retained their foreign citizenship and passports. This also applied to their children who were born in Germany.

These Yiddish-speaking newcomers were resented by many of the German Jews for they feared that the new arrivals would hinder the progress of integration. Some of the new arrivals had come to Germany to find better living conditions, while others, the family of this writer included, were seeking safety as the war in the East had turned their home communities into battle zones. Most were poor and without any skills. Gradually their lot improved, but a long time would have to pass before they stopped being "outsiders." When David Horowitz, a decorated sergeant of the Austrian Army and an articulate spokesman of the *Ostjuden*, urged a greater voice for his group within the Jewish community in 1919, he received the following rebuttal from Dr. Caesar Hirsch, a native: "People who cannot speak proper German, let alone Swabian, have no right to speak in a German community."[16] But a step toward greater acceptance was a provision in the 1924 constitution, which reduced the waiting period for membership in the Jewish community for foreigners from five to three years. Still, not until 1932 did an *Ostjude* become a candidate for the community board.

In Stuttgart there were two synagogues for *Ostjuden*, also called *Polnische Juden*, although not all carried Polish passports. These synagogues were known by the streets where they were located. The larger and more liberal group met in a courtyard building at the Marienstrasse; a smaller and extremely pious group prayed in a small loft in a *Hinterhaus* at the Weberstrasse which could only be reached by climbing a steep staircase. It was here where this writer's family worshipped.[17]

The heart of the total Jewish community was undoubtedly Max Meyer, who had come from a small town in Saxony and served in various positions from 1894 until his retirement in 1931 and beyond, until his emigration in 1939. At first, he had been the *Shochet* and teacher-cantor, but as the years went by he assumed all the responsibilities of community administration. Although he had the title *Oberrechnungsrat*, he preferred to be called *Lehrer*. Louis Hirsch in his memoirs paid Meyer a glowing tribute.[18] He writes that anyone who needed information could always go to *Lehrer* Meyer for advice and help. Meyer worked tirelessly from morning to night, for young and old, rich and poor. Among his young admirers was also this writer, who, together with young people of all Jewish backgrounds, attended Meyer's Sabbath afternoon classes which were held in his home next to the *Hauptsynagoge*. Meyer became the head of the welfare department which, with its large employment service, provided help to those in need. He also gave courses at the *Lehrhaus*, filling his lectures with love for Jews and Judaism.

In 1930, Otto Hirsch became president of the *Oberrat*. The previous year he had accepted an invitation to serve on an enlarged council of the Jewish Agency, the body recognized by the British Mandatory Power to promote the upbuilding of Palestine. Although a leading member of the *Centralverein* and theoretically a non-Zionist, Hirsch had been deeply moved by the Buber speeches at the *Lehrhaus* in Stuttgart, which advocated the strengthening of Judaism through settlement in the Holy Land.

Two important events occurred in the life of the Jews of Wuerttemberg in 1932. The first was the festive gathering in honor of the *Waisenhaus* in Esslingen, which could look back on a hundred years of continuous care for orphans, and must have been a proud day for *Oberlehrer* Theodor Rothschild, the *Hausvater* since 1899. From that year until 1931, Rothschild could report that he had taken care of 239 children and had educated them to become self-sufficient adults. At the time of the celebration, 61 children were still at the *Haus*. Most of them hailed from Stuttgart and smaller communities in Wuerttemberg, but there were also children from neighboring Baden and Bavaria as well as cities throughout Germany, such as Hamburg, Hanover, Berlin, Frankfurt and Meran. The geographical range reflects the good name enjoyed by the *Waisenhaus* in all parts of Germany.[19] In his congratulatory remarks, Hirsch attributed the success of the *Waisenhaus* to its "genuine Jewish and genuine Swabian spirit."[20]

The second festivity of 1931 revolved around the *Oberrat*, which celebrated its 100-year growth from the *Staatskirchentum* of 1831 to the *Israelitische Religionsgemeinschaft*, a corporation of public law complete with religious autonomy and the right to raise taxes. The centennial was a symbol of legal equality, a goal for which all Jews had striven for so many years. The final draft of the constitution embodying that equality had been written under the leadership of Otto Hirsch, but he would be one of the first to suffer from the legal inequalities of the Nazi regime; in 1933, he was fired from his position as Executive Director of the Neckar River Agency.

Hitler Comes to Power

On January 30, 1933, Adolf Hitler (1899-1945) was appointed *Reichskanzler* which marks the beginning of destruction and death such as the world had never seen. In reviewing his twelve years of government, this writer faced enormous difficulties, since history often turned to autobiography. Having lived and suffered from these years one cannot help but become a witness for the prosecution, which is still trying to piece together this tragic period in Germany's history. Nonetheless, the review has been made easier by a number of officially sponsored volumes prepared with great dedication over many years, bringing together documents and facts pertaining to the treatment of the Jews.[21] Our presentation then is based on their findings, and will limit itself on this gruesome period to a few main points.

Hirsch's abrupt dismissal from government service, while a personal tragedy to a loyal civil servant, proved to be a help to the 500,000 Jews living in Germany. In September 1933, Hirsch became executive of the *Reichsvertretung der deutschen Juden*, with Rabbi Leo Baeck of Berlin as its president. This body attempted to unite all Jewish organizations, both official and private, in order to deal effectively with the many problems of the new era. To quote Hirsch, its objective was: "*der Diffamierung der deutschen Judenheit ein Ende zu machen, ihrer Einordnung in den neuen Staat die Wege zu bahnen, ihre religioesen, kulturellen und wirtschaftlichen Existenzgrundlagen zu sichern.*" (To end the defamation of German Jews, to pave the way for their integration into the new state, to assure their religious, cultural and economic foundations.)[22] In retrospect, we know that only a tiny portion of these ambitious objectives was realized, and that as the weeks went by anti-Semitic harassment and legislation became stronger and stronger. The more or less orderly attempt to be rid of the Jews through emigration, evident in the early years of the Nazi régime turned, after the *Kristallnacht* of November 1938, into wholesale deportation and death in many concentration camps.

Ironically, but not coincidentally, Jewish education and cultural identification became stronger during this period. German Jewry was suddenly thrown on its own resources, which in the past had often become weak out of neglect and a desire for complete integration into German society. The spirit of *"Ja Sagen zum Judentum"* re-entered the lives of many, and led to the establishment of diversified educational and cultural activities. Ernst Simon, the noted educator and friend of Martin Buber, returned from Palestine to help set up programs for adult education. He tells us that early in the Nazi era few Jewish leaders were aware of the problems facing the Jewish community. In 1933, discussing whether there was still a future for Jews in Germany, Rabbi Leo Baeck declared: "The thousand-year history of Germany Jewry has come to an end."[23] Although he could have had many opportunities to leave, Baeck followed his congregation into the Theresienstadt concentration camp and remained in Germany to the bitter end, being fortunate enough to survive.

Perhaps Baeck harbored the secret hope that the Nazis would allow the Jewish community to dissolve itself in an orderly fashion. This may also have been the hope of Theodor Rothschild who, in 1934, stated as a comment to the curriculum of the Jewish School established in Stuttgart:

> First, the Jewish school must be a German school and follow the official curriculum of German schools . . . For all that life in the German environment demands of us belongs to the reality of our school structure. To get to know our land accurately is to learn to love it, to feel at home in it and to be deeply rooted in it.[24]

Other leaders were less hopeful. Among them was Dr. Siegfried Gumbel, a lawyer from Heilbronn, who succeeded Hirsch as president of the *Oberrat* when Hirsch became the full-time executive of the *Reichsvertretung* and had to transfer to Berlin.

As early as 1933, Gumbel advised a large manufacturer, who employed 3,000 workers, to sell his plant and to emigrate. When asked why his view was so different from that of Hirsch, he replied: "You will see—the position of the Jews in Germany is untenable."[25] Tragically, both leaders perished in concentration camps: Hirsch in Mauthausen on June 19, 1941, and Gumbel in Dachau on January 27, 1942.

Indeed, the serious application of Nazi doctrine was evident in September 1935, when the Nuremberg race laws were announced and blood became a condition of German citizenship. A person with Jewish blood was impure and degenerate; he could never aspire to become a citizen of the German Reich. In the eyes of the Nazis, the term "German Jew" was no longer proper; henceforth the title of the *Reichsvertretung* referred to "Jews in Germany." The Jew's legal status reverted to that of the "unwanted stranger," one that he had been prior to emancipation in the early nineteenth century. Moreover, new race laws should not have come as a surprise to anyone, for ever since 1920, the Nazi party had announced its program of elimination of Jews from the German body politic.[26] Sadly, the free world did not apply pressure upon the Nazis for their flagrant violation of human rights, and this, in turn, encouraged the Nazis to intensify their drive to remove Jews from Germany.

Emigration

Emigration was the only way out of the German trap, but this was easier said than done, for no country awaited the Jews with open arms. Statistics help describe the emigration process as it unfolded, but readers should understand that behind each number there was a human being, and behind each human being there was a story, in most cases a tragic story that defies the writer's pen. The period of emigration is normally defined as the years between 1933 and 1941; after

October 1, 1941, emigration from Germany was forbidden. It is estimated that approximately 300,000 of the 500,000 Jews in Germany managed to reach countries of refuge, either in Europe or overseas. The figures for Baden-Wuerttemberg are given in the appendix together with other relevant statistics.[27] The question arises where did they go, and which countries took them in?[28] The two major countries absorbing emigrants overseas were Palestine and the United States of America. For America, the figures between 1933 and 1945 are estimated at 132,000 and for Palestine, between 1933 and 1941, at 53,200. Admission to Palestine was controlled by Great Britain, the mandatory power charged by the League of Nations in 1922 with providing a national home for the Jewish people. The principle guiding admission was "absorptive capacity of the country," an ambiguous criterion often subject to political expediency. Permits for admission, called certificates, were issued by the British government to the Jewish Agency, the officially recognized body handling the affairs of the Jews in Palestine, and an intricate system of categories was devised by which applicants were selected. Offices established in major cities, including Stuttgart, assisted in the choice of people with skills useful to the development of Palestine, while Zionist organizations arranged for special agricultural farms to prepare youngsters for life in Kibbutzim. Emigrants who owned one thousand pounds or more were allowed to enter the country as "capitalists." By special arrangement with the Jewish Agency and German authorities, these people could deposit their funds in Germany and collect them in Palestine. Emigration to Palestine went along at a fair speed until 1937 when, due to Arab opposition, the British government reduced the number of certificates. At the same time, some Nazi leaders began to fear that the "hochzivilisierte" (highly civilized) Jews in addition to the influx of capital could lead to the creation of a Jewish state: this was not only opposed by the Arabs but was also not considered in the best interests of Germany itself. The decrease of certificates caused the increase of illegal immigration, during which period many Jews were arrested and interned by the British.

Shavei Zion Settlement

Of the 2,873 Jews who made their way to Palestine from Baden-Wuerttemberg between 1933 and 1941 a special group stands out: These were villagers from Rexingen in the Black Forest, together with other Jews from Southern Germany, who founded an agricultural settlement on the Mediterranean coast between Akko and Nahariya.[29]

Family and Jewish tradition[30] had always been ingrained in the lives of the rural community of Rexingen. In 1933, when other rural settlements in Wuerttemberg had been weakened by emigration to the cities, Rexingen still had 262 Jews — approximately thirty percent of the total population. Community organizations were active, and included a Zionist group, recorded as early as 1924: this at a time when few Jews in Wuerttemberg actively identified with Zionist ideas. Since 1824, the Jewish school of Rexingen had functioned without interruption and continued to exist after 1933, when it was converted to a private school, until the outbreak of World War II. During the 1930's, this community became the center of many youth activities, and established a hostel in order to accommodate the frequent visitors. While most Jews derived their living from cattle dealing, when the Nazi boycott started to undermine their economic existence, serious thought was given to emigration.

However, the Rexingen Jews did not want to leave as individuals, but rather as a group that would continue their communal identity. As a result, a delegation was dispatched to Palestine to investigate the possibilities of an agricultural settlement. In this regard they approached Dr. Manfred Scheuer, a lawyer from Heilbronn who was active in Zionist affairs. He encouraged them, but due to a general shortage of certificates—most of which had been earmarked for those already actively preparing themselves for life in Kibbutzim—difficulties arose. But another Wuerttemberger came to the rescue, the aforementioned Otto Hirsch, who induced the Berlin authorities of the Jewish Agency for Palestine to take a fresh look at the villagers' proposal of group settlement. A special commission was dispatched to Rexingen for an on the spot examination regarding the fitness of the applicants to perform farm work. The story is told that the Rexinger, many of whom owned small farms of their own, received the Berlin visitors in their farm clothes and with shoes covered with soil. The rustic appearance helped to convince the commission to approve the project and to grant the necessary certificates. On February 13, 1938, a first group of thirty-eight left for the Holy Land and, joined by others from Southern Germany, started their cooperative enterprise on April 13 of the same year. Their first and longtime Mayor was Dr. Scheuer. More settlers followed. Many difficulties had to be overcome, but through hard work they succeeded in creating a thriving community for more than four hundred people. Today, Shavei Zion is a favorite spot for many visitors with former ties to Rexingen, who admire the transplantation of the old into the new land of Israel.

United States of America

As the immigration to Palestine declined, the United States came to the fore as the country of refuge. That the first four years of the Nazi regime produced only a small number of German Jewish immigrants can be explained by the history of the United States, rather than that of Germany.[31] In the 1920's, America, which had been the haven for millions of immigrants, turned to a quota system based on national origin, defined as country of birth. This restricted the influx of nationals from Eastern and Southern European countries, mostly Catholics, Slavs and Jews, who were considered by a majority of the U.S. Congress to be undesirable. In the 19th century large-scale immigration from Germany caused the

German quota to be relatively high—25,000 persons each year—but unfortunately, in the years from 1933 to 1938[32] the Jews from Germany were unable to fill this quota. This was, in part, due to complicated administrative requirements, which demanded proof that a prospective immigrant was "not likely to become a public charge." Thus, immigrants had to provide affidavits of support from relatives or friends in the United States. As a result, a frantic search began for persons who were not only willing, but also financially able, to provide documents satisfactory to the strict immigration authorities. This search was frequently expedited with the assistance of American organizations, such as the Hebrew Immigrant Aid Society (HIAS) and the National Council of Jewish Women. Since there had been a large number of immigrants from Southern Germany in the 19th and 20th centuries, Jews from Southern Germany, including Wuerttemberg, were somewhat more fortunate in their search. Julius Wissmann, the last secretary of the *Oberrat* left a vivid report of the feverish drive to obtain visas from the United States consulate in Stuttgart.[33] He also tells of a meeting in Zuerich, Switzerland, with Karl Laemmle, head of the Metro-Gold-wyn-Mayer Film Studio in Hollywood. Formerly a native of Laupheim, Laemmle had issued three hundred affidavits to needy relatives and friends from Wuerttemberg. When Wissmann presented another affidavit of his, he was told by the consular staff: *"Wir wissen ja, dass Herr Laemmle sehr reich ist, aber einmal muss es doch ein Ende haben, denn fuer ueber 300 Familien zu garantieren, is doch zu viel."*[34] ("We know, of course, that Mr. Laemmle is very rich, but this has to come to an end once, for guaranteeing three hundred families is too much.")

The feverish drive to leave Germany, legally or illegally, increased even more in the wake of two events in late 1938. First there was the deportation of between 15,000 and 17,000 Polish Jews—about 300 lived in Baden-Wuerttemberg—in late October.[35] At that time, the Polish government decided to cancel the passports of all Polish Jews living in Germany, unless they were especially extended. This extension was denied to all Jews who had had no connection with Poland during the previous five years. It should be remembered that many Jews, born in the area restored to Poland after World War I, had been living in Germany even before the war; established in Germany, they had little or no contact with the country of their birth, thus their principal reason for not becoming German citizens was the administrative difficulties in obtaining German citizenship. But the Nazis used the Polish decree as an excuse to round up all Polish Jews and deport them to the border, which had been closed. There in no-man's land, they were stranded for weeks, until the border was finally opened up. They had to live in squalid conditions, receiving assistance from the American Joint Distribution Committee, which also found accommodations in border communities. In a few instances, Jews were allowed to return to Germany to fetch their families, while others succeeded in emigrating. However, the bulk were trapped, rounded up, and sent to their death in concentration camps with the outbreak of World War II.

Kristallnacht[36]

The second event to influence flight from Germany was directly related to a shooting incident: a young Jew who wanted to avenge the deportation of his parents fired at a Nazi embassy official in Paris. This shooting triggered a carefully prepared action by the Nazis, during which hundreds of businesses, homes and synagogues were destroyed. This rampage on November 9 and 10, 1938, came to be known as the *Kristallnacht* when about 30,000 Jews were arrested and sent to the concentration camps, while a fine of one billion marks was imposed upon the Jewish community.

A particularly horrible incident involved the Jewish

Waisenhaus in Esslingen. On November 10, during the noon hour, a horde of people armed with axes and hammers stormed the dining room, ransacked the building and the synagogue and burned the Torah scrolls and books in the courtyard. The teachers were beaten up, and many children fled into the streets while others were kept under guard and warned that they too would be burned, like the books. All this took place with more than 1,000 local residents standing idly by. The children were placed in different homes, but returned for a few short months when the *Waisenhaus* was reopened in 1939. With the outbreak of World War II on September 1, 1939, the Nazis converted the *Waisenhaus* into a hospital. Rothschild and his wife moved into Stuttgart, where they headed the Jewish school. Many of the children were also placed there, but they were soon deported and never heard from again. Theodor Rothschild himself died in 1944 in Theresienstadt, a father to the needy as long as he lived.[37]

The "Final Solution"

Despite all these "successful" destruction measures—in Wuerttemberg alone the Jewish population decreased 15 percent between October 1, 1938 and March 1, 1939—185,000 Jews still remained in Germany,[38] and ever more severe policies were now put into effect to expedite matters: food was restricted and transportation and medical attention were curtailed. From September 1, 1941 on, each Jew had to wear a yellow star, and the door to his apartment had to be identified by the same symbol; persecution drove many to suicide. Eventually, large deportations were organized to expedite the "Final Solution." From 1940 until 1945, more than twelve transports originated from Baden-Wuerttemberg alone affecting a total of 8,337 persons. They ended up in camps such as Gurs, Riga, Izbica, Auschwitz and Theresienstadt.[39] While their destinations may have been different, they all faced inhumane living conditions, brutal treatment and death for the sole crime of being Jews. Outside of this Southern Germany area, there were numerous shipments from other parts of Germany and Europe which ultimately resulted in the destruction of six million men, women and children. No matter how painful this story may be we must never forget it, and make certain that such atrocities will never occur again.

7. | THE POSTWAR PERIOD

The Aftermath of the Holocaust

On May 8, 1945, the combined efforts of the Allies finally succeeded in defeating Germany on the field of battle, and the war in Europe came to an end. Now the Allies faced an equally difficult task: restoring a semblance of order in a totally disrupted civilian population. Again, we have to resort to the unsatisfactory method of statistics to describe, at least in part, the chaotic conditions within Germany. In addition to a German population of approximately 70 million, there were now more than eight million Displaced Persons (DPs), many of whom had been brought from all parts of Europe to supply the Nazi war machine with labor. One of the first assignments of the Allied armies was to assist in the return of these millions to their homelands. Indeed compared with these tremendous numbers, the care of the approximately 90,000 Jewish survivors of the concentration camps would almost seem like a minor problem. However, nothing could have been further from the truth: these survivors were all that were left of the six million Jews whom Hitler and his henchmen had systematically destroyed over a period of twelve years. Whenever the armies came upon them, whether in camps, on marches or in hiding, they were more dead than alive. For instance, in Buchenwald, the average inmate's weight amounted to no more than 60-80 pounds, the result of a subsistence of 600 calories daily. Shortly after the liberation, in Bergen Belsen, 23,000 mass burials took place, 80 percent of which were Jews who had succumbed due to either starvation or overeating.[1] Nobody could have anticipated the conditions that would need to be faced in these concentration camps; moreover, it is to the everlasting credit of the military forces that they spontaneously extended all the help they could in matters of food and medical attention. By previous agreement, Germany had been divided and controlled by four military zones: British, French, Russian and the United States troops respectively. As the situation unfolded, sixty percent of the Jewish DPs (54,000) found themselves in the American zone of occupation.

In the Stuttgart area, it was the U.S. 100th Infantry Division with its Jewish Chaplain, Captain Herbert S. Eskin, who assisted the thousands of Jews in, and out of, camps. He was instrumental in setting up a synagogue, hospital wards and kitchen facilities at Reinsburgstrasse 26, a building which had formerly belonged to Jews killed in concentration camps.[2] This building became the center of Jewish life in the Stuttgart area until the new synagogue was dedicated in 1952 at Hospitalstrasse 36, the same site of the former synagogue destroyed in the *Kristallnacht*. Of course, Eskin and the military could only provide initial help. A few months following the liberation, the first teams of the American Joint Distribution Committee (Joint) and the United Nations Relief and Rehabilitation Administration (UNRRA) began to arrive and assume responsibility. Initially, Jewish survivors had been placed in camps together with others from their native country. But a major factor in the improvement of the Jewish DP situation was America's official recognition that they must be housed in separate camp facilities. In the eyes of the military, Jews did not have any separate status and were considered nationals of the countries of their birth; however, this often resulted in their being placed with people who had been their worst persecutors during the war. It took until August 22, 1945—three and a half months after liberation— when General Dwight D. Eisenhower (1890-1969), at the direction of President Harry S. Truman (1884-1972), ordered the establishment of special camps for Jewish DPs.

A very small number of deportees from Stuttgart had survived the war and had returned to their home community. They were the ones who were endeavoring to reestablish themselves into a new Jewish community structure. Thus, we learn of a first anniversary of the *Interessenvertretung juedischer Gemeinden und Kultusvereinigungen* which took place in Stuttgart on April 13, 1947. One of the speakers was Dr. Benno Ostertag, an attorney prior to the war, who scolded the authorities for their tardiness in restoring legal and property rights to Jewish survivors. The speaker was specific in including Displaced Persons in his plea, since their miserable situation was a direct result of the Nazi régime. In actuality, the Displaced Persons did not consider themselves a part of the *Gemeinde*. For them, Germany was only a country of transit, to pass and leave as soon as possible. While they were forced to remain they were busy forming their own communities, complete with religious, educational and social activities. Their groups were loosely organized under the Central Committee of Liberated Jews, whose principal offices were situated in Munich, the capital of Bavaria. By the end of 1947 their numbers had increased to approximately 250,000 men, women and children, many of whom were Polish nationals who had survived the war in Russia. When they returned to Poland, they encountered a vicious anti-Semitic climate, and even a pogrom at Kielce where 43 Jews were killed. This triggered their exodus into the American zone of Germany, where they hoped to find opportunities for emigration. There had also been arrivals from other countries of Eastern Europe.

Ever since liberation many, if not most survivors, had hoped to make a new home in the Holy Land. However, the British Mandate government only permitted legal entry for a small number of applicants. This, in turn, caused an underground movement to reach Palestine "illegally." We know that in the short period of December 15, 1945, until September 15, 1946, the total number of arrivals in Palestine included 9,296 "illegals." No matter how difficult and dangerous the journey, they kept coming. Those that were intercepted by the British were interned on the island of Cyprus, and these numbers ultimately exceeded 16,000. Another tragic story involved the ship "Exodus 1947" which tried to reach Palestine with 4,000 DPs aboard, but was forcibly returned by the British to Germany. It is no small wonder that the tension among the DPs in Germany was the highest in 1947, until May 14, 1948, when the State of Israel was created. This started an orderly immigration and emptying of DP camps in Europe. By December 31, 1950, the new state had provided a haven for over 120,000 wretched survivors of war and persecution.[3] Moreover, the plight of Jewish DPs was further alleviated by the easing of the strict U.S. immigration laws through President Truman, which allowed the entry by 1951 of 77,500.[4]

Unfortunately, we do not know how many DPs, upon liberation, found themselves in the Wuerttemberg area. Reliable figures date from March 1949, when the general exodus to Israel and the United States had been well under way. At that time, out of a total of 1,441–265, or 18.4 percent, were German Jews and 1,176, or 81.6 percent, Displaced Persons.[5] The next reliable figure lists the total of *Gemeinde* members for 1955 as 557.[6] At that time there was no longer any justification for listing German Jews and DPs separately, for on June 30, 1950, the International Refugee Organization (IRO), successor to UNRRA, had ceased to function. Henceforth, the care for DPs and their integration into the republic had become the responsibility of the newly-established Federal Republic of Germany, as stated in its Declaration of August 11, 1950.[7]

Reconstruction

Symbolic of Stuttgart's Jewish vitality was the dedication of its synagogue and administrative building on May 13, 1952. With the active support of all government authorities, headed by the *Bundespraesident* Dr. Theodor Heuss and many friends, the buildings were erected to serve as a memorial to the past, and as an expression of hope for a better future.[8] As it developed, it would be the only synagogue rebuilt in Wuerttemberg, and as such, assumed added significance for Jews living and visiting Stuttgart. Shortly after the dedication, the community was indeed fortunate in obtaining the services of a rabbi who stayed with them for more than twenty-five years. This was Rabbi Dr. Fritz Elieser Bloch (1903-1979), a native of Munich and a graduate of the Jewish Theological Seminary in Breslau; he had also studied at the Talmudical academies of Lithuania and been a rabbi at Aschaffenburg from 1932 to 1938. He had emigrated to Palestine and had worked in education in the new state of Israel.

In attempting to understand the immense difficulties facing Rabbi Bloch in trying to be a leader in Stuttgart, we will have to familiarize ourselves with the general Jewish situation. First, we must understand the various backgrounds of those 500-odd members of the community whom Bloch would have to serve as a spiritual guide. For this analysis we follow, in part, the findings of Dr. Nathan P. Levinson, *Landesrabbiner* in Baden, whose long service in Germany has earned him the right to be heard.[9] Levinson gives 30,000 as the approximate number of Jews living in Germany.[10] A few of these had survived the Nazi persecution by living in hiding, while others had remained alive because they were married to non-Jewish spouses and had not raised their children as Jews. The Nazis had called them "privileged Jews," privileged not to die! As pertains to Stuttgart, we know that two transports of Jews living in mixed marriages, were sent to Theresienstadt in 1944—rather late in the war— from where a considerable number returned at war's end. A third group included concentration camp survivors, some of whom had lived in Germany before the war, and others who had never seen German soil. A fourth group was made up of former German Jews who had emigrated while there was still time, but had returned to their native place for personal reasons. The above may give us an idea of some of the people that made up the Jewish community of Wuerttemberg. It would have been a difficult task for any rabbi, no matter how understanding and dedicated, to forge them into a united group.

Reasons of age are at the root of other problems besetting all Jewish communities in postwar Germany. In 1971, Kuschner records an exceedingly high number of persons in the over-sixty bracket and a very low number in the 0-20 categories.[11] Moreover, the inner stability of the communities was further weakened by the large number of intermarriages. while those youngsters who rejected mixed marriages had to emigrate, in order to find suitable spouses.[12] Still, in spite of losses from emigration, death due to old age and mixed marriages, Germany's Jewish population shows an increase from 17,825 in 1955 to 23,070 in 1959 and 26,226 in 1967.[13] This large increase was due to a number of factors: First, there was a political strengthening of all communities through the establishment of the *Zentralrat der Juden in Deutschland* in 1951. This body was elected by the communities and *Landesverbaende*, and over the years assumed an increasingly important role as the official spokesman of Jews in Germany. Its Wuerttemberg delegate is Henry J. Ehrenberg, a very successful industrialist, with plants in Germany as well as in other European countries, the U.S.A. and Israel.[14] Another factor was the German-Israel reparations agreement of 1952, during the political leadership of Chancellor Konrad Adenauer (1876-1967) and Prime Minister David Ben Gurion (1886-1973). This brought about increasing traffic in trade between the two countries, and led to diplomatic relations in 1965. In addition, this agreement was also the beginning of individual payments to victims of Nazi Germany; it caused the return of many, especially those of advanced age, who felt that it would be easier to live in the old country. Finally, the economic boom of the 50's and 60's attracted a large number of returnees as well as of newcomers.

The Stuttgart Jewish community also shows an increase in membership from 557 in 1955 to 795 in 1974, although now, in 1982, it has declined to 703. The Jewish community programs include those for youth, adults and senior citizens, while religious services are of the Orthodox-Chassidic tradition, reflecting the background of most worshippers. A *kosher* restaurant was also established on the premises of Hospitalstrasse 36. The education of the young, both in Stuttgart and throughout the state where Jewish families resided, was accomplished with the assistance of teachers who were brought over from Israel. At a time when local needs took a big bite of the budget, there were also large fundraising efforts in behalf of Israel. All these activities were accomplished by few professionals and many volunteers.[15]

What of the Future?

Ever since Jews began living in Germany after Hitler's defeat, the question has been asked: Is there a future for Jews in Germany? As yet, no one has found a satisfactory answer to this question which is almost forty years old. Thus, we have to turn to some opinions of people who have been on the inside. First there is Leo Baeck (1873-1956), the courageous Rabbinical leader who had survived Theresienstadt:

> I have loved Germany so much that it could break my heart. Not only its people, its language and its culture, but also its countryside . . . But when I visited Germany in 1946 and now again in 1952 and had to admire, what an industrious and ambitious people achieves in reconstruction, I said to myself nevertheless: This land is no longer my land . . . My Germany has perished forever.[16]

Then our own Rabbi Bloch of Stuttgart had this to say in

connection with Jewish education: "We too educate the children for Israel. There is still no future here."[17] There were also other views. In 1972, Werner Nachmann, president of the *Zentralrat*, is quoted: "The duty is imposed upon the Jews to live and work in Germany."[18] And finally a quote from Nachum Goldmann (1895-1982), the long-time Jewish leader, on the occasion of the 40th anniversary of the *Kristallnacht*: "I have never counted myself among those who were of the opinion that Jews should no longer live in Germany."[19] These differing views have one thing in common. They show an awareness of the sensitive situation for Jews living in Germany today, for it is common knowledge that many Jews, who have become well-established in their economic lives, still do not feel completely at home in the new Germany. They send their children abroad to complete their education, and are happy if they, in turn, find a new home for themselves in different countries. It is also well-known that former residents, who were fortunate enough to emigrate in time, refuse to set foot again on their native soil. The leaders, both Jewish and German, are trying hard to produce a better climate all around.

One of the essential duties for present-day Jewish leadership is to provide rabbis, teachers and administrative personnel for the existing congregations. There is a great urgency to train people within Germany and not to remain dependent, as in the past, upon professionals from abroad. This has led to intensive discussions between Jewish and government authorities, with the result that, in 1979, an Academy for Jewish Studies (*Hochschule fuer Juedische Studien*) was established in Heidelberg, the picturesque city on the Neckar river and seat of one of Germany's oldest universities. The Academy announced a series of diverse courses which would lead to the academic degree of Magister (Master) of Jewish Studies. Since its inception, however, this ambitious program has been handicapped by the shortage of German-speaking scholars who would want to serve as faculty members for any length of time. Until now, most of the instructors had to be recruited from among academics living in Israel or the United States. In view of the limited number of Jewish youth in Germany today, it is not easy to attract many to a program in Jewish studies. On the other hand, the Academy serves a large body of students of all faiths who are interested in deepening their knowledge of Judaism, while it also provides a forum for academic discussion on topics of Jewish concern. Its future success is intimately connected with, and dependent upon, Jewish life in Germany generally.

A very important nationwide movement is the "*Gesellschaft fuer christlich-juedische Zusammenarbeit,*" which has as its aim the bringing together of men and women of the Christian and Jewish faiths to further better understanding among all people. Soon after its foundation in the early 1950's, Elliot E. Cohen, the renowned editor of the United States magazine *Commentary,* who happened to be in Berlin, addressed the group. At that time, he urged Germans to undergo a harsh school of moral and political self-examination, in order to learn about freedom of religion and diversity of opinion.[20] This writer believes that Cohen's advice is still relevant today, though teaching new generations calls for different methods. In Stuttgart, the *Gesellschaft* is headed by the very energetic Heinz M. Bleicher who, with the help of dedicated volunteers, is trying hard to further the cause of education and information.[21] A case in point is the Freudental synagogue project.[22] Here in this rural community not far from Stuttgart, a group of men and women, none of the Jewish faith, have banded together and bought the building of the former synagogue which they are now busily engaged in restoring to its former dignity. In the process, they are also collecting all the memorabilia which are still available, and hope that eventually, a museum will be attached to it as a memorial to Jewish life in Wuerttemberg.

Somewhat different, but in the same spirit of good will, the city of Stuttgart is sponsoring exhibits showing the adverse impact of the Nazi period on life in general, and on Jews in particular. This same city, like many cities throughout Germany, has embarked on a program of inviting former residents to visit their old home town. Statewide efforts of education and information are the domain of the *Landeszentrale fuer politische Bildung* Baden-Wuerttemberg. Its director, Heinz Lauber, told this writer of the great impact that the American television series "Holocaust" made upon the German public, particularly its youth, which led to many productive dialogues between Jewish survivors and Germans. He feels that such meetings are the best methods of education towards democracy.

This writer too feels that only a vibrant democracy can create a bulwark against the kind of extremism which produced a Hitler. The world still gropes for an answer to how and why such a civilized nation as Germany could submit to a leadership which killed six million Jews whose only crime consisted of belonging to the Jewish faith. Today, the Federal German Republic is trying hard to extend a hand of friendship to the 30,000 Jews in its midst, and the Jews know this and appreciate it. At the same time, they realize that the battle for democracy is an ongoing one, and that they are in the forefront of it. In order to be a good fighter in this battle, they will have to be strong in their faith and loyal to their tradition; their close ties with the state of Israel will help them, spiritually and physically, to overcome the isolation in which they often find themselves. If their German neighbors, conscious of their country's past, will continue to work for living democracy, there is hope that the tiny Jewish sapling may become a sturdy tree in a forest of humanity.

NOTES

CHAPTER 1

1. For an overview until the 19th century see Paul Sauer, *Die juedischen Gemeinden in Wuerttemberg und Hohenzollern*, (Stuttgart, 1966) p. 1ff.; also Paul Taenzer, *Die Rechtsgeschichte der Juden in Wuerttemberg, 1806-1828*, (Stuttgart, 1922) p. 67.
2. Christian Wilhelm Dohm. *Ueber die Buergerliche Verbesserung der Juden* (Berlin and Stettin, 1781). For a general description of the period see: Reinhard Ruerup, "Emancipation and Bourgeois Society" *LBIYB*, XIV (1969) p. 67ff.
3. Dohm, p. 28.
4. *Ibid.*, p. 34.
5. Utz Jeggle, *Judendoerfer in Wuerttemberg* (Tuebingen, 1969) p. 108.
6. *Ibid.*, p. 113.
7. *Ibid.*, p..107.
8. Aron Taenzer, *Die Geschichte der Juden in Wuerttemberg* (Frankfurt-Main, 1937) p. 32ff.
9. *Festschrift zum 50 Jaehrigen Jubilaeum der Synagoge zu Stuttgart*, hrsg. vom Israelitischen Kirchenvorsteheramt (Stuttgart, 1911) p. 12.
10. Aron Taenzer, p. 38ff; see also Jeggle, p. 127f., and Bernard Theil, "*Die Israelitische Oberkirchenbehoerde und ihre Kritiker*," *Zeitschrift Fuer Wuerttembergische Landeskunde*, Vol. 39, (1980) p. 206ff.

11. Isaak Hess, Denkschrift An die Hochansehnliche Staende-Versammlung (Stuttgart, 1821). *Stunden der Andacht Fuer Israeliten zur Befoerderung Religioesen Lebens und Haeuslicher Gottesverehrung, Neue Ausgabe*, (Ellwangen, 1867).

12. See title page of a "*Vorschlag zu einem Lehrplane Fuer die Israelitischen Schulen in Koenigreich Wuerttemberg*." HS E207c, Bue 78.

13. Carl Weil, *Ueber die Zulaessigkeit der Juden zum Buergerrecht* (Stuttgart, 1827).

14. In 1834, this paper changed its name to *Deutscher Courier*. see *Biographisches Lexicon des Kaisertums Oestreich*, Vol. 54 (Wien, 1886) p. 8f.

15. On the new Rabbinic training see Ismar Schorsch, "Emancipation and the Crisis of Religious Authority: The Emergence of the Modern Rabbinate," *Revolution and Evolution 1848 in German-Jewish History*, W. E. Mosse, A. Paucker and R. Ruerup eds. (Tuebingen, 1981) p. 205ff.

16. He was a teacher at the Jewish *Realschule* (Philanthropin) of Frankfurt. His son Theodor, also a teacher there, was a leader of the reform. See Monika Richarz, *Der Eintritt der Juden in die Akademischen Berufe*, (Tuebingen, 1974) p. 125.

17. *Ibid.*, p. 109 ff.

18. Anton Bettelheim, *Berthold Auerbach*, (Stuttgart, 1907) p. 56.

19. Schorsch, p. 207.

20. Paul Taenzer, *Rechtsgeschichte*, p. 76ff.

21. Jeggle, p. 128 considers this figure too high.

22. Taenzer, p. 70 states that the six retained were appointed without examination. This does not hold true for Gabriel Adler and Jacob Kaufmann, whose tests are in the *Staatsarchiv* Ludwigsburg, E212,Bue 94; for the examinations themselves see HS E201c, Bue 94.

23. Taenzer, p. 77f.; for subjects and score see *Staatsarchiv* Ludwigsburg, E212, Bue 94.

24. About 100 years later, German had become the language of tradition for the Jewish villagers of Bohemia. When the Czech authorities insisted on the use of Czech, the older Jews admonished the younger ones: "*Wenigstens am Schabbes sprich Deutsch*" (At least on the Sabbath talk German). Infor-

mation from lecture of Professor Fred Hahn at the Leo Baeck Institute, New York, November 1981.

25. Geiger called him a *"Kuehner"* (courageous) in his letter to Berthold Auerbach of December 25, 1843. *Abraham Geiger's Nachgelassene Schriften,* Vol. IV (Berlin, 1876) p. 173.

26. *Gottesdienst-Ordnung Fuer die Synagogen des Koenigsreichs Wuerttemberg,* (Stuttgart, 1838). See also Jacob J. Petuchowski, *Prayerbook Reform in Europe,* (New York, 1968) p. 112ff. and Steven M. Lowenstein, "The 1840's and the Creation of the German-Jewish Religious Reform Movement" *Revolution and Evolution 1848 in German-Jewish History,* p. 255ff.

27. Custom to express disapproval of Haman, the villain of the story.

28. Symbolic punishment for the repentant sinner.

29. It came to light during the debate at the Rabbinic Conference of Braunschweig in 1844. *Protocolle der Ersten Rabbiner-Versammlung,* (Braunschweig, 1844) p. 22. Adler was a cousin of Nathan Marcus Adler, Chief Rabbi of England and a teacher of Berthold Auerbach.

30. Heinz Moshe Graupe, *The Rise of Modern Judaism,* (New York, 1978) p. 168.

31. *Rede bei dem Antritt seines Amtes als Rabbiner zu Stuttgart,* 1835. For a listing of his sermons see *Festschrift,* p. 72 n.1.

32. a. *Lehrbuch der Biblischen Geschichte,* (Frankfurt-Main, 1828).
    b. *Spruchbuch, eine Sammlung von Bibelspruechen zum Gebrauch bei dem Religionsunterricht in den Israelitischen Schulen des Koenigreiches Wuerttemberg,* (Stuttgart, 1835).
    c. *Gesangsbuch, zum Gebrauch bei dem Unterricht in der mosaischen Religion und zur oeffentlichen und zur haeuslichen Gottesverehrung,* (Stuttgart, 1836).
    d. *Confirmations-Handlung, nebst dem Konfirmanden-Unterricht,* (Stuttgart, 1836).
    e. *Lehrbuch der Israelitischen Religion zum Gebrauch der Synagogen und Israelitischen Schulen,* (Stuttgart, 1837).

33. *Rabbinische Gutachten, ueber die Vertraeglichkeit der freien Forschung mit dem Rabbinatsamte,* 2 volumes, (Breslau, 1842-43); see also Petuchowski, p. 33ff and Schorsch, p. 224ff.

34. *Rabbinische Gutachten*, Vol. II, p. 45ff.
35. Maier had published some of his sermons jointly with those of Gotthold Salomon, the preacher of the Hamburger *Tempelvereinigung* and an early leader of Reform.
36. Philippson, in his review of the conferences, forty years later (*Allgemeine Zeitung des Judentums*), Vol. 48 (1884) p. 214, states that Maier was elected because he was the oldest member present. However, he was the second oldest, born 1797, the oldest was Gotthold Salomon (1784-1862).
37. Petuchowski, p. 34f. In Germany the term "Reform" came to designate everything that was not "Orthodox." By the end of the 19th century the advocates of Reform referred to themselves as "Liberal." See also Graupe, p. 173 f.
38. Lowenstein, p. 284 speaks of Reform communities. Besides Maier who attended the first two conferences there was Michael Gueldenstein of Buchau, who attended all three and Maier Lowengard of Lehrensteinfeld, who attended only the second and third. The latter wound up his rabbinic career as *Dayan* in Basel, Switzerland. See Taenzer, p. 73.
39. a. *Protocolle der ersten Rabbiner-Versammlung.* (Braunschweig, 1844).
    b. *Protocolle der zweiten Rabbiner-Versammlung.* (Frankfurt, 1845).
    c. *Protocolle der dritten Rabbiner-Versammlung.* (Breslau, 1847).
40. *Protocolle*, 1845, p. 285 ff.
41. Joseph Maier, *Die erste Rabbiner-Versammlung und ihre Gegner*, (Stuttgart, 1845).
42. *Ibid.*, p. 34.
43. Zacharias Frankel, *Zeitschrift fuer die religioesen Interessen des Judentums*, 1. Jhrg. (Berlin, 1844) p. 166. In 1854, Frankel became the head of the first academic rabbinical college in Germany, known as the Breslau Seminary. It represented the positive historical school of Judaism combining tradition with the principle of evolution. See Graupe, p. 154ff. and Ismar Schorsch, "Zacharias Frankel and the European Origins of Conservative Judaism," *Judaism* (Summer, 1981), p. 344ff.

44. *Ibid.*, p. 35f.
45. *Protocolle*, 1845, p. 86ff.
46. *AZJ*, (Mainz, 1845) p. 216f.
47. *Ibid.*, May 6, 1845, p. 358.
48. Other anonymous letters appeared in the *Treue Zions Waech-ter*, 3. *Jhrg.* 1847, p. 207f. and 4. *Jhrg.* 1848, p. 53 pointing to the religious activities of many communities as proof that "the Jews of Wuerttemberg were better than their reputation abroad."
49. *Sha'ar Haskenim*, Part 2, Bayit Melo (Sulzbach, 1830) p. 170ff.
50. Taenzer, p. 70ff. Muehringen in the Black Forest was a very prestigious community, having been the one-time seat (1745-1750) of Rabbi Nathaniel Weil, author of the Talmudic commentary *Korban Netan'el*.
51. *AZJ*, April 1847, p. 306f and 317f.
52. Joseph Maier, *Ueber den Judeneid* (Stuttgart, 1852).
53. *Israelitisches Gebet-und Andachtsbuch* (Stuttgart, 1848). It served as a sample to the American Union Prayerbook (Reform) published fifty years later. Petuchowski, p. 141ff and 159ff.
54. *Ibid.*, p. 1ff.
55. *AZJ*, August 1855, p. 14ff.
56. Joseph Maier, *Die Synagoge* (Stuttgart, 1861) p. 21.
57. Orthodox became the term for traditional Judaism in Germany which is really not adequate as it emphasizes creed, leaving out deed. See Joseph Wohlgemuth, *"Etwas ueber die Termini Orthodoxes und gesetzestreues Judentum," Festschrift zum siebzigsten Geburtstage David Hoffman's, hrsg. von* S. Eppenstein und M. Hildesheimer, (Berlin, 1914) p. 435ff.
58. *Israelit*, 1863, no. 34, 35, 47; 1864, no. 10, 18, 21.
59. a. *Wohin kommen wir? Ein Wort an die gesetzestreuen Is-raeliten Wuerttembergs von Gabiah ben Psisa*, (Mainz, 1863).
    b. *Antwort an Gabiah ben Psisa auf dessen Frage: Wohin kommen wir? Von seinem Zeitgenossen Rabbi Schimon Hazaddik*, (Leipzig, 1864).
    c. *Offene Zurechtweisung des Rabbi Schimon Hazaddik,*

      sonst Haman der Agagi genannt, von Gabiah ben Psisa, (Mainz, 1864).

    d. *Was wollen wir? Ein Wort fuer die gesetzestreuen Israeliten Wuerttembergs von Gabiah ben Psisa,* (Mainz, 1864).

60. Theil, p. 216 suggests this connection with another petition against the Oberkirchenbehoerde.

61. *Israelit*, 1863, no. 47, p. 576.

62. *Antwort an Gabiah ben Psisa*, p. 16.

63. *Ibid.*, p. 21.

64. Taenzer, p. 90ff.

65. Theil, p. 216f.

66. *Israelit*, December 18, 1870, p. 2ff.

67. For a history of this institution see *Ilba, Israelitische Lehrerbildungsanstalt Wuerzburg, 1864-1938,* Max Ottensoser and Alex Roberg eds. (Huntington Woods, Michigan 1982).

68. Marbach, September 24, 1873, HS E201c, Bue 13.

69. *Israelit*, September 10, 1873.

70. For a history on Wasermann see *Festschrift*, p. 66f; Adolph Kohut, "Zum Andenken an den Kirchenrat Dr. M. v. Wassermann," *AZJ*, vol. 75, (1911) p. 329ff. and Taenzer, p. 75ff.

71. *AZJ*, 1896, p. 213, letter of A. Geiger to J. Derenbourg.

72. "Gutachten" by M. Wassermann, *Rabbinische Gutachten ueber die Vertraeglichkeit der Freien Forschung mit dem Rabbineramte*, (Breslau, 1842) p. 190ff.

73. Translated into English by H. W. Mayer under the title Judah Touro, *A Biographical Romance* (New York, 1923).

74. *Festschrift*, p. 48ff.

75. *Ibid.*, p. 52.

76. For his history see Jeggle, p. 137ff and Bruno Stern, *Meine Jugenderinnerungen*, (Stuttgart, 1968) p. 51f.

77. *Israelit*, 1866, p. 327f.

78. *Ibid.*, 1875, p. 217ff.

79. *Ibid.*, 1875, p. 301 ff.

80. See HS E 201c, Bue 53.

81. *AZJ*, 1884, p. 686.

82. Stern, p. 52.

83. *Israelit*, 1892, "Erste Beilage zu No. 83."

84. This book, published in Muenster, in 1871, was subsequently

refuted by the most important scholars of its day, see Joseph S. Bloch, *Israel und die Voelker* (Berlin, 1922).

85. *Israelit*, 1881, p. 378.
86. *Festschrift*, p. 73; see also Ismar Schorsch, *Jewish Reactions to German Anti-Semitism*, 1870-114 (New York, 1972) p. 79ff.
87. HS E201c, Bue 13.
88. HS E201c, Bue 55.
89. *Schwaebische Chronik*, 1893, Nos. 69, 73.
90. *Israelit*, 1893, p. 625ff.
91. *AZJ*, January 6, 1893, p. 3.
92. *Ibid.*, June 15, 1894.
93. Alfred Gunzenhauser, *Sammlung der Gesetze, Verordnungen, Verfuegungen und Erlasse betreffend die Kirchenverfassung und die religioesen Einrichtungen der Israeliten in Wuerttemberg*, (Stuttgart, 1909) p. 295ff.
94. *AZJ*, November 2, 1894, p. 2f.
95. *Israelit*, 1895, pp. 669, 719 and 761.
96. *Ibid.*, 1899, pp. 723f and 752.
97. Young Kroner, born in 1870, was a substitute rabbi from 1895-1897 in Goeppingen and then the rabbi of Oberdorf until his death in 1930. He became a well-known scholar of Moses Maimonides.
98. Theodor Kroner, *Enstelltes, Unwahres und Erfundenes in dem "Talmud-juden" August Rohlings* (Muenster, 1871).
99. *Israelit*, 1897, *"Zweite Beilage zu Nos. 44 and 45."*
100. HS E201c, Bue 13, reprint of *Der Beobachter*, Blatt No. 81, April 9, 1902.
101. *Ibid.*, No. 117, May 23, 1902.
102. Theodor Kroner, *"Das Religioese Leben in der Israelitischen Religionsgemeinschaft," Wuerttemberg unter der Regierung Koenig Wilhelms II*, ed. V. Bruns (Stuttgart, 1916) p. 395ff.
103. *Ibid.*, p. 399.
104. HS E201c, Bue 6, November 1905.
105. Hans Franke, *Geschichte und Schicksal der Juden in Heilbronn*, (Heilbronn, 1963) p. 81f.
106. HS reports to the Ministry of Church, July 4, 1910, *Festschrift*, p. 88.

107. Abraham Schweizer, *Gedenkschrift zum 25 jaehrigen Jubi-laeum des Vereins Wuerttembergischer Rabbiner*, (Berlin, ohne Datum).
108. The term "Neolog" was an import from Hungary where the non-orthodox were called Neolog.
109. HS E201c, Bue 33, "*Der Beobachter*," No. 269, November 15, 1907; No. 288, December 7, 1907 and report of *Israelitische Oberkirchenbehoerde*, January 7, 1908.
110. Habermaas served from 1900 to 1910, then became head of the Protestant consistory and finally Minister of Church and School Affairs. He drew great praise for his work on behalf of the new church constitution of 1912. *AZJ*, January 3, 1913, p. 3 and Taenzer, p. 47.

CHAPTER 2

1. Moritz Guedemann, *Quellenschriften zur Geschichte des Unterrichts und der Erziehung bei den deutschen Juden*, (Amsterdam, 1968) p. xxv.
2. B. Strassburger, *Geschichte der Erziehung und des Unterrichts bei den Israeliten*, (Breslau, 1885), p. 250ff.
3. Paul Taenzer, *Rechtsgeschichte*, p. 55.
4. Taenzer, p. 37.
5. *Ibid.*, p. 84.
6. Strassburger, p. 264f.
7. *Amts-Instruction fuer die Vorsaenger*, (Stuttgart, 1841).
8. Strassburger, p. 266f.
9. *Treue Zions Waechter*, 1847, p. 390, lists the ten communities and teachers of traditional orientation.
10. *Israelitischer Volkslehrer*, 1855, p. 51f.
11. For a detailed history see *Festschrift aus dem Anlass des 100 jaehrigen Bestehens der Israelitischen Waisen-und Erziehungsanstalt Wilhelmspflege in Esslingen a.N. 1831-1931*; also, Helmut Dreher, *Geschichte der Israelitischen Waisen und Erziehungsanstalt Wilhelmspflege in Esslingen, Zulassungsarbeit zur 1. Dienstpruefung fuer das Lehramt an Grund-und Hauptschulen*, (Moehringen, 1970).
12. Dr. Samuel Dreifuss, 1831-1853; *Hofrat* Adolf Levi, 1853-1883;

M.H. Goldschmidt, 1883-1907; *Landesgerichtsdirektor* L. Stern, 1907-1934; *Rechtsanwalt* Dr. Alfred Schweizer, 1934-1938.

13. For a description see Ina Rothschild, wife of Theodor R. in: Paul Sauer, *Die Schicksale der juedischen Buerger Baden-Wuerttembergs waehrend der Nationalsozialistischen Verfolgungszeit 1933-1945*, p. 420f. See also Chapter V.

14. *Israelit*, 1875, *Erste Beilage Zu No.* 51.

15. Adolf Kober, "Jewish Emigration from Wuerttemberg to the United States of America (1848-1855)," *Publication of the American Jewish Historical Society*, Vol XLI, March 1952, p. 225ff.

16. See the carefully detailed work of Aron Taenzer, *Die Geschichte der Juden in Jebenhausen und Goeppingen*, (Stuttgart, 1927) p. 89ff.

17. Monika Richarz, "Jewish Social Mobility in Germany during the time of Emancipation (1790-1871)," *Leo Baeck Yearbook* (New York, 1975) Vol. XX, p. 73.

18. HS *Oberamt* Esslingen, July 24, 1899 and Ludwigsburg, February 16, 1904.

19. Abraham Schweizer, "*Die Israelitischen Konfessionsschulen (Elementar-schulen) in Wuerttemberg,*" *Israelit*, November 1911, Nos. 2, 6, 23 and 30.

20. *Festschrift*, p. 47ff.

21. Dillmann was also an early member of the Stuttgart chapter of the "*Verein zur Abwehr des Anti-Semitismus*" organized in 1891. Other prominent members included: Friedrich Payer (1847-1931), president of Wuerttemberg's chamber of deputies and later vice-chancellor of Germany; also Robert Bosch, the industrialist (1861-1942).

22. *Festschrift*, p. 51ff.

23. Alfred Gunzenhauser, p. 117f.

24. *Festschrift*, p. 53f.

CHAPTER 3

1. Sauer, *Juedische Gemeinden*, p. 77.

2. Bruno Stern, *Meine Jugenderinnerungen* (Stuttgart, 1968).

3. The practice of men sitting downstairs and women upstairs,

prevailed even in synagogues such as the one in Stuttgart that had organs and were considered Reform.

4. On the subject of music in nineteenth-century synagogues, see also Eric Werner, *A Voice Still Heard* (University Park and London, 1976), p. 191 ff.

5. On piety in the rural community see Emil Schorsch, "*Juedische Froemmigkeit in der deutschen Landgemeinde*," *Der Morgen*, VI. Jahrgang (Berlin, 1930), p. 44 ff. Excerpts in Appendix.

6. Stern, p.40. Although incomplete, the Niederstetten order is more explicit than the one of the *Oberkirchenbehoerde* of 1838.

7. Read in the Appendix, Jacob Picard's delightful story, "The Parnes is Taught a Lesson," *The Marked One*, Ludwig Lewisohn transl. (Philadelphia, 1956), p. 73 ff.

8. *Sepher Minhagim*, Israel ben Mordechai Gumpel, comp., (Fuerth, 1767).

9. See Herman Pollack, *Jewish Folkways in Germanic Lands* (1648-1806) (Cambridge, Mass., 1971), p. 15 ff. and Rosa Dukas, "*Aus dem Leben der badischen Juden*" (Hebrew), *Edoth*, 1947, p. 91 ff.

10. Dukas l.c. reports that this custom gradually disappeared and was replaced by the expectant woman having a Yiddish prayerbook (*Tchinebichle*) for her times of stress; further that the custom of biting off the petiole of an *Etrog*, one of the symbolic species used during the Feast of Tabernacles, was also no longer practised as an aid to childbirth.

11. The etymology of this word is dubious; some see in it a mixture of the Hebrew *Chol*, meaning secular, and the German *Kreischen*, meaning to call. Others derive it from the French *haler la crèche*, meaning to lift up the crib. See Pollack, p. 27 f.

12. The etymology of this word is also not clear. Pollack p. 33 connects it with the German "*spinnen*," meaning to weave, as a symbol of the bride's ability to perform homely chores; the *Jewish Encyclopedia* (London, 1904), Vol. 8, p. 340, derives it from the Latin "*sponsalia*," meaning betrothal feast.

13. All celebrations are mentioned in the *Sepher Minhagim*, including minute details concerning the order of the *Aliyot* and the clothing worn.

14. This was a custom to honor the dead. See Rabbi Judah Ashkenazy's commentary, *Ba'er Heitev, Orach Chayim*, No. 224.
15. See Herman Schwab, *Jewish Rural Communities in Germany* (London, 1956); Jacob Picard, "Childhood in the Village," *Publications of the Leo Baeck Institute*, Yearbook IV (London 1959), p. 273 ff.; Jeggle p. 257 ff.
16. "*Challah*" was the portion of dough donated in the time of the Temple to the priest. In post-Temple times, the Rabbis ordained that the "*Challah*", which was at least the size of an olive, had to be separated and burnt. It gave the Sabbath bread its most common name; in southern Germany, however, the term "*berches*," from the Hebrew "berachot," meaning blessings, was used.
17. "*Cholent*," possibly derived from the French "*chaud lent*," meaning warm slowly.
18. Jeggle, p. 260 f.
19. "*Sarjenes*" is derived from the old-Italian "sargano" meaning linen cloth, (*Leintuch* in German). See F. Guggenheim, *Yiddish auf alemannischem Sprachgebiet* (Zuerich, 1973), p. 50.
20. The synagogue order of 1838 had ruled out such a procedure, but obviously the Niederstetten people did not pay any attention to it.
21. For more on this organization see next chapter.

CHAPTER 4

1. Taenzer p. 56 f.
2. *Juedisches Leben in Deutschland, 1780-1871*, Monika Richarz ed. (New York 1976) p. 33 f.
3. Jeggle p. 146 f.
4. Jacob Toury, *Der Eintritt der Juden ins deutsche Buergertum* (Tel Aviv 1972) p. 102.
5. *Ibid.*, p. 236.
6. A. Taenzer, *Die Geschichte der Juden in Jebenhausen und Goeppingen* (Stuttgart, 1927) p. 109 ff; F. Loser, "Die Bedeutung der Haendler und Hausier Gemeinden fuer die wuerttembergische Industrie," *Jahrbuch fuer Statistik und Landeskunde*, VIII, 1964, p. 8; Monika Richarz, "Jewish Social Mobil-

ity in Germany during the time of the Emancipation, 1790–1871," *LBI Yearbook* XX, 1975, p. 73 f; Sauer p. 82 ff.

7. Pauline, daughter of Julius Koch, married Hermann Einstein from Buchau and they became the parents of Albert Einstein, the great mathematician.

8. See appendix.

9. *Juedisches Leben in Deutschland*, l.c. p. 302 ff.

10. Richarz, "Jewish Social Mobility," l.c. p. 72.

11. Karl und Arnold Weller, *Wuerttembergische Geschichte im Suedwestdeutschen Raum*, 6. Ausgabe (Stuttgart 1971) p. 246.

12. Maria Zelzer, *Weg und Schicksal der Stuttgarter Juden*, (Stuttgart, 1964) p. 37 ff.

13. For general conditions see *Juedisches Leben in Deutschland, im Kaiserreich*, Monika Richarz ed. (New York 1979) p. 32 ff; for Wuerttemberg see "*Die Staatsbuergerliche Gleichberechtigung in Wuerttemberg*," article signed: "By a Protestant," *AZJ*, 1887, p. 357 ff.

14. *Juedisches Leben in Deutschland*, l.c. p. 283 ff.

CHAPTER 5

1. Michael A. Meyer, *German Political Pressure and Jewish Religious Response in the Nineteenth Century*, (New York 1981) p. 18 f.

2. *Ibid.*, p. 20.

3. For general information see Margarita Pazi, "Berthold Auerbach and Moritz Hartmann, Two Jewish Writers of the Nineteenth Century," *LBI Yearbook* XVIII, (New York 1973) p. 201ff; Jacob Katz, "Berthold Auerbach's Anticipation of the German-Jewish Tragedy," *Hebrew Union College Annual*, vol. LIII, (1982), p. 215 ff.

4. In a letter to his cousin Jacob, on October 29, 1837, he described the location with the Hebrew words *Har Haggeboah* (High Mountain) to avoid trouble with the censor. Berthold Auerbach, *Briefe an seinen Freund Jacob Auerbach* (Frankfurt, 1884) vol. I p. 30.

5. Berthold Auerbach, Spinoza, *Ein Historischer Roman*, (Stuttgart, 1837) and *Dichter und Kaufmann, Ein Lebensgemaelde*, (Stuttgart, 1840).

6. Pazi p. 203.
7. *Briefe*, vol. I p. 38 f.
8. *Ibid.*, p. 52.
9. *Ibid.*, p. 53 f.
10. Anton Bettelheim, *Berthold Auerbach, Der Mann*, Sein Werk —Sein Nachlass, (Stuttgart, 1907) p. 169.
11. *Ibid.*, p. 179.
12. *Ibid.*, p. 201 ff.
13. Bettelheim, p. 211, attributes Auguste's premature delivery to her anxiety over these events.
14. *Ibid.*, p. 257.
15. *Briefe*, Vol. II p. 133.
16. *Ibid.*, p. 251.
17. *Ibid.*, p. 262
18. *Ibid.*, p. 266ff.
19. *Ibid.*, p. 425 "*Traurig bleibt's, wie ein Mann wie Treitschke sich so unter den Poebel begeben konnte. Ich kann nicht mehr in unsere Donnerstag Gesellschaft gehen, weil ich ihn nicht dort begegnen und ihn begruessen mag.*"
20. *Ibid.*, p. 269.
21. *Ibid.*, p. 442.
22. *Ibid.*, p. 451f.
23. *AZJ*, 22 August 1890.
24. George L. Mosse, *Germans and Jews*, (New York, 1970) p. 43.
25. Jehuda Reinharz, *Fatherland or Promised Land*, the Dilemma of the German Jew, 1893-1914 (Ann Arbor 1975) p. 73f.
26. *Israelit* 1885, p. 1162.
27. *Ibid.*, 1888 p. 1270.
28. Theodor Rothschild, *Bausteine*, (Frankfurt-Main 1927) p. 138f. The original reads as follows:

   Ich erinnere mich nicht, dass das gute Verhaeltnis der beiden je ernstlich getruebt worden waere. Wir hatten am Ende des Dorfes ein gemeinsames Schulhaus. In demselben waren zwei Schulzimmer und zwei Lehrerwohnungen mit gesonderten Eingaengen. In dem einen Zimmer wurde die christliche Jugend gross und stark und mit den Kuensten des Lesens und Schreibens vertraut gemacht, und in dem anderen sassen die juedischen Buben und Maedels und wuchsen empor zu reifen, vollen Menschen. Am

Samstag war unser Schulzimmer geschlossen. Wir zogen fest-
lich gekleidet zur Synagoge, die auf einer Anhoehe stand und
uns allen ein Heiligtum voll Heimlichkeiten und Geheimnis-
sen war. Dagegen schritten wir am Sonntag mit dem Buecher-
ranzen wieder zur Schule, wenn unsere christliche Kamera-
den zur Kirche gingen. Diese lag auf dem entgegengesetzten
Berge. Kirche und Synagoge standen friedlich ueber dem
Tal einander gegenueber als zwei Staetten menchlicher
Gottesverehrung.

29. Information from article in the "*Stuttgarter Beobachter*" as
    reported in *Israelit*, 1892, p. 925.
30. Schorsch, p. 82ff.
31. *Mitteilungen*, 1892, p. 46, 96, 350f.
32. *Israelit*, 1892, *Beilage zu No* 83.
33. *Mitteilungen*, 1892, p. 202ff.
34. *Ibid*., 1893, p. 416.
35. Taenzer, p. 164.
36. Schorsch, p. 67. The German original reads as follows:
    "Da lebt man wieder freudig auf, da sieht man, die Sache
    der Juden ist nicht ihre eigene Sache, sondern zugleich die
    der Freiheit und Menschlichkeit, und was wir lange und
    immer wuenschten und immer hofften, dass nicht wir
    Juden uns zu wehren haben, sondern dass Christen die
    Initiative nehmen, das ist geschehen und in der besten
    Weise." Briefe II, p. 440.
37. Schorsch, p. 96f. and 238 n. 62; on the Christian attitude see
    also Uriel Tal, *Christian and Jews in Germany* (Ithaca and
    London, 1975).
38. Quoted from Paul Rieger, *Ein Vierteljahrhundert im Kampf*
    um das Recht und die Zukunft der deutschen Juden (Berlin
    1918) p. 14f. The original reads as follows:
    "1. Wir sind nicht deutsche Juden, sondern deutsche
    Staatsbuerger juedischen Glaubens.
    2. Wir brauchen und fordern als Staatsbuerger keinen
    anderen Schutz, als den der verfassungsmaessigen
    Rechte.
    3. Wir gehoeren als Juden keiner politischen Partei an. Die
    politische Anschauung ist, wie die religioese, die Sache
    des einzelnen.

4. *Wir stehen fest auf dem Boden der deutschen National-itaet. Wir haben mit den Juden anderer Laender keine andere Gemeinschaft, als die Katholiken und Protestan-ten Deutschlands mit den Katholiken und Protestanten anderer Laender.*

5. *Wir haben keine andere Moral als unsere andersglaeubi-gen Mitbuerger.*

6. *Wir verdammen die unsittliche Handlung des einzel-nen, wes Glaubens er sei; wir lehnen jede Verantwort-ung fuer die Handlung des einzelnen Juden ab und verwahren uns gegen die Verallgemeinerung mit der fahrlaessige oder boeswillige Beurteiler die Handlung des einzelnen Juden der Gesamtheit der juedischen Staatsbuerger zur Last legen."*

39. Schorsch, p. 119.
40. A. Taenzer, *Geschichte der Juden in Jebenhausen und Goep-pingen*, p. 537.
41. *AZJ*, 11 Juli 1902.
42. *Festschrift*, p. 116.
43. Taenzer, p. 104 ff.

CHAPTER 6

1. Taenzer, p. 114ff.
2. *Juedisches Leben in Deutschland*, Vol. 2 (Stuttgart, 1979) p. 445ff.
3. Reinharz, p. 224.
4. *Mitteilungen*, February 17, 1919, p. 29.
5. The first two presidents were Dr. Carl Noerdlinger (1925-1929) and Dr. Otto Hirsch (1929-1935); the theological member was *Stadtrabbiner* Dr. Paul Rieger, who served until his retirement in 1936.
6. He served until his emigration in 1939. His report, "Zur Ge-schichte der Juden in Wuerttemberg," is an appendix to Paul Sauer, *Die juedischen Gemeinden in Wuerttemberg und Ho-henzollern*, p. 196ff.
7. *Juedisches Leben in Deutschland*, Vol. 3 (Stuttgart, 1982) p. 196ff.

8. *AZJ*, April 25, 1919.
9. Hermann Vogelstein und Paul Rieger, *Geschichte der Juden in Rom, 2 Bde*, (Berlin, 1895 & 1896).
10. See Chapter IV, Note 53.; also his exchange of letters with Rabbi Abraham Schlesinger of Buchau who argued against Rieger in favor of Zionism. *GZ*, 4. Jhrg., Nr. 5, June 1, 1927, p. 140ff.
11. Leo Baeck, "In Memory of Two of our Dead," *LBIY* I, (London, 1956) p. 51ff; Max Gruenewald, "The beginning of the *Reichsvertretung*" l.c. p. 57ff; Ernst Simon, *Aufbau im Untergang*, (Tuebingen, 1959) p. 38f; Otto Hirsch, *Ein Lebensweg*, (Berlin, 1957); Leopold Marx, "Otto Hirsch-Ein Lebensbild," (Bulletin LBI, 6. Jhrg. 1963) p. 295ff; Alfred Marx, "In memoriam Otto Hirsch," *Gemeindeblatt der Israelitischen Kultusvereinigung Wuerttemberg und Hohenzollern*, (Stuttgart, April 1965).
12. A family history, written by Louis Hirsch is in the archives of the LBI, New York.
13. Report by Otto Hirsch, *GZ*, No. 1. April 15, 1924, p. 3.
14. On Leopold Marx see Werner P. Heyd, *Schwaebische Koepf*, (Gerlingen, 1980) p. 93ff.; also the "in memoriam" in the appendix. A very important role was also played by Marx's brother-in-law, Karl Adler, Director of the Stuttgart Conservatory of Music until his removal by the Nazis in 1933. Adler's activities as artistic leader greatly lifted the morale of the Jews not only in Wuerttemberg, but also throughout Germany. Born in Buttenhausen 1890, he served as a Professor of Music, after his arrival in the USA, at Yeshiva University, New York. He died 1973.
15. Information courtesy of Julius Kahn, whose father Siegfried was a president of the congregation.
16. *AZJ*, April 18, 1919; Zelzer, p. 102f. and 192. See also *GZ*, 3, Jhrg., December 16, 1926 and November 18, p. 455.
17. A nostalgic description of this group has been recorded by Professor Chanan Lehrmann; see Zelzer p. 394ff.
18. Leo Baeck Institute, New York.
19. *Festschrift aus Anlass des 100 jaehrigen Bestehens der israelitischen Waisen-und Erziehungsanstalt "Wilhelmspflege,"* p. 34.
20. Sauer, *Gemeinden*, p. 77.

21. For Baden-Wuerttemberg see *Dokumente ueber die Verfolgung der juedischen Buerger in Baden-Wuerttemberg durch das nationalsozialistische Regime 1933-1945, 2 Baende, bearbeitet von Paul Sauer*, (Stuttgart, 1966); *Die juedischen Gemeinden in Wuerttemberg und Hohenzollern. Denkmale, Geschichte, Schicksale. Bearbeitet von Paul Sauer*, (Stuttgart, 1966); *Die juedischen Gemeinden in Baden. Denkmale, Geschichte, Schicksale. Bearbeitet von Franz Hundsnurscher und Gerhard Taddy*, (Stuttgart, 1968); *Die Schicksale der juedischen Buerger Baden-Wuerttembergs waehrend der nationalsozialistischen Verfolgungszeit 1933-1945. Bearbeitet von Paul Sauer*, (Stuttgart, 1969), zitiert als Sauer, Schicksale; *Die Opfer der nationalsozialistischen Judenverfolgung in Baden-Wuerttemberg 1933-1945. Ein Gedenkbuch*, (Stuttgart, 1969). For Stuttgart see Maria Zelzer, *Weg und Schicksal der Stuttgarter Juden*, (Stuttgart, 1964).
22. *GZ*, X Jhrg. Nr. 13, Stuttgart, *Oktober*, 1933, S. 135ff.
23. Simon, *Aufbau im Untergang* S. 70f. See also Max Gruenewald "Education and Culture of the German Jews under Nazi rule," *The Jewish Review*, Vol. V, 1948, p. 56ff. and Leonard Baker, *Days of Sorrow and Pain*, Leo Baeck and the Berlin Jews, (New York 1978).
24. *GZ*, Stuttgart, X Jhrg., Nr. 20, 14 Januar 1934, S. 182f; Stuttgart was one of a number of Wuerttemberg communities in which Jewish schools were established because Jewish children were forced out of public schools as a result of the Nazi regime.
25. Wissmann in: Sauer, *Gemeinden*, S. 198.
26. *The Jews in Nazi Germany*, American Jewish Committee, (New York, 1933), p. 40.
27. Sauer, *Schicksale*, p. 345ff. followed the fate of 31,901 Jews of whom 20,617 lived in Baden and 10,023 in Wuerttemberg. Both states were joined into one in 1952 with Stuttgart as its capital.
28. For a detailed analysis see Herbert A. Strauss, Jewish Emigration from Germany Nazi Policies and Jewish Responses (I), *LBIYB*, XXV, 1980, p. 313ff and (II) *LBIYB*, XXVI, 1981, p. 343ff.
29. See Guenther und Leslie Petzold, *Shavei Zion, Bluete in Israel aus schwaebischer Wurzel* (Gerlingen 1978); also Utz Jeggle

und Manfred Grohe, "Shave Zion," *Illustrierte Wochenzeitung*, Nr 28, Stuttgart, 28 Mai 1978, p. 6ff.

30. See Sauer, *Gemeinden*, p. 151ff.
31. Sauer, *Schicksale*, p. 202ff. and Strauss, *LBIYB*, XXVI, p. 358ff.
32. See appendix Statistics.
33. Sauer, *Gemeinden*, p. 196ff.
34. *Ibid.*, p. 204f.
35. Sauer, *Schicksale*, p. 251ff.
36. On events in Wuerttemberg see Hartmut Metzger, *Kristallnacht*, (Stuttgart, 1978). Information courtesy of Dr. Wilhelm Quenzer. Of special interest is Pfarrer von Jan's courageous sermon of November 16, 1938. On Germans hiding Jews see Max Krakauer, *Lichter im Dunkel*, (Stuttgart, 1975).
37. Ina Rothschild in: Sauer, *Schicksale*, p. 420f; also Helmut Dreher, *Geschichte der israelitischen Waisen-und Erziehungsanstalt Wilhelmspflege in Esslingen*, (Moehringen, 1970), p. 62ff. On November 15, 1983 the State renamed the institution in his memory as: *Staatliches Waisenheim Esslingen— Theodor-Rothschild-Haus*. (State Orphans' Home Esslingen— Theodor Rothschild House)
38. Sauer, *Schicksale*, p. 110f.
39. *Ibid.*, p. 268ff. and 393. The transport of December 1, 1941 to Riga included the parents of this writer.

CHAPTER 7

1. On the DP problem see Kurt R. Grossmann, *The Jewish DP Problem* (New York, 1951); also this writer's article "The US Army and Jewish Displaced Persons," *Forum*, Vol. 19, Nr. 4, (Chicago, 1961) p. 290ff.
2. For a brief description of Eskin's work see Craigh Pugh, "Rabbi, Teach Us," *Airman*, Vol. XXVI, Nr. 12, (Kelly Air Force Base, Texas) Dec. 1982, p. 36ff.
3. Grossmann, *The Jewish DP Problem*, p. 23.
4. *Ibid.*, p. 27.
5. Harry Maor, *Ueber den Wiederaufbau der juedischen Gemeinden in Deutschland seit 1945*, (Mainz, 1961) p. 19.

6. Information courtesy office of Israelitische Religionsgemein-schaft which covers all of Wuerttemberg. It may be assumed that the number was higher since not all Jews were registered members.
7. Grossmann, l.c.p. 30.
8. *Festschrift zur Einweihung der Synagoge in Stuttgart*, hrsg. von der Israelitischen Kultusvereinigung Wuerttemberg und Hohenzollern, (Stuttgart, 1952).
9. This writer is indebted to him for furnishing his many publications on the subject, including an unpublished lecture dated September 1, 1965, dealing with Jews in contemporary Germany. Levinson, a native of Berlin (1921), graduated from the Hebrew Union College, Cincinnati, Ohio, and was encouraged by Rabbi Leo Baeck, his teacher, to return to Germany.
10. Levinson's estimate includes all Jews living in Germany while the 25,466 cited for 1965 by Doris Kuschner, *Die juedische Minderheit in der Bundesrepublik Deutschland*, (Koeln, 1977) p. 170 reflects those registered with the communities.
11. *Ibid.*, p. 62.
12. *Ibid.*, p. 235.
13. Maor, 1.c.p. 53 and Encyclopedia Judaica, Vol. 7, p. 499.
14. In 1983 the German government decorated him for his contributions to the economy of the country, while in 1977, the University of Tuebingen bestowed upon him the title of *Ehren-senator*, for his efforts in behalf of better understanding between Germans and Jews.
15. At the risk of omitting deserving men and women, this writer will list names of only those whom he met personally. First is *Landesrabbiner* Joel Berger, in office since 1981; then Jakob Fern, for many years the synagogue's *Gabbai* (Elder). The present members of the Presidium are: Henry Ehrenberg, Albrecht Isaack and Arno, son of Jakob Fern. Josef Warscher served in an executive capacity until 1960 and then Zwi-Hermann Wollach as administrator for seventeen years until his retirement.
16. Quoted in Kuschner, p. 92.
17. *Ibid.*, p. 90.
18. *Ibid.*, p. 92.
19. *Deutschland Berichte*, Vol. 14, No. 12, December 1978, p. 13.

20. Elliot E. Cohen, "What do Germans propose to do?" *Commentary*, September 1950, p. 225ff.
21. On the Stuttgart branch and its leaders see *Zeichen setzen fuer die Zukunft, Eine Festschrift zum 30 jaehrigen Bestehen, CJZ,* (Stuttgart, 1980).
22. On the importance of Freudental in the 19th century see Chapter 1.

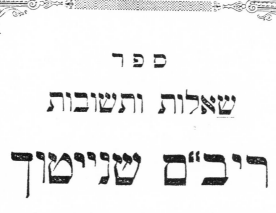

ס פ ר

שאלות ותשובות

ריב״ם שניטוך

תשובת שאלות נכבדות, נחוצות יקרות ונחמדות, בראי׳ מוצקים ולבנון מוסדות,
ברוח חכמה ותבונה עומקות, אשר עלה ונסתפק אשר שאל ואשר השיב לשואליו דבר
ה׳ זו הלכה ופלפולים בכמה פינות התורה, והעמידן בקרן אורה, האי גברא רבא
ויקירא, הוא הרב הגאון הגדול מעוז ומגדול הצדיק מוהר״ר **יוסף שניטוך**
זצ״ל, בן הרב מוהר״ם **מאיר** ז״ל, טילידי עיר המהוללה פ׳ י׳ ר׳ ד׳ א, וכא־בעים שנה
ישב על כסא ההוראה בק״ק פ ר י י ד ע : מ ה א ל א״ך אשכנז, מדינת ווירטעמבערגן,
(אשר יצק מים חים מימי הדעת ע״י רבותיו שני הכהנים הגדולים, קודש הלולים,
היה הגאון המפורסם חסיד שבכהונה וכו׳ וכו׳ בקש״ת מוהר״ר **נתן אדלער**
מפפד״ם זצ״ל והיה הגאון המפורסים וכו׳ בעהמ״ס שו״ת בנדי בהונה
זצ״ל) **ויוסף** הוא השליט בחכמתו, זבר עשה לתיירתה, למלאכת שטם כתם
והשאיר אחריו ברכה חדושים מתיקנים, יקרים מפז וגניגים, יהו שפתותיו דובבות
וזברו לדורות אחרונים, עד נעלה לציון ברננים:

הובא לבהדיס ע״י העוסק באמונה הק׳ ש מו א ל ז א נ ו ו י ל בהבנה מוה ר׳ מ ש ה ב״ם ז״ל
תתן הש״ק החסיד הפנח מוה ר׳ ד ו ד כ״ץ ז״ל בק״ק יאֲֿרֿטֿאֿ׳שֿלֿא.

ד ר א ה א ב י ט ש

ברפוס המשובח של אהרן צבי זופניק נ״י.

בשנה **אהיה כמל לישראל** לפ״ק

Denkschrift

an die

Hochansehnliche Stände-Versammlung

des

Königreichs Württemberg,

die Verhältnisse
der Israeliten und ihre bürgerliche und
moralische Bildung betreffend.

Von

J. Heß,

Vorsteher der israelitischen Gemeinde in Laudheim,
Oberamts Eilwangen.

Stuttgart,
gedruckt bei den Königl. Hof- und Kanzlei-Buchdruckern
Gebrüdern Mäntler.
1821.

2. Title page of Isaac Hess' Memorandum, Stuttgart 1821

תוכחת מגלה

Zurechtweisung

(Offene)

des Sendschreibens

Haman der Agagi genannt

von

Gabiah ben Psia.

Motto: כל המתגאה אינו בא לכלל גדולה
(Sotah 118, 82.)

Mainz.
Verlag der Le Roux'schen Hofbuchhandlung.
1864.

3. Title page of Tochachat Megillah by Gabiah ben Pesisa (Ludwig Stern), Mainz 1864

5. Rabbi Dr. Aron Taenzer (1871–1937)

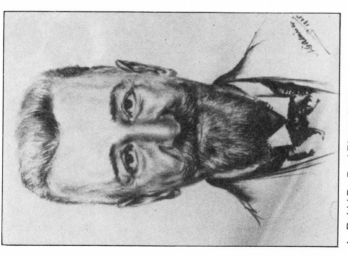

4. Rabbi Dr. Paul Rieger (1870–1936)

6. Rabbi Dr. Fritz Bloch (1903–1979)

7. Rabbi Dr. S. Bamberger (1900–1957) and wife Trude (1896–1972)

9. Siegfried Kahn (1879–1932)

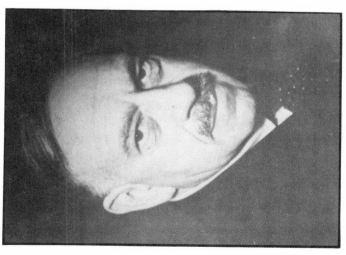

8. Dr. Otto Hirsch (1885–1941)

10. Rabbi Dr. Emil Schorsch (1899–1982)

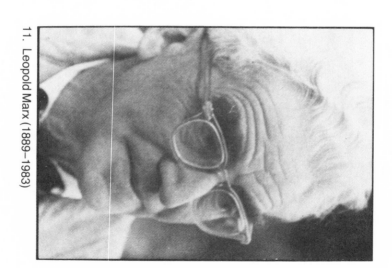

11. Leopold Marx (1889–1983)

12. Jewish school in Baisingen, 1925: Lehrer Stein (at desk), Leoni Marx, Heini Kahn, Bella Erlenbacher, Erna Kahn, Sally Erlenbacher, Ilse Wolf, Julius Marx, Senta Kahn, Milly Erlenbacher, Hermann Kahn, Viktor Gideon, Victor Schweitzer, Erwin Kahn, Siegbert Erlenbacher, Herbert Haarburger, Max Gideon, Hans Kahn, Fritz Erlenbacher, Frieda Erlenbacher, Ruth Erlenbacher, Hedy Erlenbacher

13. Chametz-burning in Baisingen, 1916

14. Harry Kahn, Cattledealer, Baisingen, with a pair of prize steer

15. Anna Lazar and Klara Kahn, hay-gathering in Baisingen

Seit 250 Jahren
Wohnsitz der
Familie Stern.

Wegen Abbruch
des Gebäudes Adolf-Hitlerstr. 71
in Niederstetten verkaufe ich

**einige Tausend Ziegel,
ca. 30 Fenster, Türen,**
Verschläge, altes Bau-
holz, Bretter, Beleuch-
tungskörper usw.
Anmeldungen erbittet

Albert Kleinhans, Saifersweiler
Niederstetten.

H A U P T S T R 71

März 1939

16. Announcing the demolishing of the Stern
house in Niederstetten, 1939

17. Stern family portrait, Niederstetten, 1870

Gemeinde-Zeitung
für die israelitischen Gemeinden Württembergs

Bezugspreis:
einschließlich Botenlgeld (sährlich 5 ℛℳ, halbiährlich 2.50 ℛℳ
vierteljährlich 1.25 ℛℳ Einzelnummer 20 Reichspfennig
Postscheck Konto 36758
Erscheint monatlich zweimal, am 1. u. 16.

Verlag:
Israelitische Verlagsanstalt G. m. b. H.
Fernspr. 23328 ☆ Stuttgart ☆ Kaiserenstr. 13
Schriftleitung:
Stadtrabbiner Dr. Rieger, Stuttgart.

Anzeigenpreis:
die einspaltige Nonpareillezeile 30 Reichspfennig
Umschlagseiten und Vorzugspläne nach Tarif. Familienanzeigen
und kleine Anzeigen die Millimeterzeile 20 Reichspfennig
Reklamezeile 1.50 ℛℳ
Bei Wiederholungen Vergünstigung

VIII. Jahrgang   Stuttgart, 16. Januar 1932   Nr. 20

Amtl. Bekanntmachungen.

Stadtrabbinat Stuttgart.

Einsegnung der Mädchen.

Die Einsegnung der Mädchen findet in diesem Jahre am Freitag, den 10. Juni, statt. Der auf diese Feier vorbereitende Unterricht beginnt Mittwoch, den 3. Februar, nachmittags 3 Uhr. An diesem Unterricht, der im Gemeindehaus erteilt wird, können nur Mädchen, die das 14. Lebensjahr vollendet haben, teilnehmen. Anmeldungen zu diesem Unterricht werden in der Gemeindepflege, Hospitalstr. 36, vormittags von 9–12 Uhr und nachmittags von 3–5 Uhr entgegengenommen.
Dr. Rieger.

SPENDEN
Dezember 1931
Spenden, eingegangen bei der Israel. Gemeindepflege:

Verlag Max Osterberg & Co., aus Max Osterbergs Kalendersammlung für sieben Vereine.

Anläßlich des Aufrufens zur Thora:

Rel.-Oberl. Leo Adler (2mal); Hermann Apt; Otto Bamberger; Adolf Baruch; Samuel Ebstein (2mal); Julius Einstein; Ludwig Einstein; Simon Einstein; Karl Ellenberg; Walter J. Engländer; Alfred Eppstein; Vorsteher Arthur Essinger; Julius Essinger; Max Gundelfinger, Cannstatt; Jakob Gutstein; Ludwig Haas; Heinrich Henoch (2mal); Max Jacobs; Rel.-Oberl. Jakob Jaffé; Joseph Jüdell; Isidor Karlsruher (anl. d. Gelähnen-Gedenkfeier); Simon Krautkopf; Albert Levi, Hermannstr. (2mal); Joseph Levi, Kanonenweg; Leopold Levi; Wilhelm Levi, Hermannstr.; Moritz Lieblich; Heinrich Löwenthal; Rudolf Marx, Reinsburgstr.; Paul Mayer, Lindenspürstr.; Max Merzbacher; Adolf Metzger; Justin Neumann; Ludwig Neumann (3mal); Hermann Rosenfeld; Sigmund Rothschild, Cannstatt; Siegfried Schottländer; Josef Schwarzschild; Julius Simon; Julius Stern; Moritz Strauß; Julius Uhlman (2mal); David-Wälder u. Sohn; Jakob Weill; Marcel Weil; Moritz Wildmann; Emil Wolf, Cannstatt; Ignatz Ziegler.

Anläßlich der Hundertjahrfeier des Oberrats:

Amtsrichter Dr. Ernst Einstein; Rechtsanwalt Dr. Alfred Gunzenhauser; Louis Hirsch; Ministerialrat Dr. Otto Hirsch; Leopold Levi; Stadtrabbiner Dr. Rieger; Julius Rothschild, Marienstraße 50; Konsul Max Straus; Vorsteher Eduard Weil.

Spenden, eingegangen bei den Vereinen:

Brautausstattungs-Verein:
Aus der Isak Schocken-Stiftung; Frau Lina Gerstle; Frau Oberkirchenrat Dr. J. Kroner.

Israel. Frauenverein:
Frau Fritz Benario; Dr. Gustav Loewenstein;

Frl. Sophie Oppenheimer; Frau Komm.-Rat Rosa Wolf.

Isr. Männer-Verein für Krankenpflege und Leichenbestattung:
Aus Max Osterbergs Kalendersammlung; Adolf und Paula Kohn, anl. ihrer Silbernen Hochzeit.

Spenden für das Isr. Fürsorgeamt:
N. N. Jahrzeitspende; N. N. zu Chanukka; Konsul Edgar Pick; N. N. (2mal); Landgerichtsrat Walter Richheimer; Frau Bertha Rosenfeld, zu Chanukka; Leo Rosenfeld, zu Chanukka.

Martin Buber über „Jeremia, ein Künder für unsere Zeit".

Jeremia
Aus den Bibelholzschnitten des Stuttgarter Malers Hermann Fechenbach

Martin Buber hat in Stuttgart eine treue Gemeinde, die sich stets vollzählig einfindet, zumal wenn er die Behandlung eines Themas ansagt, das auf einen großen Interessentenkreis rechnen darf. Im letzten Jahre ist seine feinsinnige Uebersetzung des Propheten Jeremia erschienen. Aus der Vertiefung in Jeremias Weistümer sind die beiden Vorträge entstanden, in denen er die zeitlose Bedeutung dieses Propheten dartun wollte.

In dem ersten Vortrag, veranstaltet vom Jüdischen Lehrhaus, den am Samstag, den 9. Januar, gehalten wurde, sprach Buber vom Leben und der Botschaft Jeremias auf Grund der tagebuchartigen Aufzeichnungen des alten Propheten. Er ging von der Frage aus, was ein Prophet sei. Er beantwortete sie dahin, daß der Prophet „auf die Umkehrenden hin" gesprochen hat. Seine Zukunftsverheißung ist in die Entscheidung des Menschen gestellt, an die er sich wendet. Die Katastrophe, die er voraussagt, ist von der Wegwahl abhängig, welche die Menschen einschlagen werden. So ist der Prophet Künder der von den Menschen selbst gewählten Schicksals.

In der Tätigkeit des Jeremia sind drei Perioden zu unterscheiden. In der ersten warnt er Israel, sich in das weltpolitische Geschehen einzumischen. Er fühlt den kommenden Weltensturm, die nahende Katastrophe, voraus. Denn er ist nicht nur Prophet Israels, sondern auch zum Künder der Weltstämme und Königreichen seiner Zeit berufen worden. Diese erste Periode erfüllt die Jahre 627–622.

Die zweite Zeit seiner Prophetenwirksamkeit ist das Zeitalter des Josia, der den Kult in Jerusalem neu zentralisiert, den Gottesdienst abgeschafft und so scheinbar eine Reform der Umkehr eingeleitet hat, die aber in Wirklichkeit den politischen Nebensinn erfüllen sollte: die Loslösung von Assyrien. Im Kampf mit Aegypten fällt Josia, und mit seinem Nachfolger Jojakim beginnt die zweite Redeperiode des Propheten um das Jahr 604 und seine Verfolgung durch den König. Seine Rede gegen den Tempel, in der er Israels Zusammenbruch voraussagt, stellt ihn in Gegensatz den herrschenden Kreisen seines Volkes. Er durchleidet das furchtbare Prophetenschicksal, ungehört zu bleiben. Er sieht die Weltentscheidung greifbar vor Augen. Er weiß, daß Israels Sein oder Nichtsein von seiner Entschließung abhängt, und muß gleichsam mit gebundenen Händen das nahende Unheil erschauen.

Die dritte Periode in Jeremias Wirksamkeit ist das Zeitalter Zedekias. 597 ist Jojachin als Rebell nach Babylonien geführt worden. Zedekia ist sein Nachfolger von Babylons Gnaden. In den einzelnen Phasen der letzten Tage Israels greift aus Wort Jeremias ein. Der König und das Volk brechen das Versprechen der Freilassung, das sie den Sklaven gegeben. Jetzt weiß Jeremia, daß das Schicksal Israels besiegelt ist. Der Eidbruch ist gleichsam seine Entscheidung zur Sünde gewesen. Und über das zerstörte Jerusalem tönt das Klagelied des Jeremia. Gedaljas Statthalterschaft und sein Mord sind ein neuer Episode nach dem Zusammenbruch Jerusalems. Jeremia und sein Sekretär Baruch ziehen mit den Flüchtlingen nach Aegypten. Hier verliert sich die Spur des Propheten.

Die knapp und eindringlich erzählte Lebensgeschichte des Propheten belebte der Redner durch eingestreute Bibelworte aus seinen Reden. Er schuf so in seinen Hörern ein plastisches Bild des Jeremia und rückte ihm die Grundlage für seinen zweiten Vortrag, der die Frage beantworten sollte, was das Ewige, das Bleibende, das für unsere Zeit Bedeutsame am Leben und Wirken des Propheten ist.

*

19. Stuttgart Synagogue (interior)

20. Stuttgart Synagogue in ruins after Kristallnacht

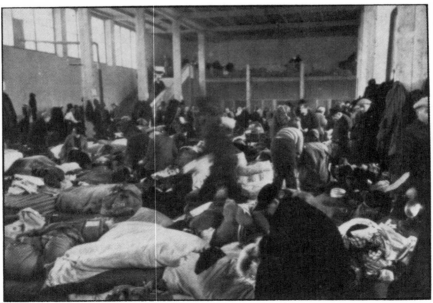

21. Before deportation

22. Interior of the new Stuttgart Synagogue, 1953

23. Karl Adler recites Kaddish at the unveiling of
the Buttenhausen memorial, 1961

24. Monument to the Jewish martyrs of Stuttgart

PART II

THE PEOPLE

BERTHOLD AUERBACH

*For information on Berthold Auerbach (1812-1882)
see Chapter 5 of this volume. The story "Eine Stunde
ein Jude" appeared in Zur guten Stunde,
Hoffmannsche Verlagsbuchhandlung (Stuttgart no
date), Vol. I, p. 442ff. and was translated
by this writer.*

A JEW FOR AN HOUR

It was in the year 1775, the year when the general empire calendar appeared for the first time, that a happy student departed from the city of Erlangen for home. Nobody foresaw, least of all he himself, that this student would one day become the best known calendar man; for it was the young Protestant theologian, Peter Hebel who, after a two-year stay at the University of Erlangen, was on his way home to join the life of the Philister, as it is commonly known. The student, a pack on his back and a staff in his hand, probably carried many a new song and jolly anecdote in his head; that day he did not feel like singing or joking, for whosoever had once worn the multicolored student cap (and Hebel had also worn one since he belonged to the Mosellaner group), had dedicated himself in his happy youth, fresh and frank, to studies and youthful pranks and knows the meaning of the old song: I return home and become a Philister again. Yes, this saying contains a lot. Whosoever says A, must say B and so on until Z. From the moment that childhood ends and one has a first A in school, learning and studying never end. Just as the mood of a child that goes to school for the first time — he cannot explain to himself why his heart beats down on him — so it is, only much stronger when a young man, knowing what it is, leaves the university and moves into the higher school of life. Now the second phase of carefree youth has passed, everything greets you more seriously: the trees, streets, fields, villages and cities, and now you yourself have to help, build, rule, order and teach. There goes an office clerk with a pile of records — soon he will bring you some to work on; there children go to school—soon they will come to you and you will have to be with them for a fixed hour; there the bell rings and the pastor goes to the Church in measured steps, clad in his vestments, soon you yourself will walk like him and enter the pulpit. But so what? There are rosy girls' faces looking out through flower-covered windows; soon you will take one of them home to be yours, and soon you will be a world yourself and you will have a new one around you. Where will be the one who will one day fill your life? Have patience! For now enjoy yourself and cheerfully visit the pub. The world is always beautiful and new, if only you open your eyes. Yes, two worlds struggle within a homecoming student: a carefree, pleasant one and a worried, serious one, and in some this struggle never ends. This too is good, for he who does not have an immortal student within him does not possess a fresh heart.

Hebel, the student, traveled quietly on the road, at times happy and then again serious, at times remembering happy days and then dreaming about the future. Suddenly he was challenged. "Stop, Jew! Pay Toll!" Hebel found himself standing before the gate of Seegringen, then the Ansbach border town. He looked around, and then at the caller. For whom is this? Who is meant by it? "Why do you stand like that, damn Jew! Do you believe that you can cheat on the toll?" thus called the one-eyed toll collector at the gate, making a fist at Hebel through the window. At the same time the dog ran out of the door and barked at Hebel. The dog understood what his master had shouted out and he could release his anger without fear and, if he wanted to, tear at Hebel's clothes. Only then did Hebel realize that the call was meant for him.

Suddenly Hebel stopped as if in a dream: believing he was in a forest surrounded by the eternal wonders of nature, then suddenly attacked by a wild animal or worse still, hit by a human hand with a hammer. Is that the world into which one should enter to preach the word of love? After the first fright Hebel instinctively reacted: "I am not a Jew." "Is that so," shouted the toll collector, "you are still lying? Wait, I will show you," and he came out, heading straight towards Hebel, wanting to grab him, with the dog ready to assist.

"I am capable of going by myself, and I will come with you," replied Hebel with an expression mixed with sadness and mischief. Suddenly, he became aware of the joke and irony of the present situation, and he was ready to enjoy it thoroughly. I have to see once, he thought, how a Jew gets along in this world, since he understood the Hebrew language well, he said: "Must I perhaps pay Jew-toll, because I have learned Hebrew? It flatters me that you think me such a good Jew, as if I had been born one;" and with a sly expression he added: "After all, I pay nothing. Take me to the judge." Smilingly, he let himself be escorted through the town where everybody made fun of him, and where the children shouted after him: "Hep. Hep!" as if they had learned it in school by rote. But Hebel smiled, and continued to smile, even when he stood before the silly judge who wanted to treat him to a sound thrashing at once; then give him a free shelter.

But now the joke started to assume serious proportions, and Hebel presented his university certificates and passport. The judge hesitated, but was not yet convinced; he wanted to punish the student for having pretended to be what he was not. However, Hebel knew how to be superior, for the toll-keeper had to be interrogated first, since Hebel had not pretended to be someone that he was not. But the judge did not want to do anything against the tollkeeper: one crow does not scratch out the eye of another crow; here it would have been worse, for the tollkeeper had only one eye. Hebel was sent on his way with coarse words.

Upon approaching the town the student had been very thirsty, but he would not drink one drop in any pub; his tongue tasted only gall and bitterness. Soon he left through the other gate, but upon looking back he said to himself: "Seegringen, I will never forget you." And he did not forget. In later years, he transferred most of his silly pranks, those hatched in cheerful moments, to the town of Seegringen. Further, on his journey home, Hebel thought a great deal of a world in which a toll is demanded from a human being because of his different faith, like a piece of cattle, except the cattle is still better off, for it does not have to pay the toll itself, and does not have to blush over the shame inflicted upon it.

Hebel lived to see the day, and beyond, when the toll on Jews—one can hardly believe that it ever existed—was abolished. However, during that one hour when he himself was thought of as being a Jew, he learned the whole deep pain which has been the lot of the Jew in society. The physical toll was abolished while the spiritual toll remained, and in many circles continues to remain. Even when not viewed with prejudice, at every new encounter and in every new situation, the Jew must prove himself a straight and honest person, loving his country and his fellow man. Hebel attached himself with special affection to Jews, and always learned anew of their sincerity, gratitude and goodness of heart. It did not disturb him that many were driven by a spirit of petty trading for all religious groups have such people in different forms. Through his calendar Hebel reported, in word and print, many jokes and anecdotes by and with Jews. He was one of the most eager writers who, through his essays about Moses Mendelssohn, the Sanhedrin of Paris and other topics, continued to enlighten his fellow Christians about Jews, in order to show that this is the genuine love which one shows human beings of different belief and thought, provided they want to do the right thing, in their own way.

If only everybody who still harbors a prejudice against Jews—and there are countless with prejudice without admitting it to themselves — if everybody for only one day, for one hour, would have considered himself a Jew, then he would give up his prejudice and convert it to justice and love.

(Postscript) The reader who is interested in the source of this story, may look it up in Hebel's works, 1843 edition, Vol. I p. 113. There it is!

JACOB PICARD

Jacob Picard (1883-1967), lawyer and author, was born in Wangen, a small village of South Baden, where Jews had lived since the seventeenth century.[1]
A decorated frontline officer during World War I, Picard had practiced law in nearby Konstanz until the arrival of the Nazi regime ended his legal career in 1933. In 1940 he managed to reach New York City via Japan, where he remained until after the end of World War II. He then returned to Holland and later died in an old age home at Konstanz.
A most sensitive writer, Picard's stories center around the life of Southwest Germany's rural Jews. His delightful "The Parnes is Taught a Lesson" is taken from his collection of short stories published in 1936 under the title, Der Gezeichnete. In 1956, the Jewish Publication Society of America published an English translation by Ludwig Lewisohn entitled, The Marked One.[2] *Picard's short autobiography, "Childhood in a Village," appeared in the Leo Baeck Institute Yearbook, vol. 4 (1959) p. 273ff.*

1. For a short history see Franz Hundsnurscher und Gerhard Taddey, *Die juedischen Gemeinden in Baden,* (Stuttgart, 1968) p. 284ff.
2. "The Parnes is Taught a Lesson" is being reprinted with the kind permission of the Jewish Publication Society of America.

THE PARNES IS TAUGHT A LESSON

They were both named Moishe, the proud *Parnes*, Moishe Levy, with his big farm and his six daughters, of whom he had already married off three with proper dowries, two of them as far away from home as Baden—whence you may learn concerning his prosperity—and also the little man Moishele, who was so poor that people had forgotten his family name and whose age no one knew. He might have been forty or even sixty, or, if you like, more. And it seemed to everyone as though he had always been around.

You may well ask why the two were called Moishe and not Maushe, as everywhere in Germany, especially in the South. Well, it is because of the dialect spoken in Upper Alsace, not too far from Basle, and the name derives from the French word Moise, which is the name of Moses, our great teacher. Yes, the scene of the story which is to be told here is in Upper Alsace; it is to be the image of happy and serene days and also as a sign of the possibility of a Christian teaching a lesson to Jewish people as a rare recompense for that which our Holy Commandments have given them through the millennia, and how the Jews involved were grateful for the lesson and glad of the oneness and community of moral attitudes.

It was in that part of the country which was the homeland of that good and true poet Johann Peter Hebel, the same in which, on the other shore of the Rhine, there was born several centuries ago that good man and great helper of our ancestors, Jossele von Rosheim, and whence he set forth whenever it was necessary to protect his Jewish brethren anywhere in the great realm of the Germans. And the time of the story is that period of French dominance when the second Napoleon, who called himself the third, and his vain wife Eugenie, produced turmoil in his great country, to which

Alsace belonged at that time and brought trade and activity to it but also restlessness and finally the misfortune of war, as his uncle had done before him. But the Jewish people of Alsace lived very well. They cultivated the land just like their fellows and had had time by virtue of many decades of peace and freedom and equality to attain prosperity. Nevertheless, though no one was in want, yet there were some who had no more than what was barely necessary, no more and also no less; and it is ever thus among us that there are those who, despite pains and industry, have no particular luck. They never truly prospered, and this applies to whole families who seem to lack luck and the favor of Heaven. Thus, while most members of the *Kehilla* were able annually to lay aside several hundred golden Napoleons, yet there were a few who managed just to live and not to go hungry. This was the best they could do and ready money was always lacking to them. To the latter group belonged Moishele, as you may have suspected.

Ready cash? He was the village barber, the barber of the Jews. What is that? Well, to put it precisely, he was the hairdresser. But even that does not define it correctly, as must be done if the people of today are not to receive a false impression. If you imagine that he ever used a razor, you are wrong. A pious Jew and a razor—those things don't go together. So what am I telling you? Yet you must know. But if you imagine that in those days and in that village even the most *bekoved* man in the *kehilla* employed the barber on weekdays, on ordinary weekdays, you are mistaken. Not even the *Parnes* indulged in such luxury. It was on *Erev Shabbos* that this thing was done, and then only with a bent, dull pair of scissors which rattled through the thick beards of the men.

They could always see Moishele coming from afar in his wooden boots and his blue linen smock which reached down to his knees and which had two wide-open pockets on his chest from which one could see protruding the scissors and a whitish yellow comb of bone. First he went to the house of the

Parnes Moishe Levy, and this was the little man's most important moment of the week. He seemed to himself indispensable then and was delighted when the mighty president of the congregation asked him: "Well, what is there new among the people, Moishele?" And he could answer and tell all he had heard. He always made a point of knowing something, even if he had to make it up. To come back to the practical matter, you will realize that there wasn't much ready cash involved in this service which Moishele rendered. He was, in fact, the poorest man in the *Kehilla*, if you omit the two feeble-minded sisters Bloch who, like himself, lived in the Bach alley in little one-storied huts. So he could barely buy himself garments, although those he had lasted for decades; far less could he indulge in any luxuries, not even in tobacco in order to use it, as the others did, in a clay pipe or to roll cigarettes.

One day, it was the first day of the *Chol Hamoed Succaus*, Moishele sat early in the morning on the milestone that stood in the bend of the road which led from the lower to the upper village on the way to the synagogue. It was a solid white piece of sandstone from the Champagne country. He sat there in his blue smock, his hands on his knees and gazed before him. He wasn't cheerful, to be honest, under the black pointed cap which they all wore in those days. His hair fell down a little over his forehead and his gaze was absentminded. It needn't have been the good Hans Brohme, the *Maire* of the village, as they call the burgomaster in that part of the country—who was placed above both Jews and Christians by the Prefect and who took notice of everything, even as his office demanded—it needn't, I say, have been he. Anyone else would have turned to Moishele and asked him why he looked so miserable and downcast. But the *Maire* considered it his official duty to find out what was wrong and approached the little man with mighty tread. "Well, Moishele, what ails you? What's the matter with you? You sit there as though the hail had killed your crops."

To begin with, Moishele was silent. He just sat there and looked up at the *Maire* with melancholy eyes. After a little while he shook his head and struck his knees repeatedly with the palms of his hands.

"Well, come on! Answer me, man!" the *Maire* said impatiently.

Finally the other replied:

"They didn't call me up to the *Tauro* on *Yontef*, not on *Rosh Hashono* and not now again on *Succaus*."

"Why didn't they, Moishele? You're a Jew, the same as the others."

"That's true. But it is because I can't make a contribution for good causes, because I have no *mesumen*, like the other people, the rich ones."

"Because you have no *mesumen*! But that won't do at all! Our dear Lord doesn't care about that; what He cares about is the heart and faith. Aren't you a pious Jew?"

"That I am. But there's nothing you can do about it."

The *Maire* reflected briefly.

"Oh yes, there is something to be done about it. Let me see to it. And don't tell anybody that I know. Are there are more days of *Yontef*?"

And Moishele with a dazed look at the *Maire* told him that on the next Thursday it would be *Shemini Atzeret* and the following day *Simchas Tauroh*. And the *Maire*, who was a peasant, had a pretty good idea of this festival and its meaning, because for nearly a week now the *Succaus* had been standing in front of the Jewish houses, covered with foliage and adorned within by the fruits of the harvest. He patted the shoulder of Moishele, who had risen, and said:

"Have patience, Moishele, we'll attend to that!" And he went on his way.

Now came the penultimate day of the festival and next that happy day on which we rejoice in the Law and hopefully seek to forget all evil. From all the streets men and women walked to the *shul* that morning. So, also, came Moishe Levy, the *Parnes*. He wore a broadbrimmed, gray, top hat, which grew narrower at the peak, the black coat with the high collar that reached almost to his ears behind, and the trousers checked in gray and black. It was the Parisian fashion before the last. The top hat he had recently bought in Strasbourg when his daughter, who knew how to manage horses, had driven him there for the purpose of selling his wheat in the big city. Next to him strode his wife Henriette, a member of the Bloch family in Gebweiler, known to everyone in the land, with her distinguished, broad East Indian shawl over her shoulders, which was held together by a great brooch of twisted gold woven like a bird's nest and from under whose wig hung down the appropriate earrings of blue enamel on gold like handsome heavy fruits. And the others were clad, even as these were, in more or less sumptuous garments. They were all in a happy mood. And it seemed to the men as though they were still carrying the festive *lulav* with the green willow wands from the edges of their own brooks, as well as the rare *esrogim* in their silver bowls. For there had been a rich harvest this year, which was equally favorable for trade. The grapes had had enough sun as well as rain at the proper time, so that the clusters had become sweet all over the land and as far as Baden; the ears of the wheat had been fuller than for long and the maize and hops had been rich. On the slopes of the nearby hills the foliage was still green and as far as eye could reach were the pines and fir trees on the dark summits of the Vosges mountains. Moishele, the barber, also had donned his *Yontef* garment which wasn't even of the fashion before the last.

In happy mood they stood between the pews of the *shul*. And who can describe their amazement when suddenly—the *chazan*, Shloime Ruef, had just begun to intone the prayer—they saw a strange and yet familiar figure enter the House of God with their own people. Unquestionably, it was Hans

Brohme; it was the *Maire*. For a moment they were of two
minds, hesitating between the scruple of a Christian in the
House of the one and only God—a thing much rarer in those
days in the country than in the cities, although Christian and
Jews were not ill-informed concerning each other's customs
—and, on the other hand, their satisfaction in that the *Maire*
considered it important to stand with them before God on an
important holiday. In the end their pleasure in the community of faith overcame their scruples. They smiled and nodded to him, especially his friend Moishe Levy who was, next
to him, the most important man of the community. And, as
they observed, Hans Brohme, too, was festively attired and,
moreover, had about his neck the silver chain of his office and
in the buttonhole of his black morning coat the gleaming red
ribbon of the Légion d'Honneur.

Had anyone ever heard of such a thing? In no other
village, in no other country was that possible. Only among
them, where all men lived in peace with each other. And how
tactful, how significant it was that for this sign of good will
the *Maire* had chosen precisely the feast of *Simchas Tauroh*.
They were not likely to forget this.

The service proceeded. Brohme stood with a serious and
even solemn expression near the door, while the Jewish men
about him, led by the *chazan*, sang the old holy prayers with
such fervor that he, too, was moved.

Then the Torah scrolls were lifted from the ark in their
white silk coverings and were carried about the synagogue
with the ringing of bells and with singing and finally there
began the reading of the Scripture portion of the day. The first
one called to the Torah was naturally Moishe Levy. Slowly
and loudly he sang the *berocho*, as one had not heard it done
for a long time, as though it were a question of showing their
friend and through him the whole of Christendom how the
Jews here in this village, and indeed everywhere, praised the
greatness of God. Already the rich *Parnes* had named his

contributions: five *livres* for the Chevra Kaddisha and five *livres* for this and five *livres* for that, so that they all looked at each other and nodded at each other because they had so generous a *Parnes*. Already the *chazan* was calling: "*Ja-amaud sheini*," and the latter, the second one called up, was the fat Jacques Brunshwig with his little black Napoleonic beard, who was the second most powerful member of the *kehilla*, needless to say. He was already on his way to the *almemor*, when a sudden voice arose:

"Why don't you call up Moishele? Moishele must be called up. I'll contribute for him. He can contribute today as much as Moishe the *Parnes*."

It was the *Maire*. No doubt about that. Consternation seized upon them all. So that was why he had come. First they hardly knew how to treat this unheard of and painful situation, that someone interfered in the accustomed course of their service. They didn't even at that moment consider whether it was an *avere* which was being committed here. But they would not have had the best and best respected *Parnes* in the whole of Upper Alsace, if he hadn't found a way out. Swiftly he went up to Jacques Brunshwig who was about to intone the *berocho*, conferred in whispers with him and next with the *chazan*, Shloime Ruef, whereupon the former left the *almemor* with a smile and returned to his seat while the latter, commissioned by the *Parnes*, hastened to the good Moishele and whispered to him.

He had probably been the only one in the synagogue who had been morally uncomfortable during the incident, at least so soon as he felt that what was taking place here concerned him. Indeed, a feeling of guilt came over him.

But immediately the voice of the *chazan* rose again and cried: "*Jaamaud sheini*."

Nevertheless, after a moment of hesitation, Moishele, finally not without pride, walked up to the consecrated scroll and spoke—no, sang—clearly and without a trembling of the voice, the *berocho* as he had probably not sung it since his own *Bar-Mitzvo*. And the whole congregation perceived the special quality of the moment and were delighted with the experience which had been given them.

Was it because in the person of Moishele, Hans Brohme had in a sense been called to the Torah, one of the other faith and in him, too, the Prefect of the region and thus the whole government, including the Emperor Napoleon in Paris? Or was it that they received a satisfaction from this particular *Simchas Tauroh* because a Christian friend had taught them a lesson which they were bound to remember, that the value of a man was not to be gauged by his ability to contribute for causes however good, but by the sanctity of his will, by his being a pious and honorable man who did well his day's work, however humble it may be?

We would like to believe that both motivations were active.

What is certain is that, in the succeeding years on *Simchas Tauroh*, it was always the poorest man in the *kehilla* who was called third to the Torah, after a *Kohn* and the *Levi*. The *mitzvah* was bought for him by one of the rich men. But neither the name of the latter nor the amount of his contribution was ever revealed. Such was the fruit of the lesson which the *Parnes*, Moishe Levy, learned for himself and for the others and which was motivated by poor Moishele. For, when at the end of the service, the *Parnes*, with his wife between himself and the *Maire*, had proceeded on his way home and they had shaken hands all around, he had promised himself never to forget the lesson he had received.

RABBI EMIL SCHORSCH

*Emil Schorsch (1899-1982) was eminently qualified
to write about Jewish life in Southwest Germany, for
the small village of Huengheim, Baden, where he was
born, had been the home of his ancestors for close to
two hundred years. Due to the illness of his mother, he
was sent as an eight-year-old to the Jewish orphanage
at Esslingen, then headed by Theodor Rothschild,
whose daughter Fanny later became his wife.
Originally trained to be a teacher, he decided to enter
university and Rabbinical seminary. In 1925, he obtained his doctorate at the Tuebingen University and
in 1928 was ordained at the Breslau Seminary.*

*Until 1938, Rabbi Schorsch served as the associate
rabbi of Hanover, one of the largest Jewish communities of Germany. Imprisoned for a short period by the
Nazis in the Buchenwald camp, he managed to emigrate with his family to the United Sates. Here, until
his retirement in 1964, he served as the rabbi of
the community of Pottstown, Pennsylvania. Rabbi
Schorsch's article analyzes, with critical love, the
inner life of Southwest Germany's rural and city Jews,
thereby providing an authentic background of the
people described in this volume. I am grateful to Mr.
Robert S. Schine for having brought the article to my
attention.[1]*

1. Emil Schorsch, "Juedische Froemmigkeit in der deutschen Landgemeinde," *Der
Morgen*, 6. *Jahrgang*, (Berlin, April 1930) 1. Heft, S.44ff. Translated and excerpted
by this writer. For a biographical essay on Rabbi Schorsch see (his son) Ismar
Schorsch, "A German Rabbi in America," *The Rabbinical Assembly*, Proccedings of
the 1982 Convention, p. 164 ff.

JEWISH PIETY IN THE
GERMAN RURAL COMMUNITY
(Excerpts)

The following will try to show how the rural Jew's intimate connection with nature has led through special circumstances to a religious way of life distinct from city piety. These observations are based principally on rural conditions of southwest Germany in the most recent past and present. Before we speak about the religious attitude of the individual, let us first point to the differences between city and rural communities: in a rural community we have a small number of members, a greater density of settlers and, as a result, a closer living together than in the city. All these facts favor from the beginning religious life in the country in an extraordinary manner. Here, only genuine religious feeling can be shown. Thus, for example, there is no appreciation of cantorial virtuosity despite a closer connection with traditional chants than is the case in city communities. This does not mean that rural piety is deeper than city piety, but only that the outward form of rural religiosity is more genuine than in the city; it lacks an external smoothness which suggests some hypocrisy, although, to be sure, rural religious hypocrisy exists as well. Rural hypocrisy is of a different kind, however, and lies in its religious activities. For example, if one wanted to be considered pious in a rural setting, it would not suffice to come regularly to the synagogue and remain there in silent devotion; one would have to pray there with fervor, join loudly the cantor, sometimes being ahead of him, and take over every so often a religious function—in short, only through such practical behavior can a rural Jew let himself be convinced that someone else is a pious person.

In an attempt to analyze the rural Jew's attitude, particularly his strong adherence to traditional customs, one can reduce it in essence to three factors. First is the practice tying a person from his youth to the customs observed in the parental home. In the quiet rural lifestyle, belief in progress that would sacrifice custom has little or no validity. Second, the adherence to religious customs in the country also contains a deep sense of obligation, particularly toward parents. It is based not the least on an unspoken feeling that to abolish parental customs would imply that parents have lived their lives in profound error. Finally, rural piety views all religious practices, even the less meaningful ones, as protection against unpredictable blows of fate. For example, when a storm looms, one prays for protection, by way of God, against the danger of lightning. In view of these three facts one can state that rural piety appears to be more original than city piety. It is the result of an obvious connection with nature which plays a characteristic role among the rural Jews of Southern Germany. Although the Jews live in the country, they are not just peasants like their non-Jewish neighbors. Morever, the Jews are not exclusively traders and merchants, both occupations are often linked together. Their activities bring them in steady contact with their non-Jewish environment. One learns to know, understand and appreciate the calm, cautious and steady nature of the peasant. In his simple and open way of life, the peasant does not pass himself off for what he is not. One especially comes to know the genuine piety of the peasant, the honest joy of leisure earned through hard physical labor; one senses the sanctity of a Sunday filled with the sound of bells which lead the peasant families, clad in their Sunday best, to church. Somehow all this influences the Jew, and he does not withdraw himself from this genuine charm. Thus, when approached for a donation to a new church bell, the head of a Jewish family, most certainly makes a contribution. Perhaps this also explains psychologically the curiosity of a synagogue in a southern community (Buchau at the Federsee) having a bell. In addition, the influence of the non-Jewish environment is especially noticeable in customs related to ancient Jewish piety. What was there that could prevent a Jewish family from totally enjoying the quiet charm of a Friday night provided a restless city dweller would not lurk in the background with the thought one could not devote three hours to quiet solitude? In the country, the Sabbath descends upon the family in complete stillness, perhaps touched by a certain boredom which is not really considered unpleasant, allowing the total nerve-healing power of God's Sabbath to release itself.

It would be an error to believe that this stillness could only be attributed to the influence of the non-Jewish environment. Such an influence could not be that strong were it not for the helpful fact that in the country the Jews themselves live in intimate connection with nature and agriculture, the basic influences of the peasants' religious mood. The rural Jew also knows the wonderful aroma of freshly cut and loaded hay, knows the sweat of labor, experiences the satisfaction of bringing in the harvest, feels gratefulness toward the Power upon which the fruit of his labor depends and which grants him the produce of his field. Herein lies one of the major sources of rural religiosity. A city dweller, living amid an ocean of cement, forgets all too easily the incalculable background of every being; for him religion begins with the question, whether there exists a God at all.

Now, to what extent have these circumstances influenced Jewish piety in the country? First, I want to mention the sure acceptance of religious duties. When religious requirements demand everyone's presence, a rural Jew can be depended upon, and it is a foregone conclusion that everybody appears at services in the synagogue. These feelings of religious duty are shared even by young people, who, for the Holy Days, return from the religiously indifferent city to their native rural environment. Even they, who have absorbed much of the city atmosphere, feel the distinct charm of the rural home and cherish it as a welcome gift throughout their lives. The rural Jew has little room for romanticism which explains the lack of formality of his religious customs wher-

ever they may occur—within the family or in the house of
God. His religious sense of duty, for instance, compels him to
diligently put on *Tefillin* daily; should this not be possible at
home, he does it wherever he may be. In addition, the absence
of aesthetic form can often be noticed in domestic piety, be it
at the *Kiddush* that the head of the house recites as quickly as
possible in a melodic but not distinctly musical form; be it at
Grace after meals, even be it in the building of the Sukkah
which requires decorations, but in which, curiously, every
bit of artistic sophistry is avoided. This lack of formality
appears to us as the result of an inner impediment, namely a
fear that too strong an aestheticism would weaken religious
sincerity. In rural Judaism the appreciation of religious customs can assume a shape for which an outsider may easily
lack understanding. A rural Jew will often pay for the chance
of carrying out a *Mitzvah*. For example, the calling up to the
Torah reading was and is frequently sold at auction. Then,
one may honor someone else with the *Mitzvah* bought at
auction. Money is also paid for the honor of providing *Kid -
dush* wine throughout the year. Curious perhaps, but all this
is a sign that religious customs are still a reality in the country.

Another cause for the development of rural piety is its
definite, but partial magical linkage with the Infinite, the
Divine. We understand by that linkage the will, wish or even
only the feeling to influence the Divine through a definite
means of behavior. Additional and above all, there is a general conviction that only the complete fulfillment of the
Divine commandments can bring about real fortune. The
country Jew harbors the belief that through his good deeds he
collects a treasure which will act as his advocate in the
hereafter.

For instance, the commandment of affixing *Mezuzot* is
not just observed because it is written in the *Torah*, but also
due to the belief that the fortunes of the house depend upon
them. How such a belief can grow may be seen from instances
where houses passed from Jewish to Christian ownership,

and the new owner did not remove the *Mezuzot*. Although these matters border on the apocryphal, one does not encounter gross superstition. Thus, nothing is known of the ill-practice of amulets, although one is aware that such did exist in the field of popular Jewish religion. The customs at funerals also do not reach over into the field of superstition. For example, the plucking and throwing behind oneself blades of grass at the cemetery is not superstitious, but a symbolic act of profound meaning. Thus, it is not proper to devalue rural piety because it is not free of magical elements.

The emotional depth of rural piety stems also from its close link to nature. This is very evident when the end of the Sabbath approaches. The rural Jews do not look at the calendar for the exact time of its ending, but gather instead before the house of God. In cheerful conversation they await here the appearance of the stars which are the world's clock of Sabbath's end. And what of the special mood with which the new moon is greeted by the person who, in the first days of the month, steps out in the open with a burning candle in his hand? Thus, a feeling of intimacy develops with the Divine which, however, because of genuine and understandable shyness never leads to a conversation about God.

Undoubtedly, today's rural piety also has a negative side. It is not learned piety. This in itself is neither an advantage nor a disadvantage. Judaism has such a vast number of customs that only a deep knowledge of their meaning and their connections can create that clear climate whence rises the eternal, primordial religious world of Judaism. This lack of learning is also the reason why in the country Jews preserve customs, *Minhagim*, that may have made sense at one time, but make no sense today. The origin of these customs may be easily explained, however, when a community has a proper teacher and leader. The community, in obvious gratitude, accepts his authority, and, should he be active in it for decades, he will create a new partnership out of the pliable material of the rural members. Knowledge, of course, can also become a danger to religious life. It can happen if there is someone in the community who at one time or another has "learned" a bit. In certain situations, this can easily lead to feelings of superiority and dampen the spirit of religiosity. For often it is only a single individual who gives the total religious life of a community an irritating character, thereby causing a peculiar type of religious activity.

This then appears as the essence of rural Jewish piety. It is a living piety, perhaps not of the highest type, but filled with life and religious commitments. It is not piety by the hour whereby one visits an isolated synagogue once to fulfill a religious obligation. Instead, one's whole existence is inundated by religion, though not in an exaggerated form. It is an important duty of each city community not only to put its greater economic power to the preservation of the rural communities, but also to preserve the piety of the rural inhabitants absorbed by the city rather than have them crushed by its colossus.

HANS GEORGE HIRSCH

IN MEMORIAM LEOPOLD MARX
1889-1983

When Leopold Marx, adventurously, escaped from a French prisoner of war camp and returned home, in December of 1919, more than a year after the conclusion of the armistice, I was little more than three years old. Then he, together with his unforgettable Idel—later Judith—entered my life. Ever since that time, until his final greeting in December of last year, he exercised a deep influence upon me. As I grew up, he impressed me with the wide range of his interests, his strong love of nature and our home state, his dedication to Judaism and his unshakeable longing for peace.

I recall what he said at midnight of a New Year's Eve: "Let us hope that this year will be the year of real peace." And when in the late summer of that year (1926) Germany was accepted into the League of Nations, it appeared to me, in retrospect, as if that hope had been fulfilled and he had been a prophet. More than half a century later, having suffered many sorrows, he wrote in ecstatic joy how grateful he was to witness Sadat's visit to Jerusalem, and that now there was real hope for peace. His creative thinking about peace knew no bounds. Only a few years before, while Henry Kissinger was still Secretary of State, he had submitted to him, in perfect English, a proposal for an International Sinai Development Authority with the Sinai peninsula as a bridge for peace.

In February of 1926, Leopold and my father, influenced by Martin Buber and following the example of the Jewish *Lehrhaus* at Frankfurt which had been founded by Martin Buber and Franz Rosenzweig a few years before, established the Jewish *Lehrhaus* Stuttgart. It was open to Jews and non-Jews for the study of Judaism and Hebrew language through courses and lectures. Leopold served as its secretary for many years. The Jewish *Lehrhaus* Stuttgart continued its courses from 1926 on, without any interruption, while the interest of the much larger community of Frankfurt slackened, so that only one Bible course—that of Eduard Strauss—was offered. Only in 1933 did Frankfurt resume its program of courses.

The Jewish *Lehrhaus* Stuttgart became best-known through its annual dialogues on religion between Martin Buber and leading Christian theologians. The scheduling of such dialogues was not only innovative but very risky for two reasons: First, in the late Middle Ages, so-called religious dialogues were designed to force Jews to convert. As such, they entered Jewish history as hateful institutions, best to be avoided. Thus, it required the courage of a fresh start to engage in such dialogues. Second, it turned out that, while modern Christianity had given up forced conversions, it was still pursuing missionary goals. This was especially notice-able at the last of these dialogues in the middle of January 1933.

In his work, "Otto Hirsch—a Life Portrait," published by the Leo Baeck Institute in 1963, Leopold wrote about the founding of the *Lehrhaus*. But this literary work is not the only monument erected for his friend, my father. It was Leopold who initiated the move to name the bridges leading to the port of Stuttgart after Otto Hirsch. And thanks to him, an Otto Hirsch monument stands in Shavey Zion in an Otto Hirsch park. Thus, he kept faith to the memory of his friend.

Only in the fall of 1939, after the outbreak of the war, did Leopold and Idel Marx manage to emigrate. The year before, Leopold had spent some time in the Dachau concentration camp, a trying experience about which he wrote several poems. In 1939, he was arrested once more.

In Israel, despite heavy daily horticultural work, he continued the writing of poetry. His book of poems, *Hachscharah*, a collection of earlier and more recent poems, appeared in 1942. Tragic family blows followed: the death of his mother in Theresienstadt, the death of his nephew, Fritz Adler, in the Atlantic and, on January 15, 1948, his son Jehoshua, an officer in the *Haganah*, was killed in the defense of Gush Etzion, near Hebron. In his memory Leopold dedicated Bet Jehoshua, a center devoted to cultural activities in Shavey Zion. Leopold's principal literary work, "*Jehoshua, My Son*" also deals with him, his older son.

When this work was still in the manuscript stage, I had my doubts whether he would be able to find a publisher for it. In order to make it available to family and friends, I proposed in 1976 that Leopold publish it himself in offset print and I advanced concrete proposals. However, Leopold, with a stubbornness thus far unknown to me, rejected them. He insisted that this work had to be published as a regular book by a commercial publisher. It seemed to me then and still seems to me today a miracle that the meritorious Heinz Bleicher appeared and published the book with a beautiful cover designed by Grete Adler, Leopold's sister.

Already in 1964, Leopold's most popular work, his translation of the Song of Songs, was published by Reclam: last year alone 500 copies were sold. In 1976, I brought him from Europe his just published volume of poems entitled: "Es fuehrt eine lange Strasse" (It is a long road). Leopold's translation of the Psalms, unfortunately, still awaits publication. After Buber's death and the publication of his translation of the Psalms, I was astonished that Leopold would want to undertake a new translation of the Psalms. On this subject he wrote me on April 17, 1971: "I pursue the translation because the one by Buber, a work of his old age, is not only not rhythmical, but also at times difficult to understand and, in some places, controversial."

Thus Leopold overcame the loss of his beloved Judith through continuous creativitiy. She died eleven years before him, after almost 56 years of marriage. This tranquil and quiet woman, radiating goodness, love and understanding, helped Leopold time and again to retain his equilibrium. She was also an active leader in her community, doing pioneer work in the school-affairs of Shavey Zion and a founder and long-time leader of the local Zionist Women's group (WIZO).

After death had torn her from his side and with his eyesight steadily deteriorating, Miriam Strauss became his reader and writer, or as he phrased it in the dedication of his book, *Jehoshua, my Son*, the "Light of his later days." Leopold's friends owe her thanks, which I myself expressed to her half a year ago.

On the occasion of his 90th birthday, the City of Stuttgart presented Leopold with a scroll of honor and a monetary prize. With this donation he established a foundation for the benefit of Jewish and Arab schoolchildren in memory of his son Jehoshua.

Now that he is no longer among us, the memory remains. He was a true poet who had lived in our midst. He spoke to us about the tragedy of life, but he overcame this tragedy through his messianic belief in the victory of Good, in ultimate peace and in his love of the land of Israel.

Eulogy delivered by Hans Hirsch at memorial gathering held on November 13, 1983 at the Leo Baeck Institute, New York. Extracted and translated from the German by Herman Dicker.

ADOLF KOBER

Adolf Kober (1879-1958), rabbi and historian, former-
ly at Cologne, Germany, has left a rich legacy of
historical writings. His article, whose appendices are
reproduced, appeared in the Publications of the
American Jewish Historical Society, Vol. XLI, Nr. 3
(March, 1952) p. 225ff. In the course of his research on
immigration to the United States, Kober, in 1948,
approached the State Archives in Munich, Karlsruhe,
Darmstadt and Wiesbaden, but only the one in
Ludwigsburg, Wuerttemberg furnished detailed
lists of emigrants.

JEWISH EMIGRATION FROM WUERTTEMBERG TO THE UNITED STATES 1848–1855

APPENDICES I THROUGH V

EXPLANATORY NOTE

In order to facilitate the reading of these Appendices, we wish to offer the following key to them, since they are based upon a digest of the Wurttemberg records that we have consulted.

APPENDIX I

In the first column are given the name of the emigrant and his age in brackets, if it appeared in the original record of the district-clerk. Thus, under the year 1848, the first name listed, that of Gutrath Amsoll indicates that she was twenty-seven years old when she left Wuerttemberg.

In the second column, the emigrant's former place of residence is given.

In the third column, the emigrant's occupation is given as it appeared in the original record of the district-clerk.

In the fourth column, the family status of the emigrant is given as well as the data concerning those who accompanied the emigrant when he left Wuerttemberg. The abbreviations used in this column are: s. (= single); w. (= wife); m. (= male); f. (= female). Whenever a number precedes the abbreviations m. or f., it represents the number of male or female children accompanying the emigrant parent. For example, the second name appearing, under the year 1848, that of Maier Bernheimer, tradesman, who left Jebenhausen in that year to settle abroad, shows that he was accompanied by his wife Juettle (the widow of Simon Rothschild) with five children: the children consisting of two sons from Maier Bernheimer's first marriage; one boy from his second marriage; and two children, a boy and a girl, of his second wife, Juettle by her first marriage with Simon Rothschild.

Whenever any number follows the abbreviations w., m. or f., in the fourth column, it represents the respective ages of the wife, son or daughter accompanying the emigrant. For example, the first name appearing under the year 1849, that of Josef Aron Arnold, tradesman, indicates that he left Jebenhausen in that year for abroad with his wife, Deifele, age forty-six, together with their four children: consisting of a daughter, age six; a son, age eleven; a daughter, age fifteen; and a daughter, age eighteen. He took along with him 2,000 florins.

In the fifth column, information whenever recorded, is given pertaining to the assets of the emigrant, the amount of money he took along when he left Wuerttemberg. In this column appear the abbreviation, fl. (= florins); and the symbol + (= plus).

In the sixth column appear the emigrant's reasons for leaving Wuerttemberg together with additional remarks recorded by the district-clerk.

APPENDICES II, III, IV AND V

For the convenience of the reader, Appendix II lists the districts of Wuerttemberg by regions; Appendix III gives an alphabetical list of all the localities mentioned in the second column of Appendix I, together with the names of the districts in which the respective localities are situated. The captions of Appendices IV and V are self-explanatory.

APPENDIX I

RECORDS OF JEWISH EMIGRATION FROM WÜRTTEMBERG (1848–1855)

1848

Name [and Age]	Residence	Occupation	Family Status	Assets	Reason for Migrating and Remarks
AMBOLL, GUTRATH [27]	Creglingen	—	s.	125 fl.	settling
BERNHEIMER, MAIER	Jebenhausen	tradesman	JÜTTLE, widow of SIMON ROTHSCHILD (w.) and 5 children: 2 m. from his first marriage, 1 m. from his second marriage, 2 [1 m., 1 f.] from the first marriage of his w. (ROTHSCHILD)	—	settling
DETTELBACHER, PAULINE	Jebenhausen	—	s.	—	settling
HEILBRONNER, THERESE (daughter of LAZARUS HEILBRONNER) [33]	Buchau	—	s.	—	service
JOOS, FIEDEL [38]	Baisingen	carpenter	—	—	settling
JOSSE, FRIEDERIKA	Steinbach	—	s.	—	marriage
LEVI, MALCHE [30]	Freudental	—	s.	—	settling
MICHAEL, FANY [27]	Baisingen	—	—	—	settling
MIRABEAU, ISAC	Olnhausen	soap-boiler	with w.	300 fl.	settling
OTTENHEIMER, HIRSCH	Jebenhausen	tradesman	CLARA (w.) and 5 children (3 f.. 2 m.)	—	settling
SCHNATZ, ISIDOR	Binswangen	carpenter	with w. and 4 children	750 fl.	settling
STERN, RÖSLE (daughter of the cattle dealer, AARON STERN)	Lehrensteinfeld	—	—	50 fl.+travelling money	settling
STRAUSS, KAROLINE (daughter of MARX STRAUSS) [24]	Baisingen	—	—	—	settling
WOLF, SUSSEL (daughter of the church-warden WOLF)	Freudental	—	s.	100 fl.	settling

1849

Name [and Age]	Residence	Occupation	Family Status	Assets	Reason for Migrating and Remarks
ARNOLD, JOSEF ARON [53]	Jebenhausen	tradesman	DEIFELE (w.) [46] and 4 children (f. 6, m. 11, f. 15, f. 18)	2,000 fl.	settling
BIKART, METHILDE	Rexingen	—	s.	400 fl.	hopes to establish a better existence
BIKART, SALOMON	Rexingen	master carpenter	without children	1,400 fl.	better existence
EPPSTEIN, JULIUS	Rexingen	—	s.	700 fl.	settling

1849 (*Continued*)

Name [and Age]	Residence	Occupation	Family Status	Assets	Reason for Migrating and Remarks
FELLHEIMER, ABRAHAM	Jebenhausen	tradesman	RIKKELE, née ULRICH (w.) [52] and 2 children (f. 9, m. 17)	2,000 fl.	settling
GUTMANN, ABRAHAM (son of cattle-dealer JUL. GUTMANN)	Gerabronn	——	s.	175 fl.	settling
LANDAUER, SALOMON	Gerabronn	trade-apprentice	s.	100 fl.+passage cost	settling
LINDAUER, JETTE (widow of WOLF LINDAUER, née ARNOLD) [42]	Jebenhausen	——	widow and 4 children (f. 8, f. 10, m. 13, f. 17)	2,000 fl.+passage cost	settling
NEUMANN, AUGUST [20]	Knochendorf	——	s.	200 fl.	at the suggestion of his brother-in-law in North America
NÖRDLINGER, ISAK	Pflaumloch	merchant	s.	not known	settling
ROSENFELD, FEISEL (*sic!*) [61]	Jebenhausen	tradesman	with w. and 4 children (f. 12, f. 15, m. 19, m. 20)	1,600 fl.+passage cost	settling
ROSENTHAL'S, ABRAHAM 9 children: BABETH [23] SOPHIE [22] LUISE [19] ISAK [18] LAZARUS [16] MARX [14] BERTA [12] THERESIA [10] HELENE [7]	Laupheim	——	——	600 fl.	settling: ABRAHAM ROSENTHAL has escaped to North America in the previous year [1848].
SONTHEIMER, JACOB (son of the widow FRATEL SONTHEIMER)	Weikersheim	baker	s.	——	settling
STERN, SAMUEL	Gerabronn	——	s.	100 fl.+passage cost	settling
STRAUSS, LÄMMLEIN	Wiesenbach	trade-apprentice	s.	200 gulden	—
WEISS, SAMUEL	Hechtberg	baker	——	400 fl.	already in North America [Philadelphia] and wants to marry there.

1850

Name [and Age]	Residence	Occupation	Family Status	Assets	Reason for Migrating and Remarks
BLOCH, MAIER	Mühringen	journeyman cutler	s.	152 fl.	hopes to establish a better existence
BLUM, JAKOB JOSEF	Aufhausen	——	with w. and 2 children (1, 4)	800 fl.	settling
ELLINGER, ABRAHAM [20]	Pflaumloch	weaver	s.	250 fl. travelling expenses	settling, to seek better existence
FELDENHEIMER, ABRAHAM	Hengstfeld	saddler	s.	150 fl.	improvement of his condition.

1850 (*Continued*)

Name [and Age]	Residence	Occupation	Family Status	Assets	Reason for Migrating and Remarks
GRONAUER, ABRAHAM	Eschenau	quarryman	s.	travelling expenses only	already in America
GUTMANN, ISAK [17½]	Kochendorf	——	s.	150 fl.	at the suggestion of his sister in New York.
GUTMANN, SAMUEL	Oberdorf	——	s.	——	settling
HENLE, SALOMON [20]	Oberdorf	trade-journeyman	——	1,000 fl.	settling (destination: New York), to seek better existence.
HIRSCHHEIMER, LÖW [36]	Lehrensteinfeld	tradesman	with w. and 7 children and his mother HIEDEL HIRSCHHEIMER [70]	4,000 fl.	settling
JANDORF, RUFIN	Hengstfeld	shoemaker	s.	150 fl.	improvement of his condition.
KAHN, ABRAHAM	Niederstetten	——	s.	125 fl.	to learn trade
LÖWENTHAL, BARUCH	Mühringen	confectioner	s.	200 fl.	hope to establish a better existence.
MEZGER, WOLF	Wachenbach	butcher	s.	73 gulden, 28 kreuzer	settling
MICHAEL, BERNHARD	Baisingen	merchant	with w. and son (16)	700 fl.	hopes to establish a better existence.
OBERDORFER, JETTE	Oberdorf	——	s.	150 fl.	settling
RÖDELSHEIMER, HANS	Oberschwandorf	tradesman	JETTE, née DESSAUER (w.) and 4 children (f. 10, m. 12, m. 18, m. 19)	without any fortune, the state exchequer granted him 200 fl. on behalf of his emigration	settling
ROSENHEIM, MOSES	Jebenhausen	merchant	s.	his fortune of 1,200 fl. is still in Jebenhausen	settling (destination: Zanesville, Ohio)
ROSENSTEIN, JULIUS	Ödheim	tradesman	s.	——	is already in America
ROTHSCHILD, SAMUEL	Jebenhausen	tradesman	s.	——	settling (was in America before Nov. 23, 1850.)
STRASSBURGER, MOSES	Hohebach	——	s.	——	settling
THALMESSINGER, MAIER MOSES	Pflaumloch	——	——	——	to attain a better existence
WEIS, JOSEF	Hochberg	brewer	s.	800 fl.	was already in America when he renounced his former citizenship.

1851

Name [and Age]	Residence	Occupation	Family Status	Assets	Reason for Migrating and Remarks
ADLER, LEHMANN	Buttenhausen	butcher	s.	140 fl.	better living
ALTMEIER, LÖW	Oberdorf	—	—	150 fl.	settling
BEER, SORLIE	Zaberfeld	merchant	s.	120 fl.	settling
BERNHEIMER, JEANETTE (daughter of ABRAHAM BERNHEIMER)	Jebenhausen	—	s.	200 fl.	—
DESSAUER, ERNESTINE	Unterschwandorf	—	s. with 2 children (f. 11, m. 15)	200 fl.	settling
EICHBERGER, SAMUEL THEODOR	Mergentheim	merchant	s.	—	settling
EINSTEIN, EVELINE	Jebenhausen	—	married	300 fl.	settling; the husband had already escaped to America.
ELKAN, MOSES	Michelbach	ropemaker	s.	175 fl.	settling
FELDENHEIMER, SAMSON	Archshofen	butcher	s.	200 fl.	settling
FRIEDENHEIMER, BERNARD	Lehrensteinsfeld	brandy and vinegar manufacturer	with his w.	900 fl.	settling
GUTMAN, DAVID	District of Neresheim	—	—	6,000 fl.	settling (South America)
GUTMANN, HESS	District of Neresheim	—	with 4 relatives	1,400 fl.	a better existence
HARTHEIMER, LAZARUS	Igersheim	without profession	s.	113 fl.	settling
JANDORF, MOSES HAYUM	Hengstfeld	cigar maker	s.	125 fl.	improvement of his condition
JUNG, ELIAS	Pflaumloch	—	—	150 fl.	settling
JUNG, LAZARUS	Pflaumloch	—	—	200 fl.	settling
LEDERMANN, ISAK	Berlichingen	soap-boiler	with w. and 1 child (f.)	800 fl.	settling
LEVI, ISAAK	Laudenbach	butcher	s.	155 fl.	settling
LICHTENBERG, HELENE (widow)	Dörsbach	—	with 3 children (2 m., 1 f.)	—	settling
LINDAUER, DAVID HIRSCH	Jebenhausen	butcher	s.	300 fl.	to work at his occupation
MARX, ANSCHEL MARX	Weikersheim	clothmaker	with w.	unknown	is already in America
MARX, DANIEL and DELZEL	Baisingen	—	both s.	2,000 fl.	establishing a better existence
MARX, MORDOCHAI	Hohebach	—	s.	—	settling
NEUBURGER, DAVID [17] and his sister, REGINE [21]	—	—	—	each 150 fl. travel-money [together 300 fl.]	to seek a better existence
NÖRDLINGER, ISAK	Pflaumloch	—	—	—	striving after a better existence.
PHILIPP, FANNY	Baisingen	—	s.	150 fl.	founding of a better existence
RIES, MARX	Michelbach a. L.	soap-boiler	s.	150 fl.	settling
ROSENHEIM, JETTLE	Jebenhausen	—	s.	1,400 fl.	marriage

1851 (Continued)

Name [and Age]	Residence	Occupation	Family Status	Assets	Reason for Migrating and Remarks
ROSENHEIM, DAVID	Jebenhausen	——	s.	200 fl.	to take over service
ROSENHEIM, MORITZ MOSES	Jebenhausen	farmer	with his w.	1,000 fl.	domestic settlement (destination Philadelphia)
STRASSBURGER, MOSES	Hohebach	——	s.	150 fl.	settling
STRAUSS, HOHNA	Markelsheim	butcher	s.	150 fl.	settling
STRAUSS, SIGMUND	Wachbach	——	s.	150 fl.	settling
WASSERMAN, DAVID	District of Neresheim	butcher	s.	150 fl.	settling
WEIL, ISAK	Buttenhausen	shoemaker	s.	150 fl.	better living
WOLF, ESTHER	Craintal	——	s.	116 gulden 27 kreuzer	marriage

1852

Name [and Age]	Residence	Occupation	Family Status	Assets	Reason for Migrating and Remarks
ADLER, SIMON	Laupheim	——	s.	125 fl.	settling
AUGSBURGER, ISAK	Unterschwandorf	——	s.	18 fl. (from the community of Unterschwandorf)	settling
BÄR, MANASSE	Mulfingen	merchant	s.	1,000 fl.	settling (is already in America)
BLOCH, MINA (widow)	Mühringen	——	with 4 children	700 fl.	better existence
BLUM, MARUM	Aufhausen	——	s.	130 fl.	settling
FALK, SOLOMON LÖW	Braunsbach	butcher	s.	300 fl.	settling
FELDENHEIMER, JOSEF	Hengstfeld	shoemaker	s.	100 fl.	settling
FRANK, ABRAHAM MOSES	Nordstetten	retailer	with w. and 2 children	1,800 fl.	better existence
FRANK, HEINRICH MOSES	Nordstetten	soap-boiler	with w. and 4 children	2,000 fl.	better existence
FRÖHLICH, LEOPOLD	Aufhausen	——	s.	130 fl.	settling
GIDEON, LINA	Rexingen	——	s.	72 fl. (50 fl. from the Jewish community, 22 fl. from private individuals)	settling
GRONAUER, Louis	Eschenau	mechanic	s.	only travel money	settling
GUGGENHEIMER, SARA	Laupheim	——	s.	130 fl.	settling
GUTMANN, ABRAHAM HIRSCH	Dörzbach	merchant	——	15,000 fl.	settling (is already in America)
GUTMANN, HEINRICH	Kochendorf	tradesman	with w. and 2 daughters	400 fl.	settling

1852 (*Continued*)

Name [and Age]	Residence	Occupation	Family Status	Assets	Reason for Migrating and Remarks
GUTMANN, JEANETTE (married)	Oberdorf	—	mother of 2 children	600 fl.	settling
GUTMANN, JONAS	Oberdorf	—	s.	100 fl.	settling
GUTMANN, THERESE and CLÄRE	Oberdorf	—	—	400 fl.	settling
HESS, DAVID	Dörzbach	shoemaker	s.	—	settling
HIRSCH, GISEL	Niederstetten	—	s.	300 fl.	improvement of his condition
HOFHEIMER, HIRSCH	Laupheim	—	s.	125 fl.	to seek his luck
JANDORF, PFEIFER	Hengstfeld	farmer	s.	200 fl.	improvement of his condition
JUDA, JETTLE	Lehrensteinsfeld	—	s. with 2 brothers	only travel expenses	settling
KAHN, ARON JUDAS	Freudental	—	s.	150 fl.	settling
KATZ, SAMSON	Unterschwandorf	optician	s.	18 fl. from the community of Unterschwandorf	settling
KUBITSCHEK, HEINRICH	Aufhausen	—	—	120 fl.	settling
LAUCHHEIMER, HEINRICH	Jebenhausen	merchant	s.	400 fl.	settling
LIEBMANN, LEVI	Jebenhausen	retired school-teacher	with his w. REBEKKA, née EINSTEIN, and 4 daughters	1,000 fl.	settling
LÖWENBERG, JOSEF	Hohenbach	saddler	s.	—	is already in America
MARX, MARIE and JAKOB	Mühringen	—	s.	300 fl.	better existence
MEYER, MAXIMILIAN [14]	Crailsheim	—	—	100 fl.	settling
NEUHAUSER, JULIUS	Mühringen	—	with w., mother and 4 children	1,100 fl.	better existence
NÖRDLINGER, JAKOB	Pflaumloch	—	s.	5,000 fl.	settling
NÖRDLINGER, LAZARUS	Pflaumloch	—	s.	200 fl.	settling
ROHRBACHER, LEOPOLD	Jebenhausen	merchant	s.	150 fl.	settling
ROSENBERGER, ISAK	Aldingen	baker	s.	140 fl.	slackness in his occupation
ROSENBERGER, MÄNDEL	Eschenau	tradesman	with w. and 3 children	only travel expenses	settling
ROSENFELD, BÜSSLE (widow)	Hohebach	—	with 11 children (3 m., 8 f.)	—	settling
ROSENFELD, MARIE	Mühringen	—	s.	140 fl.	better existence
ROSENHEIM, ULRICH	Jebenhausen	—	s.	1,000 fl.	settling, is already in America
ROSENTHAL, SALOMON	Weikersheim	shoemaker	s.	100 fl.	settling
ROTHSCHILD, HERZ	Lehrensteinsfeld	without occupation	s.	only travel expenses	settling
ROTHSCHILD, MOSES, widow of	Mühringen	—	with 2 children	400 fl.	hope to establish a better existence

1852 (*Continued*)

Name [and Age]	Residence	Occupation	Family Status	Assets	Reason for Migrating and Remarks
SÄNGER, LINA	Oberdorf	—	s.	150 fl.	settling
SCHLESINGER, NATHAN	Unterschwandorf	—	s.	18 fl. from the community of Unterschwandorf	settling
SELIGMANN, EMMANUEL	Hochberg	—	s.	130 fl.	better existence (destination New York)
SELIGMANN, SIMON	Hochberg	without a profession	s.	140 fl.	better existence (destination New York; already in America)
STEINHARDT, ISAK	Olnhausen	innkeeper	with his family, 3 children (f.)	2,000 fl.	settling
ULMANN, ABRAHAM, widow of	Olnhausen	—	with 5 children	500 fl.	settling
WERTHEIMER, SAMUEL and IMMANUEL	Aldingen	—	s.	300 gulden	slackness in occupation

1853

Name [and Age]	Residence	Occupation	Family Status	Assets	Reason for Migrating and Remarks
ADLER, ISAC (son of the tradesman BERNHARD ADLER) [18]	Aldingen	weaver	—	150 fl.	settling
ARNOLD, BERNHARD	Jebenhausen	—	s.	200 fl.	settling
BAER, JUDITH (widow of ISAAC BAER who died in 1852, née HAUSSMANN) [52]	Buttenhausen	—	with her 7 children (f. 14, m. 17, m. 19, m. 22, f. 24, f. 27, m. 29) and 1 grandchild (f. 3).	300 fl.	settling; all children with exception of two are already in U. S. A.
BAMBERGER, LOUIS (son of ABRAHAM BAMBERGER)	Crailsheim	lacemaker	—	300 fl.	settling
BERGHEIMER, ANNA	Brackenheim	—	with son	150 fl.	settling
BUXBAUM, JOSEPH	Ernsbach	soap-boiler	—	400 fl.	settling
EICHBERGER, MAINDLE	Hengstfeld	tradesman	with w. and 4 children (m. 23, f. 24, f. 25, f. 26)	300 fl.	settling; 3 children are already in in U. S. A.
FRIEDBERGER, MAJER BARUCH (son of the tradesman BARUCH FRIEDBERGER) [16]	Laupheim	—	—	160 fl.	settling
GEISSENDORFER, JOHANNE	Kochendorf	—	with her child (m. 1½)	travel-expenses	settling
GIDEON, JOSEF [36]	Rexingen	—	with w. and 1 child	600 fl.	settling
GIDEON, LIPPMANN [19]	Rexingen	shoemaker	s.	140 fl.	settling
GUTMANN, SIMON	Dörzbach	—	s.	—	settling; is already in U. S. A.

1853 (*Continued*)

Name [and Age]	Residence	Occupation	Family Status	Assets	Reason for Migrating and Remarks
GUTSMANN, SIGMUND [19]	Dörzbach	——	s.	——	settling; is already in U. S. A.
HEIDENHEIMER, ISAC	Archshofen	——	s.	200 fl.	settling
HIRSCHFELDER, AARON [17]	Rexingen	butcher	——	150 fl.	settling
HIRSCHFELDER, BERTA [22]	Rexingen	——	s.	150 fl.	settling
HIRSCHMANN, LAZARUS (son of horse-dealer JACHIEL HIRSCHMANN) [20]	Freudental	butcher	——	travel-expenses + 100 fl.	settling
HOPPER, LEOPOLD [19]	Rexingen	shoemaker	s.	140 fl.	settling
IMANUEL, PAULINE [16]	Hochberg	——	s.	120 fl.	settling
KAHN, MAYER (son of the farmer ABRAHAM KAHN)	Hengstfeld	——	——	——	settling
KOHN, SAMUEL [26]	Freudental	goldsmith	s.	2,000 fl.	settling
LANDAUER, ALEXANDER [18]	Buchau	linen-weaver	——	140 fl.	settling
LANDAUER, CAROLINE (sister of MOSES LANDAUER)	Gerabronn	——	——	100 fl.	settling
LANDAUER, MOSES	Gerabronn	tradesman	——	100 fl.	settling
LEVI, ALBERT (son of the master shoemaker KASIMIR LEVI) [20]	Esslingen	——	——	——	settling; is already in Hartford, Conn.
LEVI, ELIAS [49]	Nordstetten	peddler	with w. and 4 children	500 fl.	settling
LEVI, JONATHAN	Archshofen	——	s.	773 fl., 55 kreuzer	settling
LEVI, MORITZ (son of the peddler LEOPOLD LEVI) [17]	Nordstetten	butcher	——	200 fl.	settling
LEVI, MOSES [32]	Lehrensteinsfeld	ragpicker	——	travel-expenses	settling [he returned in 1884].
LEVISON, LOUIS LEHMANN [18]	Mühringen	——	——	140 francs	settling
LIEBMANN, LIEBMANN	Wankheim	merchant	with w. 27 years old, and 3 children (f. 2, f. 4, m. 6)	1,000 fl.	settling
LIMBURGER, JEANETTE (daughter of tradesman JOSHUA MOSES LIMBURGER)	Hall	——	——	350 fl.	settling
LÖWENTHAL, ABRAHAM [17]	Buttenhausen	——	——	140 fl.	settling
LÖWENTHAL, SIMSON [20]	Buttenhausen	cotten-weaver	s.	200 fl.	settling
LOSER, FRIEDRICH	Mergentheim	——	s.	200 fl.	settling

1853 (*Continued*)

Name [and Age]	Residence	Occupation	Family Status	Assets	Reason for Migrating and Remarks
MARX, MOSES (son of tradesman ABRAHAM MARX) [20]	Hohebach	—	—	120 fl.	settling
MEINHOLD, ABRAHAM [14]	Massenbach-hausen	—	—	100 fl.	settling; was assigned again to the community on Aug. 6, 1856.
MEINHOLD, KAROLINE [16]	Massenbach-hausen	—	s.	100 fl.	settling; was assigned again to the community on Aug. 6, 1856.
OBENHEIMER, ABRAHAM	Wachbach	—	s.	250 fl.	settling
OCHS, NAFTALI [32]	Nordstetten	butcher	with w. 24 years old and 1 child (m 2)	1,000 fl.	settling
OTTENHEIMER, EMANUEL [19]	Nordstetten	butcher	s.	travels with his cousin Ochs who is said to have 1,000 fl. travel-expenses	settling; his father already migrated to America.
OTTENEHIMER, JETTE	Jebenhausen	—	s.	1,000 fl.	settling
POLACK, MAIER	Mühringen	tailor	with FRIEDERIKA (w.) and 4 children (f. 4, m. 9, m. 10, m. 18)	350 fl.	settling
RIESER, SAMUEL [16]	Buchau	merchant's clerk	—	300 francs	settling
RÖDELHEIMER, ABRAHAM [17]	Laupheim	merchant	s.	150 fl.	settling
ROSENFELD, JAKOB	Massenbach-hausen	—	s.	100 fl.	settling
ROSENHEIM, MOSES [20]	Jebenhausen	—	s.	150 fl.	settling
ROSENHEIM, ULRICH	Jebenhausen	—	—	200 fl.	settling
ROSENTHAL, EPHRAIM	Hohebach	—	with his w.	150 fl.	settling
ROTHSCHILD, IMANUEL [16]	Lehrensteinsfeld	—	—	travel-expenses	settling
ROTHSCHILD, SALOMO (brother of IMANUEL ROTHSCHILD) [15]	Lehrensteinsfeld	—	—	travel-expenses	settling
SCHWARZ, VEIT (son of the butcher LIPPMANN SCHWARZ)	Rexingen	weaver	with his w. and 4 children (m. 2, f. 4, m. 6, m. 8)	800 fl.	settling
SELIGMANN, MORITZ (MOSES) [19]	Hochberg	—	—	2,000 fl.	settling: is already in U. S. A.
STERN, NATAN (son of the tradesman JOSEPH STERN) [17]	Morstein	—	s.	150 fl.	settling
STRAUSS, DAVID	Markelsheim	—	—	150 fl.	settling
STRAUSS, GEORG MICHAEL	Michelbach	master shoe-maker	with w. and 6 children	650 fl.	settling
STRAUSS, LAZARUS	Wachbach	without a trade	—	200 fl.	settling
WASSERMAN, LÖW	Dunsbach	butcher	s.	150 fl.	settling

1853 (*Continued*)

Name [and Age]	Residence	Occupation	Family Status	Assets	Reason for Migrating and Remarks
WEIL, MAIER	Nordstetten	tradesman	with w. (second marriage) and 2 children of first marriage (f. 6, m. 10)	450 fl.	settling
WERTHEIMER, BELA (widow of MOSES WERTHEIMER)	Aldingen	——	with 4 children (f. 13, m. 14, f. 18, m. 18)	1,000 fl.	settling
WERTHEIMER, HENRIETTE	Wachbach	——	s.	96 fl.	settling

1854

Name [and Age]	Residence	Occupation	Family Status	Assets	Reason for Migrating and Remarks
ADLER, SAMUEL [18]	Edelfingen	butcher	s.	125 fl.	to seek a better existence.
ANSCHEL, ABRAHAM [19]	Hochberg	tradesman	s.	150 fl.	better existence
BAULAND, MORITZ [33]	Jebenhausen	butcher	s.	1,000 fl.	settling
BERLINGER, HÜNDEL	Berlichingen	——	s.	125 fl.	improvement of existence
BERLINGER, JAKOB [18]	Hochberg	——	s.	150 fl.	better existence
BERLIZHEIMER, BERNHARD	Mühringen	——	s.	250 fl.	better existence
BERLIZHEIMER, DAVID	Mühringen	shoemaker	s.	400 fl.	better existence
BLOCH, GOTTHILF [16]	Oberdorf	——	s.	200 fl.	settling
BLUMENTHAL, MORITZ	Crailsheim	tailor	s.	——	settling
BLUMENTHALER, ESTHER	Bonfeld	——	s.	150 fl.	settling
EINHORN, MARX	Goldbach	without a trade	s.	——	settling
ELKAN, ISAK	Michelbach an der Lücke	cattle-dealer	with his sister	300 fl.	settling
EMMANUEL, SAMUEL [14]	Hochberg	——	——	120 fl.	better existence
EPSTEIN, JAKOB	Mühringen	——	s.	140 fl.	better existence
FELDENHEIMER, ISAK	Hengstfeld	tradesman	s.	150 fl.	settling
FELDENHEIMER, ZILLI (widow)	Hengstfeld	——	with 3 children	500 fl.	settling
FELLHENNER, AUGUST [13]	Hochberg	——	s.	100 fl.	better existence
FELLHENNER, LOUIS [40]	Hochberg	merchant	with w. [36] and 4 children (ages 3 to 9)	4,000 fl.	better living
FRANK, LEOPOLD	Nordstetten	tradesman	with w. and 2 children	1,000 fl.	better existence
FRANKFURTER, VEIT [15]	Oberdorf	——	s.	150 fl.	settling

1854 (*Continued*)

Name [and Age]	Residence	Occupation	Family Status	Assets	Reason for Migrating and Remarks
FREIBURGER, SIMON	Rexingen	—	with w.	2,000 fl.	better existence
FRÖHLICH, MAX [15]	Aufhausen	—	s.	140 fl.	settling
FRÖHLICH, SIMON	Rexingen	optician	s.	514 fl.	better existence
GIDEON, SIGMUND	Mühlen a. N.	cooper	s.	150 fl.	hope to establish a better existence
GUGGENHEIMER, MAYER	Laupheim	weaver	with his w.	300 fl.	to seek a better living
GUTMANN, ALBERT	Gerabronn	merchant	s.	350 fl.	settling
GUTMANN, BERTA	Mergentheim	——	s.	150 fl.	better living
GUTMANN, ISAK	Oberdorf	——	s.	300 fl.	settling
GUTMANN, LAZARUS	Gerabronn	shoemaker	s.	200 fl.	settling
GUTMANN, LOUIS [15]	Dörzbach	without a trade	——	200 fl.	supposed improvement of existence and probably also fear of conscription
GUTMANN, RIEKE	Dörzbach	——	s.	200 fl.	improvement of existence
GUTMANN, SOLOMON [27]	Oberdorf	rope-maker	with w. and 1 child (m. 3¼)	6,000 fl.	settling
GUTMANN, SELIGMANN [14]	Kochendorf	——	s.	200 fl.	emigration
HAUSER, HAYUM [27]	Oberdorf	——	——	150 fl.	settling
HEIMPURTER, NAFTALI [23]	Oberdorf	——	s.	200 fl.	settling
HERMANN, JOEL	Dünsbach	merchant	——	300 fl.	settling
HERZ, ISAK [27]	Hochberg	——	s.	600 fl.	better living
HERZ, JULIUS	Poppenweiler	merchant	s.	150 fl.	to seek a better living
HESS, EZECHIEL	Aufhausen	glazier	with his w.	600 fl.	settling
HILB, EMMANUEL	Mühlen a. N.	butcher	s.	150 fl.	better existence
HIRSCH, HERMANN [15]	Wankheim	merchant's clerk	——	300 fl.	——
HIRSCH, SALOMON [16]	Hohebach		s.	25 fl.	better existence and probably also fear of conscription
HIRSCH, SAMUEL	Thalheim	without a trade	s.	200 fl.	settling
HIRSCH, SAMUEL (brother of HERMANN HIRSCH) [17]	Wankheim	merchant	——	——	is already in America since 1853
HÖCHSTETTER, SELIGMANN [18]	Buttenhausen	merchant	s.	300 fl.	settling
HÖCHSTETTER, SIMON [17]	Buttenhausen	merchant	s.	300 fl.	settling
JANDORF, ISAK	Hengstfeld	tradesman	——	150 fl.	settling
JANDORF, LÖW	Hengstfeld	butcher	——	150 fl.	settling

1854 (*Continued*)

Name [and Age]	Residence	Occupation	Family Status	Assets	Reason for Migrating and Remarks
KAHN, MARX [35]	Hochberg	—	with w. and 5 children aged 1 to 10	600 fl.	better living
KAUFMANN, ABRAHAM	Hochberg	baker	with w. [40] and 2 children aged 1 and 3	600 fl.	better living
KAUFMANN, LENE	Berlichingen	—	s.	150 fl.	improvement of existence
KUBITSCHEK, JACOB [19]	Aufhausen	butcher	s.	300 fl.	settling
KUSIEL, ASCHER [20]	Hochberg	tradesman	s.	150 fl.	better living
LAMMFROMM, SAMUEL [26]	Oberdorf		s.	150 fl.	settling
LANDAUER, ISRAEL	Gerabronn	merchant's apprentice	s.	140 fl.	settling
LAUCHHEIMER, HIRSCH [18]	Jebenhausen	butcher	—	200 fl.	settling
LAUCHHEIMER, ISR. [16]	Jebenhausen	baker	s.	300 fl.	settling
LEVI, ARON	Nagelsberg	butcher	s.	100 fl.	better existence
LEVI, EBERHARD	Esslingen	button-maker and trimmer	s.	300 fl.	better living
LEVI, ISAK HIRSCH [15]	Aufhausen	—	s.	300 fl.	settling
LEVI, JAKOB [18]	Aufhausen	—	—	250 fl.	settling
LEVI, LEOPOLD	Freudental	—	s.	50 fl.+travel expenses	settling
LEVI, ROSETTE	Berlichingen	—	s.	100 fl.	improvement of existence
LEVI, SANDEL [18]	Aufhausen	—	—	300 fl.	settling
LEVINGER, ISAK	Laupheim	peasant	s.	150 fl.	to seek a living
LEVISOHN, BARETTE and HIRSCH	Mühringen	—	s.	300 fl.	better existence
LINDAUER, DAVID HIRSCH	Jebenhausen	tradesman	s.	200 fl.	settling
LINDAUER, JOSEF [16]	Jebenhausen	butcher	s.	200 fl.	settling
LINDAUER, MAIER [17]	Jebenhausen	merchant	s.	200 fl.	settling
LINDNER, EMANUEL [17]	Mulfingen	peasant	s.	300 fl.	better existence and probably also fear of conscription
LÖB, LEVI [16]	Affaltrach	farmer	—	travel expenses	settling
LÖBSTEIN, JOSUA [16]	Jebenhausen	baker	s.	250 fl.	settling
LÖW, SAMUEL HIRSCH [19]	Ernsbach	carpenter	s.	150 fl.	settling
LÖWENGART, ELIAS [16]	Pflaumloch	—	s.	200 fl.	settling
LÖWENGART, SAMUEL [20]	Pflaumloch	—	—	200 fl.	settling
LÖWENSTEIN, LEOPOLD	Laupheim	shoemaker	—	150 fl.	to seek a living.
LÖWENTHAL, MOSES	Aldingen	butcher	—	150 fl.	to seek a better living

1854 (*Continued*)

Name [and Age]	Residence	Occupation	Family Status	Assets	Reason for Migrating and Remarks
Löwenthal, Salomon	District of Ried-lingen	—	with w. and child	—	settling
Manasse, Albert	Thalheim	without a trade	s.	200 fl.	settling
Manasse Wolf	Thalheim	butcher	s.	150 fl.	settling
Manasse, Zion, widow of	Bonfeld	—	with her 5 children	500 fl.	settling
Marx, Esther	Oberdorf	—	—	200 fl.	settling
Marx, Hayum [14]	Oberdorf	—	s.	175 fl.	settling
Marx, Marx [28]	Oberdorf	glazier	with his w. and ½ year old child	900 fl.	settling
Marx, Samuel [19]	Oberdorf	shoemaker	s.	100 fl.	settling
Michelberger, Benedikt [19]	Braunsbach	shoemaker	s.	150 fl.	improvement of existence and probably also fear of conscription
Monheimer, Hayum [15]	Oberdorf	—	—	125 fl.	settling
Moos, Julius [20]	Buchau	—	—	140 fl.	settling
Morgenroth, Maier	Ernsbach	shopkeeper	with w. and 2 daughters (14, 19)	400 fl.	settling
Neuburger, Mayer [14]	Buchau	—	—	200 fl.	settling
Nördlinger, Isak Hirsch [18]	Pflaumloch	—	—	200 fl.	settling
Ochs, Judas	Nordstetten	tailor	with w. and 6 children	650 fl.	better existence
Oettinger, Moses	Mergentheim	book-binder	s.	150 fl.	better living
Ottenheimer, Julius [20]	Jebenhausen	merchant	s.	500 fl.	settling
Ottenheimer, Karoline	Bonfeld	—	s.	200 fl.	settling
Pressburger, Nathan	Rexingen	—	s.	150 fl.	better existence
Rohrbacher, Ulrich	Jebenhausen	butcher	s.	200 fl.	settling
Rosenberger, Gabriel [15]	Oberdorf	—	—	200 fl.	settling
Rosenberger, Lipmann	Aldingen	peasant	s.	150 fl.	to seek a better living
Rosenberger, Samuel [17]	Oberdorf	—	s.	150 fl.	settling
Rosenfeld, Abraham	Mühringen	—	with w.	600 fl.	better existence
Rosenfeld, Immanuel	Wachbach	trader	s.	150 fl.	to seek a better living
Rosenheim, Therese	Jebenhausen	—	s.	1,000 fl.	settling
Rosenstrauss, David Theodor [16]	Wankheim	merchant	s.	200 fl.	settling
Rosenstrauss, Fanny [21]	Wankheim	—	s.	200 fl.	settling

1854 *(Continued)*

Name [and Age]	Residence	Occupation	Family Status	Assets	Reason for Migrating and Remarks
ROSENSTRAUSS, HERMAN [19]	Wankheim	engraver	s.	200 fl.	better living
ROSENTAL, ABRAHAM HIRSCH	Laudenbach	merchant	s.	150 fl.	better living
ROTHSCHILD, ISAK LÖW	Nordstetten	trade-clerk	s.	250 fl.	better existence
ROTHSCHILD, MARX	Nordstetten	——	s.	150 fl.	better existence
SAHM, HIRSCH	Braunsbach	tinman	s.	200 fl.	improvement of existence
SCHERNBACHER, JOEL [15]	Oberdorf	——	s.	300 fl.	settling
SCHIELE, SALOMON LEVI [20]	Jebenhausen	tradesman	——	200 fl.	settling
SCHLACHTER, ABRAHAM [17]	Braunsbach	without a trade	s.	200 fl.	better existence and probably also fear of conscription
SONTHEIMER, GÖZ	Weikersheim	lacemaker	s.	200 fl.	better living
STEINER, LÖW	Dünsbach	tradesman	s.	200 fl.	settling
STERN, ABRAHAM	Morstein	butcher	s.	140 fl.	settling
STERN, JOHANNA	Dörsbach	——	s.	100 fl.	better existence
STETTHEIMER, JAKOB	Niederstetten	——	s.	——	settling
STRASSBURGER, FANNY	Hohebach	——	s.	200 fl.	better existence
STRASSBURGER, MINA	Hohebach	——	s.	200 fl	better existence
STRAUSS, CORLATINE (widow)	Bonfeld	——	with 5 children	800 fl.	settling
STRAUSS, KAUFFMANN	Bonfeld	——	s.	150 fl.	settling
STRAUSS, LUDWIG	Bonfeld	without a trade	s.	100 fl.	settling
STRAUSS, MOSES [19]	Braunsberg	merchant	s.	150 fl.	better existence and probably also fear of conscription
STRAUSS, SAMUEL [15]	Dörsbach	——	——	150 fl.	better existence and probably fear of conscription
SÜSSFELD, LAZARUS	Hengstfeld	tradesman	s.	250 fl.	settling
TALHEIMER, SAMUEL, wife of	Bonfeld	——	with her 5 children	400 fl.	settling
TALHEIMER, ABRAHAM [13]	Affaltrach	——	——	the necessary travel-expenses	settling
THALHEIMER, SALOMON [18]	Affaltrach	butcher	——	travel-expenses	settling
THANNHAUSER, SALOMON [19]	Buttenhausen	potter	s.	140 fl.	settling
UHLMANN, MAYER and MOSES ISAK	Freudental	——	s.	200 fl.	settling
ULLMANN, ABRAHAM [19]	Buchau	merchant	s.	140 fl.	settling

1854 (*Continued*)

Name [and Age]	Residence	Occupation	Family Status	Assets	Reason for Migrating and Remarks
WASSERMANN, ARON	Laupheim	confectioner	s.	150 fl.	to seek a better living
WEIL, MARX [20]	Aufhausen	——	——	400 fl.	settling
WOLLENBERGER, JUDAS	Hausen near Massenbach	——	s.	140 fl.	settling

1855

Name [and Age]	Residence	Occupation	Family Status	Assets	Reason for Migrating and Remarks
ADLER, JULIUS	Laupheim	——	s.	250 fl.	settling
ARNOLD, ADOLF LÖB [16]	Jebenhausen	merchant	s.	200 fl.	settling
BLUM, DAVID	Aufhausen	tradesman	——	200 fl.	settling
DREIFUSS, BARETTE (widow of JEREMIAS DREIFUSS)	Steinbach	——	——	225 fl.	to seek a better living
DREYFUSS, HAYUM	Hausen	butcher	s.	140 fl.	settling
ELSASS, ISAK	Aldingen	peasant	s.	150 fl.	better living
FULD, ISRAEL	Neunkirchen	tradesman	with w. and 1 daughter	——	settling
GUNDELFINGER, DAVID	Michelbach	——	s.	400 fl.	settling
GUTMANN, LAZARUS BÄR	Oberdorf	——	s.	100 fl.	settling
HIRSCH, AKIEFE [19]	Hohebach	——	s.	25 fl.	better existence
HIRSCH, ISAK ERNST	Niederstetten	stone-mason	s.	150 fl.	settling
HIRSCH, MORITZ [14]	Wankheim	without a profession	——	200 fl.	settling
HIRSCHHEIMER, LEOPOLD	Neunkirchen	without a trade	s.	unknown	to seek a better living for himself
JANDORF, ISAK	Hengstfeld	——	s.	150 fl.	settling
JANDORF, MERG	Hengstfeld	——	s.	100 fl.	settling
JUNG, NANETTE	Pflaumloch	——	s.	150 fl.	settling
KAHN, MOSES	Dünsbach	——	s.	150 fl.	settling
KAUFFMANN, SARA [13]	Hochberg	——	s.	130 fl.	to go to relatives
KUBITSCHEK, HESS	Aufhausen	tradesman	with w. and 5 children	800 fl.	settling
LANDAUER, JAKOB	Michelbach	——	s.	400 fl.	settling (destination Australia)
LAUCHHEIMER, ABRAHAM [15]	Jebenhausen	——	s.	150 fl.	settling
LAUPHEIMER, ELIAS	Laupheim	——	s.	250 fl.	settling
LEVI, JOHANNA (widow)	Aufhausen	——	——	200 fl.	settling

1855 (Continued)

Name [and Age]	Residence	Occupation	Family Status	Assets	Reason for Migrating and Remarks
LEVI, MEIER [16]	Laudenbach	without a trade	s.	unknown	settling
LICHTENBERG, KARL [20]	Dörzbach	optician	—	—	to seek work: already in America.
LOWENBERG, DAVID [15]	Hohebach	—	—	200 fl.	improvement of existence
MAI, JETTE	Berlichingen	—	s.	100 fl.	better existence
MAINZER, ABRAHAM (son of rabbi of Weikersheim)	Weikersheim	tanner	s.	unknown	settling
MARX, ISAK [20]	Hohebach	baker	—	60 fl.	to find a better living
METZGER, OSCHER	Wachbach	without a trade	s.	100 fl.	settling
MORGENROTH, ROSA and SARA	Ernsbach	—	s.	300 fl.	settling
POLAK, ABRAHAM [15]	Wankheim	without a profession	—	150 fl.	settling
REICHENBERGER, NATHAN	Niederstetten	—	s.	250 fl.	settling
ROSENFELD, HANNE [20]	Hohebach	—	—	150 fl.	settling
ROSENTHAL, NATHAN	Michelbach	—	s.	200 fl.	settling
ROSENTHAL, REGINE	Vogelsberg	—	s.	200 fl.	settling
STEIN, NATHAN	Freudental	—	s.	300 fl.	settling: is already in America
STERN, BARUCH	Hohebach	merchant	with w.	10,000	settling, not immediately in America
STERN, ISRAEL [16] and KAROLINE	Hohebach	—	s.	200 fl.	better existence
STRAUSS, BENET	Markelsheim	without a trade	s.	100 fl.	settling
STRAUSS, JAKOB [18]	Vogelsberg	—	s.	630 fl.	better existence; not immediately to America
STRAUSS, MOSES	Dünsbach	—	s.	175 fl.	settling
UHLMAN, SALOMON	Laupheim	—	s.	150 fl.	settling
UHLMANN, SIMON	Freudental	farmer	s.	200 fl.	settling
ULLMANN, ISAK	Eschenau	—	s.	—	settling
VEIT, MORITZ [20]	Heilbronn	merchant	s.	150 fl.	settling
WASSERMAN, KARL	Lauchheim	merchant	s.	150 fl.	settling

APPENDIX II

The kingdom of Württemberg was divided into four regions: 1) Neckarkreis, 2) Jagstkreis, 3) Schwarzwaldkreis, 4) Donaukreis. These "Kreise" or regions were divided into "Oberämter" or districts. In the following "Oberämter" Württemberg's Jews registered before emigrating.

DONAUKREIS

Göppingen
Laupheim
Riedlingen

JAGSTKREIS

Crailsheim
Ellwangen
Gerabronn
Hall
Künzelsau
Mergentheim
Neresheim
Oehringen

NECKARKREIS

Besigheim
Brackenheim
Esslingen
Heilbronn
Ludwigsburg
Neckarsulm
Waiblingen
Weinsberg

SCHWARZWALDKREIS

Horb
Nagold
Oberndorf
Tübingen

APPENDIX III

LIST OF LOCALITIES FROM WHERE THE JEWS EMIGRATED
AND THE "OBERAMT" OR DISTRICT TO WHICH THE
LOCALITY BELONGED

Place	District	Place	District
Affaltrach	Weinsberg	Lauchheim	Ellwangen
Aldingen	Ludwigsburg	Laudenbach	Mergentheim
Archshofen	Mergentheim	Laupheim	Laupheim
Aufhausen	Neresheim	Lehrensteinfeld	Weinsberg
Baisingen	Horb	Markelsheim	Mergentheim
Berlichingen	Künzelsau	Massenbach-	
Binswangen	Neckarsulm	hausen	Brackenheim
Bonfeld	Heilbronn	Mergentheim	Mergentheim
Brackenheim	Brackenheim	Michelbach an	
Braunsbach	Künzelsau	der Lücke	Gerabronn
Buchau	Riedlingen	Morstein	Gerabronn
Buttenhausen	Horb	Mühlen am	
Crailsheim	Crailsheim	Neckar	Horb
Craintal	Mergentheim	Mühringen	Horb
Creglingen	Künzelsau	Mulfingen	Künzelsau
Dörzbach	Künzelsau	Nagelsberg	Künzelsau
Dünsbach	Gerabronn	Neunkirchen	Mergentheim
Edelfingen	Mergentheim	Niederstetten	Gerabronn
Ernsbach	Oehringen	Nordstetten	Horb
Eschenau	Weinsberg	Oberdorf	Neresheim
Esslingen	Esslingen	Oberschwandorf	Nagold
Freudental	Besigheim	Ödheim	Neckarsulm
Gerabronn	Gerabronn	Olnhausen	Neckarsulm
Goldbach	Crailsheim	Pflaumloch	Neresheim
Hall	Hall	Poppersweiler	Ludwigsburg
Hausen, near		Rexingen	Horb
Massenbach	Brackenheim	Steinbach	Hall
Hechtberg	Waiblingen	Thalheim	Heilbronn
Heilbronn	Heilbronn	Unterschwandorf	Nagold
Hengstfeld	Gerabronn	Vogelsberg	Künzelsau
Hochberg	Waiblingen	Wachbach	Mergentheim
Hohebach	Künzelsau	Wankheim	Tübingen
Igersheim	Mergentheim	Weikersheim	Mergentheim
Jebenhausen	Göppingen	Wiesenbach	Gerabronn
Kochendorf	Neckarsulm	Zaberfeld	Brackenheim

APPENDIX IV

AGES OF EMIGRANT JEWS AS RECORDED IN APPENDIX I[97]

Years	1 to 10		11 to 20		21 to 30		31 to 40		41 to 50		51 to 60		over 60		Total
	m.	f.	m.	f.	m.	f.	m.	f.	m.	f.	m.	f.	m.	f.	
1848	——		—	1	—	3	1	- 1	——		——		——		6
1849	—	6	4	- 5	—	2	——		—	2	2	- 1	1	—	23
1850	(3 children)		7	—	——		1	—	——		——		—	1	12
1851	——		1	- 1	——		——		——		——		——		3
1852	——		——		——		——		——		——		——		0
1853	9	- 6	29	- 6	6	- 7	3	- 1	1	—	——		——		68
1854	(11 children)		55	- 2	6	- 1	3	- 2	——		——		——		80
1855	——		12	- 2	——		——		——		——		——		14
Total	(35 children)		109	- 17	12	- 13	8	- 4	1	- 2	2	- 1	1	- 1	206

[97] The abbreviations m. represents male; f., female. Unfortunately, the Württemberg records do not always give the age of every emigrant.

APPENDIX V

OCCUPATIONS OF EMIGRANT JEWS AS RECORDED IN APPENDIX I[98]

Occupation	1848	1849	1850	1851	1852	1853	1854	1855	Total
Baker		2			1		3	1	7
Bookbinder							1		1
Brandy & vinegar manufacturer				1					1
Brewer			1						1
Butcher			1	6	1	6	13	1	28
Buttonmaker & trimmer							1		1
Carpenter	2	1					1		4
Cattle-dealer							1		1
Cigarmaker				1					1
Clothesmaker				1					1
Confectioner			1				1		2
Cooper							1		1
Cutler-journeyman			1						1
Engraver							1		1
Farmer				1	1		1	1	4
Glazier							2		2
Goldsmith						1			1
Innkeeper					1				1
Lacemaker						1	1		2
Mechanic					1				1
Merchant		1	2	3	4	2	13	4	29
Merchant-apprentice							1		1

[98] The occupations were not always given in the original records.

APPENDIX V *(Continued)*

Occupation	1848	1849	1850	1851	1852	1853	1854	1855	Total
Merchant-clerk						1	1		2
Optician					1		1	1	3
Peasant							3	1	4
Peddler						1			1
Potter							1		1
Quarryman			1						1
Ragpicker						1			1
Retailer					1				1
Ropemaker				1			1		2
Saddler			1		1				2
School-teacher (retired)					1				1
Shoemaker			1	1	3	3	5		13
Shopkeeper							1		1
Soap-boiler	1				2	1	1		5
Stonemason								1	1
Tailor						1	1		2
Tanner								1	1
Tinsmith							1		1
Trade-apprentice		2							2
Trade-clerk							1		1
Trade-journeyman			1						1
Trader	2	3	4		2	3	10	3	27
Weaver			1			3	1		5
Total	5	9	15	17	19	24	68	14	171

APPENDIX
STATISTICS
GLOSSARY
BIBLIOGRAPHY

STATISTICS

JEWISH EMIGRATION FROM
BADEN-WUERTTEMBERG 1933-1941*

Destinations	Temporary Transit Countries		
	Absolute number of	Percentage of total	Absolute number of
Emigration Countries	Emigrants	Emigration	Emigrants
1. USA	8,846	46.02%	12
2. Palestine	2,873	14.94%	132
3. Great Brittain	1,432	7.45%	843
4. France	1,307	6.80%	848
5. Switzerland	855	4.45%	66
6. Argentina	799	4.15%	20
7. Netherlands	559	2.91%	329
8. Brazil	380	1.97%	17
9. South Africa	287	1.49%	12
10. Uruguay	238	1.24%	22
11. Belgium	195	1.01%	190
12. Australia	151	0.78%	4
13. Italy	111	0.58%	345
14. Poland	93	0.48%	20
15. China	92	0.48%	8
16. Chile	88	0.45%	3
17. Canada	78	0.40%	12
18. Colombia	75	0.39%	11
19. Sweden	59	0.31%	20
20. Czechoslovakia	50	0.26%	61
21. Mexico	49	0.26%	—
22. Cuba	46	0.24%	93
23. Hungary	44	0.23%	10
24. Spain	39	0.20%	87
25. Portugal	38	0.20%	39
26. India	33	0.17%	2
27. Bolivia	32	0.16%	8
28. Luxemburg	32	0.16%	85
29. Ecuador	28	0.15%	—
30. Liechtenstein	21	0.11%	23
31. Rhodesia	19	0.10%	—
32. New Zealand	17	0.09%	—
33. Austria	17	0.09%	74

*Source: Sauer, Schicksale p. 147-149

34. East Africa-Kenya	17	0.09%	—
35. Venezuela	17	0.09%	1
36. Romania	16	0.08%	8
37. Peru	15	0.07%	—
38. Yugoslavia	14	0.07%	27
39. Paraguay	13	0.07%	18
40. Dominican Republic	12	0.06%	12
41. Philippines	12	0.06%	1
42. Iran	8	under 0.05%	1
43. Panama	8	under 0.05%	9
44. Denmark	7	under 0.05%	33
45. Soviet Union	7	under 0.05%	6
46. Tunis	7	under 0.05%	—
47. Egypt	6	under 0.05%	3
48. Dutch-Indies	6	under 0.05%	—
49. Turkey	5	under 0.05%	8
50. Finland	4	under 0.05%	3
51. Guatemala	4	under 0.05%	—
52. Iceland	4	under 0.05%	—
53. Lettland	4	under 0.05%	—
54. Trinidad	4	under 0.05%	4
55. Jamaica	3	under 0.05%	1
56. Uganda	3	under 0.05%	—
57. Ethiopia	2	under 0.05%	—
58. Algeria	2	under 0.05%	—
59. Ireland	2	under 0.05%	—
60. Japan	2	under 0.05%	2
61. Lebanon	2	under 0.05%	1
62. Thailand	2	under 0.05%	—
63. Estonia	1	under 0.05%	—
64. Haiti	1	under 0.05%	—
65. Honduras	1	under 0.05%	—
66. Lithuania	1	under 0.05%	3
67. Morocco	1	under 0.05%	3
68. Cyprus	1	under 0.05%	4
69. Africa (unknown countries)	9	under 0.05%	7
70. America (unknown countries; 15 in South America)	17	0.09%	4
71. Asia (unknown country)	1	under 0.05%	1
	19,224	100.00%	-113)

Percentage of the German-Austrian quota fulfilled, and number of German and
Austrian immigrants admitted to the United States, 1933-1944*

	Total quota	1933	1934	1935	1936	1937	1938
Per cent:	100	5.3	13.7	20.2	24.3	42.1	65.3
Numbers:	27,370	1,450	3,740	5,530	6,650	11,520	17,870

	Total quota	1939	1940	1941	1942	1943	1944
Per cent:	100	95.3	47.7	17.4	4.7	4.8	
Numbers:	27,370	26,080	13,050	4,760	1,290	1,351	

*Source: Herbert A. Strauss, "Jewish Emigration from Germany"
LBIY XXVI, 1981, S. 359.

DEPORTATIONS FROM BADEN-WUERTTEMBERG*

Transports	Number deported	Number killed	Number survived	Percentage of survivors of number deported
22 Oct 1940 to Gurs	5,362	3,3735	1,627	30.34%
1 Dec 1941 to Riga	981	939	42	4.28%
26 April 1942 to Izbica	345	345	—	0.00%
13 Juli 1942 to Auschwitz	45	45	—	0.00
22 Aug 1942 to Theresienstadt	1,100	1,049	51	4.64%
29 Sept 1942 to Auschwitz	40	40	—	0.00%
1 March 1942 to Auschwitz	44	43	1	2.27%
17 April 1943 Theresienstadt	20	15	5	25.00%
11 Jan 1944 to Theresienstadt	76	16	60	78.95%
12 Feb 1945 to Theresienstadt	177	4	173	97.74%
Other deportations	147	126	21	14.29%
Total	8,337	6,357	1,980	23.75%

Wuerttemberg Jews deported from the rest of Germany

| Total | 665 | 623 | 42 | 6.32% |

*Source: Sauer, *Schicksale*, p. 393

Percentage of Youth in Jewish Population of Germany*

	1961	1962	1963	1964	1965	1966	1967	1968	1969	1970	1971	1972
Jewish Population	21,906	22,240	22,853	23,576	25,466	26,005	26,226	26,123	26,209	26,438	26,684	26,487
Youth 0-20	3,569	3,731	3,967	4,035	4,512	4,650	4,510	4,554	4,587	4,109	4,197	4,253
Percentage	16.29	16.77	17.35	17.11	17.71	17.88	17.19	17.42	17.50	15.54	15.72	16.05

Population changes of Jewish Minority in Germany*

Date	1.10. 1961	1.10. 1962	1.10. 1963	1.07. 1964	1.10. 1965	1.10. 1966	1.10. 1967	1.07. 1968	1.07. 1969	1.07. 1970	1.10. 1971	1.10. 1972
Emigrants	128	129	60	116	110	133	117	98	133	119	133	117
Deaths	102	98	93	124	104	111	109	124	111	109	123	129
Total Immigrants	230	227	153	240	214	244	226	222	244	228	256	246
Births	234	207	233	244	347	289	274	185	226	261	276	276
Additions	13	6	8	20	14	23	16	16	16	17	22	19
Total	247	213	241	264	361	312	290	201	242	278	298	295
+ change −	+17	−14	+88	+24	+147	+68	+64	−21	−2	+50	+42	+51

Marriages in West Berlin*

	1961	1962	1963	1964	1965	1966	1967	1968	1969	1970	1971
Jewish Marriages	9	10	6	23	18	6	13	14	11	11	9
Mixed Marriages	54	59	60	57	54	46	57	50	31	51	48
Total	63	69	66	80	72	52	70	64	42	62	57

*Source: Doris Kuschner, Die juedische Minderheit in der Bundesrepublik Deutschland, Koeln 1977.

GLOSSARY

ALIYAH	Honor of being called to Torah reading
ALMEMOR	Raised platform in center of synagogue
BAL SEGON	Person in charge of Torah honors
BAR MITZVAH	Celebration of a boy's thirteenth birthday
BERCHES	Sabbath bread, name customary in Southern Germany
CHALLAH	Portion of dough given to priest in Temple days; now name for Sabbath bread
CHAMETZ	Leavened food forbidden during Passover
CHATAN BERESHIT	Aliyah at beginning of Torah cycle
CHATAN TORAH	Aliyah at end of Torah cycle
CHEDER	Jewish elementary school
CHIUV(IM)	Obligated for an honor during synagogue service
CHOLENT	Warm Sabbath food
CHUPPAH	Wedding canopy
DAYAN	Judge at religious tribunal
HAFTORAH	Prophetic portion recited after Torah reading
HAGGADAH	Story of Israel's Exodus from Egypt
HOLEGRASCH	Home ceremony upon giving baby's secular name
KABBALAH	Mysticism
KADDISH	Prayer for the dead
KIBBUTZ(IM)	Collective settlement(s) in Israel
KIDDUSH	Blessing at start of festival
KRIAH	Tear in garment as sign of mourning
KRISTALLNACHT	November 9-10, period of heavy anti-Semitic attacks
MATZAH(OT)	Unleavened bread for Passover
MEZUZAH(OT)	Doorposts for rolls of parchment with Biblical texts

MIKVAH	Ritual bath
MINHAG	Custom
MINYAN	Number, at least ten, for public worship
MITZVAH	Commandment
MOHEL	Circumciser
OVEL	Mourner
PIDYON HA'BEN	Redemption of first born
PIYUTIM	Lyrical prayers
POLTERABEND	Nuptial Eve
ROSH HASHANAH	New Year
SANDEK	Person holding child during circumcision
SARJENES	Shrouds
SHADCHAN	Marriage broker
SHAMASH	Beadle
SHAVUOT	Feast of Weeks
SHECHITAH	Ritual slaughter
SHOCHET	Ritual slaughterer
SHOFAR	Ram's horn
SHULCHAN ARUCH	Code of Jewish laws
SEDER	Home celebration on Passover
SIMCHAT TORAH	Festival of "Joy of Torah"
SOCHOR	Friday night celebration before circumcision
SPINHOLTZ	Celebration before wedding
SUKKAH(OT)	Tabernacle(s), Feast of
TALIT	Prayer shawl
TALMUD	Collected works of the oral tradition
TALMUD TORAH	Study of Torah
TORAH	Name for Five Books of Moses; in general term for "The Teachings of Judaism"
TEFILLIN	Phylacteries
TISHAH BE'AV	Ninth of Av, day of destruction of Temple
WIMPEL	Cloth used for circumcision and later for the binding of a Torah scroll
YAHRZEIT	Date of relative's death
YESHIVAH	Talmudical academy
YOM KIPPUR	Day of Atonement

BIBLIOGRAPHY

ABBREVIATIONS
AZJ   = *Allgemeine Zeitung des Judentums, 1837-1921.*
GZ   = *Gemeindezeitung fuer die israelitischen Gemeinden Wuerttembergs, 1924-1936.*
HS   = *Hauptstaatsarchiv Stuttgart*
ISRAELIT = Orthodox periodical, 1860-1938.
LBIYB = Leo Baeck Institute Yearbook, since 1956.
MITTEILUNGEN (Communications) = Periodical of Society in defense against Anti-Semitism (1891-1933).

Auerbach, Berthold
    Briefe an meinen Freund Jakob Auerbach, 2 Bde., Frank-furt-Main 1884.
Baeck, Leo
    "In Memory of Two of our Dead," LBIY vol. I, 1956, p. 51 ff.
Bettelheim, Anton
    Berthold Auerbach, Stuttgart 1907
Dohm, Christian Wilhelm
    Ueber die buergerliche Verbesserung der Juden, Berlin und Stettin 1781.
Dokumente
    Ueber die Verfolgung der juedischen Buerger in Baden-Wuerttemberg durch das nationalsozialistische Regime 1933-1945, bearbeitet von Paul Sauer, 2 Bde., Stuttgart 1966.

Dreher, Helmut
    Geschichte der israelitischen Waisen-und Erziehungsan-
    stalt Wilhelmspflege in Esslingen, Moehringen 1970.
Festschrift
    Zum 50 jaehrigen Jubilaeum der Synagoge in Stuttgart,
    hrsg. vom Israelitischen Kirchenvorsteheramt, Stuttgart
    1911.
Graupe, Heinz Mosche
    Die Entstehung des modernen Judentums, 2. rev. und erw.
    Auflage, Hamburg 1977.
    English edition: The Rise of Modern Judaism, New York
    1978.
Grossmann, Kurt R.
    The Jewish Displaced Persons Problem, New York 1951.
Guggenheim, Florence
    Yiddisch auf alemannischem Sprachgebiet, Zuerich 1973.
Gunzenhauser, Alfred
    Sammlung der Gesetze, Verordnungen, Verfuegungen und
    Erlasse betreffens die Kirchenverfassung und die religioe-
    sen Einrichtungen der Israeliten in Wuerttemberg, Stutt-
    gart 1909.
Hess, Isaak
    Denkschrift an die Hochansehnliche Staendeversamm-
    lung, Stuttgart 1821.
Hundsnurscher, Franz und Taddey, Gerhard
    Die juedischen Gemeinden in Baden, Stuttgart 1968.
Jeggle, Utz
    Judendoerfer in Wuerttemberg, Tuebingen 1969.
Juedisches Leben in Deutschland
    Selbstzeugnisse zur Sozialgeschichte 1786-1945, 3 Bde.,
    hrsg. von Monika Richarz, Stuttgart 1976-1982.
Kober, Adolf
    "Jewish Emigration from Wuerttemberg to the United
    States of America (1848-1855)," Publication of the Ameri-
    can Jewish Historical Society, vol. XLI, March 1952,
    p. 225 ff.
Kroner, Theodor
    "Das Religioese Leben in der Israelitischen Religionsge-
    meinschaft," in: Wuerttemberg unter der Regierung Koe-
    nig Wilhelms II, hrsg. von V. Bruns, Stuttgart 1916.

Kuschner, Doris
Die juedische Minderheit in der Bundesrepublik Deutschland, Koeln 1977.

Maier, Joseph
Gottesdienst-Ordnung fuer die Synagogen des Koenig-
reichs Wuerttemberg, Stuttgart 1838.

Rede bei dem Antritt seines Amtes als Rabbiner zu Stuttgart, Stuttgart 1835.

Die erste Rabbiner-Versammlung und ihre Gegner, Stuttgart 1848.

Die Synagoge, Stuttgart 1861.

Maor, Harry
Ueber den Wiederaufbau der juedischen Gemeinden in
Deutschland seit 1945, Mainz 1961.

Marx, Leopold
"Otto Hirsch-Ein Lebensbild," Bulletin LBI, 6. Jahrgang
1963, p. 295 ff.

Petuchowski, Jacob J.
Prayerbook Reform in Europe, New York 1968.

Petzold, Guenther & Leslie
Shavei Zion, Bluete in Israel aus schwaebischer Wurzel,
Gerlingen 1978.

Picard, Jacob
The marked one, and twelve other stories, Philadelphia
1956.

Pollack, Herman
Jewish Folkways in Germanic Lands (1648-1806), Cambridge, Mass. 1971.

Protocolle
Der Ersten Rabbiner-Versammlung, Braunschweig 1844.

Der Zweiten Rabbiner-Versammlung, Frankfurt-Main 1845.

Der Dritten Rabbiner-Versammlung, Breslau 1847.

Rothschild, Theodor
Bausteine, Frankfurt-Main 1927.

Sauer, Paul
Die Schicksale der juedischen Buerger Baden-Wuerttembergs waehrend der nationalsozialistischen Verfolgungszeit 1933-1945, Stuttgart 1968.

Die juedischen Gemeinden in Wuerttemberg und Hohenzollern, Stuttgart 1966.

Schorsch, Ismar

"Emancipation and the Crisis of Religious Authority: The
Emergence of the Rabbinate," in: Revolution and Evolution 1848 in German-Jewish History, W.E. Mosse, A. Paucker and R. Ruerup eds., Tuebingen 1981.

Jewish Reactions to German Anti-Semitism, 1870-1914,
New York 1972.

Schwab, Herman

Jewish Rural Communities in Germany, London 1956.

Sepher Minhagim

Israel ben Mordechai Gumpel comp., Fuerth 1767.

Signs of Life

Jews from Wuerttemberg, Walter Strauss ed., New York
1982.

Simon, Ernst

Aufbau im Untergang, Tuebingen 1959.

Stern, Bruno

Meine Jugenderinnerungen, Stuttgart 1968.

Strauss, Herbert A.

"Jewish Emigration from Germany, Nazi policies and Jewish Responses," LBIY, XXV, 1980 p. 313 ff. and XXVI,
1981, p.343 ff.

Taenzer, Aron

Die Geschichte der Juden in Jebenhausen und Goeppingen,
Stuttgart 1927.

Die Geschichte der Juden in Wuerttemberg, Frankfurt-Main
1937.

Taenzer, Paul

Die Rechtsgeschichte der Juden in Wuerttemberg: 1806-
1828, Stuttgart 1922.

Zelzer, Maria

Weg und Schicksal der Stuttgarter Juden, Stuttgart 1964.

INDEX

227